THE
ADMINISTRATION
OF CHANGE
IN AFRICA

THE
ADMINISTRATION
OF CHANGE
IN AFRICA

Essays in the Theory
and Practice of
Development Administration
in Africa

E. PHILIP MORGAN, Editor

Foreword by DWIGHT WALDO

Dunellen
New York/London

309.2
M823

International Standard Book Number 0–8424–0039–7
Library of Congress Catalogue Card Number 70–148704
Printed in the United States of America.

Martin Robertson & Company Ltd. • London
Published for the Program of Eastern Africa Studies
Maxwell School of Citizenship and Public Affairs,
Syracuse University

FOREWORD

Reviewing the essays between these covers, my reflections and speculations concern above all a
paradox: to the later-developing countries the
experience of the West is at once of central importance and of limited, increasingly questionable,
and problematic importance.

The central importance of the Western experience is obvious and indisputable. To become developed has meant in practice to approximate a
condition, commonly designated by the terms "industrialized" and "modernized," first achieved by
certain European and European-settled nations. To
do this has dictated the adoption and adaptation
of institutions (not the least the "sovereign"
state, and quite as emphatically for socialist as
for nonsocialist countries) and technologies (socialist metallurgy and genetics proved to be the
same as "capitalist") deemed to be necessary in
achieving industrialization and modernization.
The accepted indices of achievement in development
are those which measure industrialization and modernization, concerning such familiar things as
manufactures, gross national product, per capita
income, trade balances, educational institutions,
transportation facilities, and vital statistics.
Even the idea of development — which has absorbed
much of the significance of no-longer-fashionable
"progress" — is essentially Western.

This much, it seems to me, is a statement of
plain fact, the recognition of which is the basis
for any intelligent action. A statement of facts
is not to be mistaken for an argument for either
superiority or inevitability. As to superiority:
that something happens earlier to one people than
another, even if "valued," is not evidence of
superiority; that Western peoples have borrowed
(and stolen) from non-Western peoples in achieving
industrialization and modernization may be admitted;

35209

that development ought to mean, and increasingly
does mean, not a copying of some by others but a
worldwide process of mutual interchange can be enthusiastically endorsed. As to inevitability:
so many disparate and unpredictable forces are
now in motion that the idea the non-West must and
will copy an industrial, modern West is, quite
simply, absurd. For — other considerations aside —
the Western "model" has entered into a period of
radical challenge, severe stress, and swift change.
If we are indeed in the throes of transition from
industrialization to post-industrialization, what
is the practical, theoretical, and moral status of
the industrial model? Is a model now declared obsolete and in process of being abandoned a proper
goal for high endeavor? On the other hand, how
can a new model that exists only on rudimentary
foundations, and in varied and sometimes conflicting projections, serve as a goal?

Increasingly I have found my mind engaged by
the thought that in strange and ironic ways the
experiences of Western countries nowadays make
them increasingly akin to the later-developing
countries, while they are simultaneously growing
more distant from them as measured by some quantitative and qualitative criteria. If in fact so-
called developed countries are in transition to
another, essentially different condition of existence, then by definition, they are, with regard
to that different condition, underdeveloped; and
confusion and turbulence in the process of transition are to be expected. If we postulate that
massive societal change tends to be characterized
by certain recurring types of social phenomena
and to present generic types of problems in social
mechanics, then commonalities between countries
that seem to be (and in many ways are) widely disparate emerge with arresting clarity.

I believe that a perception of uniformity and
unity in the midst of diversity — a perception of
crucial theoretical and practical import — is

emerging. A shift in perspective among those concerned with development is in fact widely apparent in the literature. It is evidenced in the criticism of the "static" administrative institutions and "instrumental" administrative ideologies of developed countries; by the emergence of "change" and "system adaptivity" as central concepts, processes conceived not only as common to underdeveloped countries but as bridging between these and developed countries; and by attempts generally to construct "universal" models, particularly "dynamic" models. The shift in perspective is best revealed in a philosophical probing of development: what was taken uncritically as a "given" two decades ago now is seen as a subtle, problematic concept.

There is much evidence of the sea-change in these essays. Overtly, perhaps it is most evident in the essays of Esman and Montgomery. I refer to their often critical stance toward received or traditional Western administrative institutions and ideologies: the irrelevance (or worse) of a rigid distinction between politics and administration, the questionable utility of the doctrine of civil service neutrality under new or changed conditions, the frequently misguided emphasis upon "instrumental efficiency"; generally, to their rejection of a static, organizational-administrative "physics" and their argument for the creation of a new physics to conceptualize and manage rapid change. Much is epitomized in a metaphor proposed by Montgomery: we began with a simple subject-predicate conceptualization of development, but we are moving into a period in which development becomes a compound-complex sentence — with frequent shifts of subjects, verbs, and objects.

Sensitized to the existence of similarities regardless of differences of developmental status or of scale, to me these essays again and again become commentaries on common problems. Highly developed as well as little-developed nations are experiencing (in phrases used below) "cultural

traumas" and a "destruction of history." They too
suffer from feelings of "limited resources" and
"powerlessness in the face of destiny." They also
exhibit "structural vulnerability" and know not
whom, or what, or how, to "imitate." Granted important differences; but I argue that the similarities are real and important, much more so than
ordinarily perceived. In some ways, certainly,
the similarities become increasingly obvious, at
least at the ostensible level. Typical "development" problems of regionalism, functional articulation, ethnic relations, social equity, public
order, and even investment and productivity, once
thought solved (or at least on the way to solution
in developed countries), have reemerged with
worrying intensity. As problems of institutional
erosion or destruction become a serious concern
in the West, "institution-building" is a subject
on which any expertise is not just for export.
Problems of "nation repair" or rebuilding are, at
least in appearance, very much like those of
nation-building.

Whether repair, building, or rebuilding, the
problems of all must be addressed under the constraints of two cruel dilemmas. (1) A rising
revolution of lowering expectations, centering
on such matters as population growth, resource ex-
haustion, and destruction of the biosphere, cannot
but collide with the revolution of rising expectations, with resulting turbulence and conflict.
(2) It is increasingly questionable whether the
nation-state is an appropriate instrument for its
tasks, even a possible instrument; but the nation-
state system still shows, on balance, more evidence
of extension and intensification than of abandonment
and transition. These are not, of course, two separate dilemmas. They are intimately entwined and
synergistic.

Despite the vogue for futuristics and for all
the punditing about an emergent post-industrial
age, the future is obscure if not opaque — this at

the same time that change accelerates and it becomes increasingly clear that the future will be different. The effect is simultaneously to increase the area of uncertainty for countries at all levels of development, to make their problems of change and adjustment similar if not identical, and to draw them closer together in a train of common destiny. In this situation, developed countries can, with logic and without false humility, look to developing countries for knowledge about change and its cause-and-effect nexuses, at the same time continuing to search developed — and further "developing" — countries for ideas and technologies appropriate to their circumstances and goals. When Esman describes the "statesmanship" necessary in a developing country, he could as well be describing the statesmanship necessary in a developed country. Increasingly, development administration becomes (in Fred Rigg's nice metaphor but with a meaning he did not fully anticipate) not a mirror for us, nor a mirror for others, but a mirror for all.

Dwight Waldo

ACKNOWLEDGMENTS

Most of these papers were prepared for a symposium held at Syracuse University in May, 1970. The meeting, on development administration in Africa, marked the close of the Africa-Asia Public Service Fellowship Program, an internship program which had provided young American interns to serve transitionally in the legal and development-related departments of civil services in various South Asian and African nations. Financial support for the project came from the Ford Foundation, the U. S. Agency for International Development, and participating governments.

Although any program spanning nearly a decade inevitably involves far too many people to permit individual thanks, several groups of principals deserve recognition. Impetus for the Syracuse program came from Stephen K. Bailey, then Dean of the Maxwell School of Citizenship and Public Affairs of Syracuse University. A succession of Africa-Asia Program directors must be cited for a job well done. In the order of their tenure, they are Robert Heussler, Arthur Osteen, Robert R. Stephens, John Lindeman, Fred G. Burke, and Marshall H. Segall. The editor had the pleasure of working with each of these men save Mr. Heussler. Others who merit warm gratitude are the administrative staff of the Program, who were principally Mrs. Juanita Hazell, Robert A. Miller, Mrs. Patricia Suters James, Jeffrey A. James, David H. Koehler, Michael J. Chaput, Ladislav Venys, and Mrs. Gloria Katz.

Marshall Segall, Professor of Social Psychology and Director of the Program of Eastern African Studies at Syracuse University, has provided willing support at every stage of this effort and the editor remains in his debt for the opportunity to assemble and edit the essays that follow. For the administration of the symposium itself, and for editorial and clerical help far beyond the call of their immediate responsibilities, warm thanks go to Judith Dollenmayer, Mrs. Gloria Katz, and the staff at 119 College Place. The index was prepared by my research assistant, Judith Lightsey. My wife, Maria, also deserves note for her affectionate prodding in the face of incurable indolence.

Finally, special thanks are extended to participants in the symposium and contributors to this volume. Without their ready cooperation this collection could never have appeared. The quality of each essay speaks for itself; any errors are the responsibility of the editor.

E.P.M.

Atlanta, Georgia
October, 1972

CONTENTS

xiv

NOTES ON CONTRIBUTORS

DWIGHT WALDO Albert Schweitzer Professor in the Humanities at the Maxwell Graduate School, Syracuse University, Professor Waldo is the author of *The Administrative State, Comparative Public Administration: Prologue, Problems, and Promise,* and many other works. Presently Professor Waldo is editor-in-chief of *Public Administration Review.*

E. PHILIP MORGAN Former Coordinator of the Africa-Asia Program, Syracuse University, and Assistant Professor of Political Science, Emory University, Atlanta.

MILTON J. ESMAN John S. Knight Professor of Sociology at Cornell University and Director of the Center for International Studies at Cornell. Among Professor Esman's publications is *Common Aid Effort: The Development Assistance Activities of the OECD* (with D.S. Cheever).

DENIS A. GOULET Recently, Visiting Professor of Sociology at the Univeristy of California, San Diego, and a Visiting Fellow of the Center for the Study of Democratic Institutions, Professor Goulet is now a Fellow of the Center for the Study of Development and Social Change in Cambridge, Massachusetts.

IRVING SWERDLOW Formerly Associate Dean of the Maxwell School, Professor Swerdlow is Professor of Economics at Syracuse University. He has been a Senior Research Fellow of the Brookings Institution in Washington, D.C., and is editor of *Development Administration.*

G. OKA OREWA Head of Public Administration at the
   United Nations Economic Commission for Africa,
   headquartered in Adis Ababa, Ethiopia. Mr.
   Orewa is a Nigerian citizen and the author of
   several books, including *Local Government
   Finance in Nigeria* (Oxford University Press).

W. BEDIAKO LAMOUSE-SMITH Now Assistant Professor
   of Sociology at Syracuse University, Professor
   Lamouse-Smith has taught at the Free University
   of Berlin and at Makerere University in Uganda.
   A Ghanaian citizen, he is currently studying
   the adjustment of African migrant workers to
   urban life.

BRIAN VAN ARKADIE Development economist at the
   Institute of Development Studies, University
   of Sussex, Mr. Van Arkadie is especially interested in planning in East Africa. Several
   years ago he headed the economic planning
   group for Uganda.

JULIUS M. WAIGUCHU A citizen of Kenya, Professor
   Waiguchu received his doctorate from Temple
   University, where he was a United Nations Fel-
   low. He is currently Professor of Political
   Science at Paterson State College, New Jersey.

KENNETH L. BAER Assistant Professor of Sociology
   and Education at Emory University, Mr. Baer
   has worked extensively in Africa and has recently completed a long-term anthropological
   study of administrative institutions, culture,
   and indigenous perceptions in rural Tanzania.

ROBERT A. MILLER A doctoral candidate at Syracuse
   University, Mr. Miller worked as an Africa-
   Asia Fellow in Malawi's Ministry of Development
   and Planning from 1966 to 1968 as a District
   Development Field Officer.

NICHOLAS DANFORTH An officer in the self-help campaign under the Lesotho Ministry of Local Government during the drought of 1966, Assistant Secretary for Commerce and Industry in the Lesotho Ministry of Finance in 1967, and Assistant Secretary for Mines in 1968, Mr. Danforth also served with the Town Planning Advisory Board, the National Planning Board, and the Basutoland Factory Estates Development Board. He received an M.A. in African Studies at Columbia and is now with the Twentieth Century Fund in New York City.

HENRY J. RICHARDSON III A graduate of Yale Law School, Mr. Richardson served as an Africa-Asia Fellow in the Malawi External Affairs Ministry. He is now completing a doctorate at the U.C.L.A. African Studies Center.

JOHN D. MONTGOMERY Professor of Public Administration at Harvard University, Professor Montgomery is Secretary of the John F. Kennedy School of Government there. Among his books are *The State Versus Socrates*, *Foreign Aid in International Politics*, and *Approaches to Development* (with William Siffin).

PROGRAM OF EASTERN AFRICAN STUDIES STAFF

Judith Dollenmayer A graduate student in Social Sciences and Assistant to the Director of the Program during 1969-70, Miss Dollenmayer edited each essay chosen for inclusion in this volume and assisted in its organization.

Gloria Katz Chief administrative officer of the Program, Mrs. Katz supervised the complex logistics of both the Symposium on Development and this volume.

Sally LaMar Secretary to the Director of the Program, Mrs. LaMar prepared the manuscript for publication.

INTRODUCTION
by
E. Philip Morgan

In 1961 the Ford Foundation awarded to Syracuse University an initial grant to support a public-service internship program in Africa and South Asia. The program's chief goal at that time was to recruit bright young Americans who were likely to emerge one day in the public service or in some aspect of public life. They were engaged to spend one year or two serving in the civil service or legal establishment of one of the developing countries of Africa or Asia. The program assumed that the more experience these people gained in the problems of the world's struggling areas, the more enlightened and effective American public servants they would be.

As the program expanded, however, its scope and objectives changed somewhat. East, Central and Southern Africa became the chief geographic focus. Aid in economic planning and technical assistance came to be recognized as meeting the urgent needs and desires of African governments more directly than the work of American lawyers in general administration. This emphatic shift in focus is reflected in the selection of participants and papers for this volume.

By the time the Africa-Asia Program began to close its activities in 1969, it had supported 99 Fellows in tasks as varied as city planning in Calcutta and the distribution of powdered milk in Lesotho. It had been generously supported by well over one million dollars from the Ford Foundation and several hundred thousand dollars from the U. S. Agency for International Development. The internship program was a unique undertaking which is unlikely soon to be repeated, particularly under university auspices, given immediate political circumstances both at home and overseas.

It is very difficult now, for instance, to justify
sending expatriates to staff the civil services of
African countries, where tremendous local pressure
exists for Africanization of administrative positions. No matter how salutary might be firsthand
exposure of Americans to Africa's problems through
temporary assignments in African administration,
the aspiring local population can interpret such
American activity only as forestalling their hope
of employment by their own national governments.
The employment of Europeans and Americans as expatriate civil servants, unless it can be shown to
be a pedagogical matter of technical assistance,
requiring esoteric skills, often gives rise to
charges of neocolonialism even when the African
government in question has requested the expatriates' services.

It seems particularly questionable for universities to perpetuate arrangements which supply,
or appear to supply, an African civil service with
outside general administrative personnel who might
be obtained locally. However, even at the level
of sophisticated technical assistance, universities
now find it difficult to provide aid which will
assuredly be perceived locally as disinterested.
There is, of course, the suspicion of political
objectives implicit in joint university-U.S. government contract assistance. Many university
scholars and administrators, perhaps understandably,
feel that technical assistance should not be entirely disinterested, but for educational and intellectual rather than political reasons. Their
argument goes somewhat as follows: since a university's primary role is one of education, it might
reasonably expect to give technical assistance in
the form of training of nationals; if the technical
skill being requested is not so basic as to need
replication locally, perhaps universities can fairly expect an opportunity to do primary research in
return for their services. Of course, what is done
with that firsthand research carries many implica-

tions, but another point is emphasized here. Even granted a consensus that the use of university assistance and research contracts — overtly or covertly — for political purposes compromises the integrity of any educational institution, it is similarly probelmatical whether their primary purpose of education can be maintained if universities are asked to perform aid and technical assistance services without being able to teach or do research overseas.

Other forces also oppose university sponsorship of programs which place administrative and technical personnel in African countries. Public or private money for such efforts has dried up since 1967, which to a degree is explained above and otherwise accounted for by the general cutback in magnitude and type of United States overseas assistance. Also, the increasingly rapid localization of African civil services as a matter of political necessity entails a consequent cut in expatriate hiring. Finally, local educational facilities now bear much of the burden of training and supplying administrative and technical personnel for local institutions.

As the Africa-Asia Program was approaching an end, it occurred to some members of the staff that, though much had been learned by both interns and staff about problems of administration and change in developing countries, no insights were being recorded in any systematic way. Annual reports had been required of Fellows, with final summary evaluations as they returned from field experience. However, these documents too frequently reflected fond reminiscences rather than insights as to how a Western mind with certain perceptual patterns encountered a different culture milieu and grew conscious that it was participating in the administrative or legal process of changing local patterns of perception and behavior. The question "How was the changer changed?" rarely appeared. The relationship of one's personal task to the larger social and political processes around him was seldom placed in a perspective which would permit generalization and comparison. Localization caused by political expediency, even at the expense of efficiency, is not necessarily a bad thing even in the short run. Sooner or later each of these states must find a coherent set of political norms and institutions which coalesce into a reasonably predictable political process. So long as expatriates influence internal administrative and technical decisions, the emergence of an indigenous political process is retarded. This observation, of course, is not confined to university-sponsored interns or technical assistance personnel; it applies to foreign personnel in general.

A word should be said about the particular notion of development administration being presumed throughout this volume. B. B. Schaffer has summarized development administration in a way that approaches its meaning in this volume:

> The content of the development administration movement...has been a sense of the distinctiveness of administration for development programmes, policies, and plans in those conditions...in which there are unusually extensive needs...; precisely where there are peculiarly few resources and exceptionally severe obstacles to meeting the needs. The peculiarity of development administration lay exactly in that inconvenient combination: extensive needs, low capacities, severe obstacles.*

Such a conception may include administrative change, but we are using the broader connotation of public activity in the achievement of transformational goals,

---

*B. B. Schaffer, "Deadlock in Development Administration," in Colin Leys, ed., *Politics and Change in Developing Countries*, London: Cambridge University Press, 1969, p. 184.

so that we can address the politics as well as the administration of change.

The germ of this volume (and its parent symposium) grew from our awareness that the Africa-Asia Program compiled much practical administrative experience, but that the wealth of case material in interns' experiences meant little without an organizing effort to distill from experience a set of generalizable problems amenable to theoretical and practical solution. Therefore, several theoretical papers were solicited to address, in complementary fashion, various perspectives on development and administration. The essays which provide this analytic background are those by Milton J. Esman, Denis A. Goulet, and Irving Swerdlow.

Professor Esman's paper compares historical differences in the circumstances of modern and modernizing countries as a background to framing an appropriate set of norms for development administration in modernizing countries. In addition, this essay suggests steps for the prudent statesman concerned with applying these new development norms, a pattern of action which cannot be found in traditional Western doctrines of administration.

Denis Goulet diagnoses underdevelopment as an experience of vulnerability in economic, political, and cultural life. Two administrative problems, coercion and elitism, are examined in this light. Goulet illustrates certain nonelitist modes of administrative behavior which suggest, as does Esman, that development should be judged as a liberating enterprise. In this vein, Goulet draws heavily on the work of French social planner Robert Caillot.

Irving Swerdlow's essay uniquely attempts to integrate the fundamental assumptions of three perspectives upon development analysis: institution-building, public administration, and economic growth theory. As an economist Swerdlow is concerned mainly with the achievement of rapid economic growth in the developing countries, yet he views the inability of governments to perform ad-

equately the necessary functions in economic institutions as the "largest single proximate bottleneck to achieving rapid economic growth." He is
aware of the social scientists' skepticism of efficiency as a norm for evaluating the effectiveness
of social institutions. Nonetheless, Professor
Swerdlow argues cogently that, for specifically
economic institutions, the efficiency criterion
should be maintained, using the precepts of institution-building and public administration to illustrate his argument.

Illustrating and supplementing the theoretical
material discussed above, Part II offers African
perspectives on the context of political, economic, and social change. This group of essays, by
eminently qualified African professionals and one
British development economist, provides a setting
for the theoretical essays in Part I and some comparative reference points for the participant-
observer material in Part III. The "African context" section reflects keen African consciousness
of development problems and authenticates many of
the case study observations. At the same time,
however, these essays dissect some aspects of
ethnocentrism, if not naiveté, which characterize
Western perspectives on development problems and
Western prescriptions for modernization.

G. O. Orewa identifies some of the major administrative obstacles to development met by African
countries over the past decade. His paper high-
lights the roles of professionals and illustrates
at some length what development research is being
done in Africa. Orewa concludes with suggestions
of urgent reforms which are required in order to
improve Africa's administrative machinery. W. B.
Lamouse-Smith's essay provides a theoretical counter-
part to Orewa's statement. He points out some of
the peculiar conditions which affect public administration in Africa and attempts to show why the
resulting problems must be approached through new
administrative arrangements. If planning and ad-

ministrative problems were examined through a tentative theory of complexity, Lamouse-Smith suggests, ways could be found to reduce the complexity of the African context within which the planning and administration of development projects occurs.

Reinforcing this argument that administrative arrangements "by the book" must be altered to fit the specific context, Brian Van Arkadie systematically states what structural and institutional changes must occur in pursuit of long-term economic development. His illustrations are drawn from his experience as a development economist and planner for the three countries of East Africa. In contrast with Van Arkadie's general treatment of the need to reconcile the planner's objectives with political realities, Julius Waiguchu addresses more specifically the problem of emergent bureaucratic elitism. He concludes that a process of creating elites occurred at the expense of the development of other political institutions in Kenya. Waiguchu shows how the major political party has come to be preempted by the administration and the chief executive, until some doubt exists whether the party remains an effective political instrument.

Detailing many of the problems raised in Parts I and II, the essays in Part III offer participant observations from varied African settings. The Tanzanian strategy of rural development is amply illustrated from an original analytic perspective in the paper by Kenneth L. Baer. Professor Baer examined over a long term the perceptions of local participants in the Urambo settlement project of Western Tanzania. Given a context of European cooperative administrative structures, rural Tanzanian culture, and the new developmental ideology of self-reliance, he asks whether development administration can instill production-oriented values in the population without fundamentally modifying their culture.

Robert A. Miller describes the District Development Committees in Malawi as one means of organizing rural participation in national development. His paper attempts to treat the committees within the analytic frame of institution-building, a perspective made familiar to the reader by Milton Esman and Irving Swerdlow. Continuing to focus upon rural problems of development administration, Nicholas Danforth presents an analysis of the development prospects of the Basuto people in the context of several community development programs and the current emphasis upon industrial development in Lesotho. His piece adds a social-psychological dimension to the other two rural studies, which dramatize the influence of culture upon development projects. Finally, Henry Richardson places development administration in a broad context, which treats the idiosyncrasies of internal administration and decision-making as they interact with international political influence. Richardson writes of an external impingement on domestic policy-making. He is concerned with policy outputs in the Ministry of External affairs of the Malawi government, especially in regard to relations between Malawi and Southern Africa, and how these affect Malawi's selection of development programs.

Professor John D. Montgomery's concluding paper synthesizes the foregoing essays into a formal, heuristic statement about future trends in development administration in Africa. He presents a behavioral model of the politics of development administration, illustrating its categories with lessons from Africa as presented by the African administrators and the interns. Montgomery suggests: "The manner in which the development administrator discovers and influences the behavioral responses of citizens to new opportunities is at least as important as the conventional dimensions of bureaucratic performance heretofore used to evaluate effectiveness." The author offers a set of behavioral response-indicators which attest to citizen commitment to modernization; these may help administrators determine who will benefit most from modernization and how its benefits will be distributed.

As with any collection of essays, there is nothing conclusive in the contents of this volume, nor was having the last word in such a difficult area our aim. Ideas and suggestions have been offered — some based on systematic inquiry and others more impressionistic — about how both administrators and students of administration might act and think in a field which permits few broad generalizations. The contributors are people in diverse occupations who spend a great deal of time thinking and working with the kind of administrative problems African countries face. We hope these essays will stimulate more thought, more useful theory, and more empathic action in the administration of developmental change in Africa.

PART I

Theoretical Perspectives on Development and Administration

Administrative Doctrine and Developmental Needs

by Milton J. Esman

How relevant are classical or "Western" concepts and methods of public administration to the concerns of development administrators in the less industrialized countries? My paper will explore and assess this relationship.

"Development administration" refers to those activities of government that foster economic growth, strengthen human and organizational capabilities, and promote equality in the distribution of opportunities, income, and power. These activities inevitably involve deliberate attempts at social and behavioral changes.[1] This definition does not exhaust the functions of government. The more basic governmental functions — to maintain order, provide national defense, collect taxes, regulate access to scarce resources, and settle disputes among citizens — are essential to any ordered society and prerequisite to the developmental activities referred to above.

sible control by superiors over subordinates, and reinforcing the rule of law. Public bureaucracy would thus be governed by rigid definitions of roles, explicit procedures for processing actions, and authoritarian patterns of relationship both among officials and toward the public. While rule of law would serve democratic purposes by limiting the scope of government and assuring that political rulers determine public action, hierarchical structure would produce an essentially authoritarian regime within the administration. Clients or publics would be regarded as subjects to whom pre-programmed services were impersonally, impartially distributed. Client groups would not participate in administrative decisions, for this would compromise the objectivity of administration. Requests for deviations from or changes in standardized regulations would be processed through political channels. Political, and not administrative, structures were (and are still understood to be) the legitimate adaptive institutions of society.

3. Political neutrality of administrative personnel. Administrators served the state, not any temporary faction therein, and they were to be neutral between political parties, social classes, interest groups, and alternative policies or courses of action. Administrators provided technical expertise and continuity in exchange for career security and faithful, disinterested service. Political or policy questions lay beyond their scope; they were to be controlled instruments of responsible political superiors who were given authority over them by political processes in which the administrators themselves did not participate.

4. Instrumental efficiency. To achieve the purpose of government consistent with law and with minimum expenditure of scarce means was the distinguishing professional function of good administrators. Their discretion extended only to how, not to what; their governing criterion was efficiency.

Administrative Doctrine
and Developmental
Needs

by Milton J. Esman

How relevant are classical or "Western" concepts
and methods of public administration to the concerns of development administrators in the less
industrialized countries? My paper will explore
and assess this relationship.

"Development administration" refers to those
activities of government that foster economic
growth, strengthen human and organizational capabilities, and promote equality in the distribution of opportunities, income, and power. These
activities inevitably involve deliberate attempts
at social and behavioral changes.[1] This definition does not exhaust the functions of government.
The more basic governmental functions — to maintain
order, provide national defense, collect taxes,
regulate access to scarce resources, and settle
disputes among citizens — are essential to any
ordered society and prerequisite to the developmental activities referred to above.

The Context of
Modernization
in the West

In "Western" societies — by which we mean the
European and North American countries which first
mastered modern physical and social technologies
and through industrialization converted themselves
into welfare states — governments performed many
developmental activities while they were in the
process of industrialization. While allowing for
substantial variations from country to country,
the context surrounding Western modernization
included three factors that do not hold for countries which became politically independent after
World War II or which failed to industrialize
before that time:
  1. The Western countries had a reasonably
secure political base for modernization. Major
governmental and political structures were in
place, a sense of national identity linked individuals and intermediate groupings to the political system, and the processes of rulership were
sufficiently legitimate and deployed sufficient
authority to command generalized compliance.
Political processes produced non-bureaucratic
ruling groups who were reasonably competent to
govern.
  2. Within society were widespread entrepreneurial and other organizational capabilities which
were able to perform a wide variety of developmental functions. While these related particularly to
economic growth, they also included welfare and
educational activities that could be entrusted to
voluntary organizations and local governments.
This limited the financial and organizational bur-
dens on the state and its agencies.
  3. Societal demands for public services, though
they appeared to be intense at the time, were modest by modern standards. The pace of public affairs
was leisurely, and the proportion of national economic and trained manpower resources claimed by

4

government was small. Whether the regime was mer-
cantilist or Smithian in economic policy, authoritarian or democratic in its political doctrines
and behavior, demands on governments were moderate
and well within their capacities to handle.

The Major Elements of
Classical Western
Administrative Doctrine

Under these circumstances, a body of administrative doctrine developed which emphasized, far
more than the realities of public life warranted
even in those days, the limited role of government
Differing from country to country, these streams
of administrative doctrine nevertheless contained
the following common themes:[2]
 1. The importance of controlling administrative discretion through the rule of law. Rule of
law stipulated that the acts of administrators and
other agents of the state must be determined and
limited (programmed, to use the current concept)
by explicitly written rules; procedures must be
available to citizens for redress when administrators acted outside the rules or applied them abu-
sively. Rule of law was intended to achieve three
objectives: to insure the control of administrative personnel by responsible political representatives of the state, and control of the latter
by judicial and quasi-judicial tribunals; to guarantee equitable, consistent, and fully predictable
treatment to the public; and to limit strictly the
activities of governments to those duly authorized
by law. Under the norms of the rule of law, administrators were expected to enforce regulations and
distribute services precisely as prescribed by law.
The ideal was to limit discretion to the utmost so
that administrators would behave as controlled ex-
ecutors of public policy.
 2. The organization of public authorities in
hierarchical structures, thus guaranteeing respon-

sible control by superiors over subordinates, and reinforcing the rule of law. Public bureaucracy would thus be governed by rigid definitions of roles, explicit procedures for processing actions, and authoritarian patterns of relationship both among officials and toward the public. While rule of law would serve democratic purposes by limiting the scope of government and assuring that political rulers determine public action, hierarchical structure would produce an essentially authoritarian regime within the administration. Clients or publics would be regarded as subjects to whom pre-programmed services were impersonally, impartially distributed. Client groups would not participate in administrative decisions, for this would compromise the objectivity of administration. Requests for deviations from or changes in standardized regulations would be processed through political channels. Political, and not administrative, structures were (and are still understood to be) the legitimate adaptive institutions of society.

3. Political neutrality of administrative personnel. Administrators served the state, not any temporary faction therein, and they were to be neutral between political parties, social classes, interest groups, and alternative policies or courses of action. Administrators provided technical expertise and continuity in exchange for career security and faithful, disinterested service. Political or policy questions lay beyond their scope; they were to be controlled instruments of responsible political superiors who were given authority over them by political processes in which the administrators themselves did not participate.

4. Instrumental efficiency. To achieve the purpose of government consistent with law and with minimum expenditure of scarce means was the distinguishing professional function of good administrators. Their discretion extended only to how, not to what; their governing criterion was efficiency.

A set of techniques was identified, principally from industrial practice, as universally applicable to the pursuit of economy and efficiency in government. Thus tight organization, close supervision, smooth procedures, tidy budgetary and financial controls — in sum, the technologies of "scientific" business-like management — became the test of good administrative practice, particularly in American doctrine. The rationalistic focus on progressive efficiency was embodied in the standard staff functions of budgeting, personnel, and organization and methods. Thus the outputs of government were displaced by efficiency criteria as the principle concern of professional public administration.

These Western precepts of public administration produced emphasis on written rules, precedent, predictability, consistency, equity, routine, efficiency, and technique. They depoliticized administration, deemphasized program outputs, and relegated the public to the status of subjects. They put policy initiatives, programmatic innovation, and clientele involvement outside the legitimate purview of administrative personnel. It was a doctrine for system maintenance, laissez-faire government, and the provision of modest public services, not an administrative prescription for development or innovation. Political acts, including the humanization of administration and the exoneration of the rigidities of rule-of-law bureaucracy, were to be performed by politicians. Politicians made policy; administrators implemented; clients complied.

This body of doctrine operated in defiance of much observable behavior, particularly in the United States, where administrative law and career bureaucracy developed more slowly than in Europe, where bureaucratic structures were readily penetrated by organized interest groups, and where symbiotic relationships grew up between bureaucratic agencies and their clienteles (e.g., the Army Engineers and public works contractors, state extension services and the Farm Bureau, the I.C.C. and the railroads).

Yet these institutional and behavioral realities
did not significantly undermine the intellectual
sway of such administrative doctrines during the
half century or more of rapid industrialization
preceding World War II. Though this body of ideas
has come under severe attack since World War II,
as received notions they continue strongly to influence administrative thinking in the West. They
have formed the nucleus of technical assistance in
public administration which has been exported to
developing countries by bilateral and international agencies for the past 25 years.

Some Themes in
Contemporary
Administrative Thought

    Before commenting on the relevance of the con-
cepts and practices to the less developed countries,
let me set forth a few of the properties of public
administration recognized by more recent research
and thinking.[3] This may help to evaluate whether
the received tradition of Western administrative
doctrine addresses the current needs of developing countries.
    1. Administration is a plural phenomenon.
This is true in two senses. First, national leadership operating on behalf of the state has several options about the instruments it will deploy
in pursuit of programmatic objectives. It may
use bureaucratic agencies — the only ones, incidentally, that Western administrative doctrine
seriously contemplates — but it is not limited
to them. The national leadership may pursue its
purposes through private enterprise, pure or modified market mechanisms, voluntary organizations,
associational groups, political party channels,
mass media, or local governments. It may use
these instruments in a variety of combinations
created by appropriate inducements and sanctions.

These organizations may already exist, or they may be strengthened or even created by the regime.

Second, it is dangerously simplistic to speak of "the bureaucracy" of any modern or modernizing nation. A public works agency is not the same and will not behave the same as a foreign office, an education ministry, veterinary service, central bank, or police department. Their professional orientations, their clienteles, their work methods, and the technologies they deploy differ profoundly. Though they may be more or less integrated by the norms and styles of the polity on which they depend — by common personnel, financial, and supply procedures, and even by a common core of generalist administrators — each is a separate subculture and interest group. At any point in time, different agencies may be embroiled in conflict and any one of them may be at the forefront of innovation, while others may greatly resist change.

2. Administration is deeply implicated in political choices. Administrators both control access to scarce resources and participate in their differential allocation and distribution. Despite much self-deception and self-serving humility, administrators in all modern societies participate in the shaping of public policies and manage action programs which involve political decisions. They perform communication functions linking client groups to government agencies and to one another. Thus administrators become involved in processing claims on government — some of which they help to generate — and in mediating and managing conflict. That they do not engage in partisan politics does not foreclose these substantive political activities. Political demands are frequently transmitted through administrative channels; administrators are involved in the processing of these demands and participate in their resolution. Political choices are required not only in responding to demands that originate in society but also in inducing clients to use new public services and to comply with government policies. The im-

9

plementation of policies through programmatic action involves numerous choices that have differential political effects; since they can be only
partly preprogrammed by law, many are perforce
determined within administrative channels. Administration is simultaneously a political and an
instrumental process.

3. Administration is complex. It handles
large volumes of resources and converts them through
complex technologies, delivers services over large
distances to clients facing different problems, me-
diates among competitive interests, and operates
through sophisticated organizations under conditions
of uncertainty. Thus holistic prescriptions for
administrative problems are likely to be deceptive
and useless. Widely heralded nostrums such as comprehensive planning, decentralization, public corporations, market mechanisms, performance budgeting,
community development, strengthening non-bureaucratic institutions, computerization, and aerospace
technologies may help in some situations but be
entirely futile and even damaging in others. Moreover, there are no final "solutions" to administrative problems. Every structural and programmatic
improvement produces second-generation problems.
Thus the creation of independent agencies or corporations (enclaves of development), free from civil
service and treasury controls, soon entails problems of programmatic integration; the organization
of client groups to enhance participation often
generates self-serving pressures for expanded and
expensive public services which escalate conflict
beyond the capacity of government to manage; the
successful distribution of fertilizers and miracle
seeds generates problems of credit, storage, pric-
ing, marketing, and the distribution of benefits
among landlords and tenants.

10

The Context in Developing Countries

As we look at countries not attempting to modernize, it is clear that most do not share the conditions that characterized "Western" countries during the period when classical administrative doctrines were formulated.

1. Many of them do not enjoy a secure political base for modernization. The cement of nationhood is fragile — indeed, the structures of the state are not firmly in place. National symbols command little support; the polity is riven by ethnic, religious, and regional cleavage; the criteria of legitimacy for rulers and procedures for succession have not been fixed; and the regime's capacity to extract compliance is as weak as the social disciplines that so tenuously bind individuals and groups to the modern polity. Because political leadership has frequently been ineffective, military and civil bureaucracies often perform rulership functions. These bureaucratic structures and personalities become the principle symbols and representatives of the modern state. Thus not only is the distinction between political and administrative functions blurred, but the classical distinction between politicians and administrators is obscured as well. Administrators, often by default, become the principle adaptive agencies of their societies.

2. Entrepreneurial, managerial, and professional skills are in acutely short supply; and there is little experience of voluntary organization for modern economic and civic activities. Traditional organizations convert slowly, if at all, to modern economic and governmental purposes. A very high proportion of trained and experienced managers and professionals is associated with public administration. Relatively few reserves of entrepreneurial or organizational capability exist in the society for modernizing governments to

draw on or even to co-opt for developmental purposes. Yet governments frequently decline to encourage the organizations that bespeak such capability because these are controlled by ethnic mi-
norities or other groups whom the ruling elites distrust. The rulers are disinclined to entrust resources to or rely for the fulfillment of policy
objectives on groups that might become competitive.
    3. Demands on government for public services
are intense — far in excess of administrative or
economic capabilities. These demands are generated by social and economic interests which have
been mobilized by post-independence politics and
the extension of modern communications, by governmental elites eager to gain domestic political support or overcome national backwardness, and by the
influence of international organizations and foreign
aid programs. The claims for services cover every
section of life from infrastructure — roads, power,
irrigation, and telecommunications — through assistance to agriculture and industry, to peremptory
demands for education, welfare, employment, and
housing. These demands are superimposed on expanded needs for traditional governmental activities, such as public order, national defense,
collection of revenue, and the maintenance of an
expanded civil service.
    These circumstances create burdens for govern-
ments in contemporary developing countries which
their Western predecessors did not have to face
with nearly the same urgency and intensity. Among
these responsibilities are the following:
    1. Guiding economic development, not only by
facilitating private enterprise, where this is
considered a socially desirable policy, but also
by deploying fiscal, monetary, and price policy
instruments, by planning and carrying out large
public investment projects, and in some cases by
managing major industrial and commercial enterprises.
    Classical administrative concepts and methods
are most appropriate and most transferable to de-

veloping countries in the construction and management of major public works and business enterprises.
In ports, highways, telecommunications systems,
electric power installations, and public sector
industries — where technology largely determines
behavior and makes it reasonably predictable, where
there is broad consensus on goals and means — where,
in effect, efficiency concerns are dominant — modified versions of Western management technologies
apply. The problem is to determine through observation and experimentation what modifications are
necessary in any country to adapt rationalistic
managerial technologies in procurement, scheduling,
production, costing, and quality control to local
conditions.

2. Modernizing elites are attempting to foster
behavioral changes among groups of citizens — to
induce farmers to use fertilizers, to persuade
rural women to practice birth control, to provide
incentives for manufacturers to produce for export, to encourage teachers to revise classroom
methods. Promoting social change brings agents
of government into different patterns of relationship with clientele groups than were comtemplated
by classical Western administrative theory. The
latter implied the delivery of clearly defined
services through fixed, impersonal procedures to
essentially passive clienteles. In developing
countries there may be no significant societal
demand for certain services because of ignorance,
distrust, or the disincentives of existing institutions. Clients must be made aware of new opportunities and convinced of the benefits of changing
their behavior in order to employ new technologies
such as miracle seeds and programmed learning, or
to use new public services such as irrigation and
family planning, or to invest their energies or
funds in developmental activities such as marketing cooperatives or new professional societies.
Often citizens must be organized in order to participate in public services and to interact ef-

fectively with administration. This kind of involvement with clients cannot be accomplished by the formal, rule-bound, command procedures of classical bureaucracy. It requires the initiation of dialogue with clients; and because of uncertainty about the methods that are likely to be effective with specific client groups, no standard packages of services can be offered. Administrators with general goals in mind must be prepared to experiment with different patterns of services and methods of delivery, to learn from experience and feedback from clients, and to adapt their activities until they begin to see results.

This style of administration involves changes both within bureaucracy — away from hierarchical command and toward patterns that permit greater initiative and discretion at operating levels — and in relationships between administrators and clients — requiring greater involvement of clients in shaping programs of action that accommodate the objectives of government to clientele needs. In the assistance and guidance role, the administrator is a teacher, experimenter, and negotiator as well as a technician. These new patterns of interaction with clients are a hallmark of development administration, a relationship that was not contemplated in the highly structured, efficiency-oriented models of Western administration.

3. The pervasiveness of social conflict in developing countries and the weak institutions and procedures for mediating conflict place these polities in constant jeopardy. Economic growth and political development tend to generate conflicts among social, economic, regional, and ethnic groups faster than they produce methods and institutions for conflict management. In the allocation of resources, both financial and symbolic, and in the distribution of the costs and benefits of public policies, administrators must calculate the implications for ethnic, regional, class, and generational conflict. Policies and actions of govern-

14

ment must be oriented to the need to avert and regulate conflict, even at some cost to other objectives, such as economic growth and instrumental efficiency. Government energies must be invested in
anticipating and diverting destructive conflict by
policy measures, new structures, negotiation, and
the deployment, when necessary, of sufficient force.
This political function is one which contemporary
development administrators cannot avoid, though the
classical Western administrative doctrine makes
scant provision for it.

4. Most of the social and technological innovations and reforms which accompany modernization
must be deliberately induced and must be based in
organizations.[4] These organizations, intended to
produce changes in the society to which they belong,
combine diverse skills, foster and protect innovative practices or patterns of behavior, and
guide their acceptance by other organizations and
groups which must incorporate these changes into
their ongoing activities. Whether the innovation
be program budgeting, development banking, family
planning, or service-oriented agricultural education — examples of the dozens of new technologies
and new patterns of interpersonal and intergroup
relations that must be incorporated into new or
existing organizations — the organization must become technically viable, its staff must be committed to the innovations, and its leadership must
manage relations with complementary organizations
until the latter accept and use the innovations,
to which they may originally have been indifferent
or even hostile. Thus, a new service-oriented
school of agriculture is becoming an institution
when it is able to do a competent job of teaching
and research, when its graduates are readily accepted by the government's department of agriculture,
and when adequate funds are available because its
clients — the department and farm organization —
support its requests for appropriations. The limited organizational capabilities of most modernizing

15

countries mean that much of the initiative, planning, support, and actual guidance of developmental institutions must come from public administrators.

These functions of modern development administration — innovation, experimentation, active intervention in the economy, major involvement with clients, building new capabilities, and conflict-management activities — cannot be accommodated within the norms of classical Western models of administration. This does not mean that the classical norms are irrelevant for some classes of activities — as we have indicated — but that a different emphasis is required to make them responsive to needs that were not contemplated in Western theory.

New Norms for
Development
Administration

Let me suggest what some of these new emphases ought to be.

1. Performance tests. To abandon rule of law as a normative ideal would have dangerous consequences, exposing senior officials to loss of control over subordinates and the public to arbitrary, abusive, even predatory official behavior. Indeed, for many government activities, routine, equity, and predictability are highly desirable. Yet if rule of law is equated with rule of precedent and absolute predictability in the distribution of governmental services, little innovation and only very sluggish adaptation to clientele needs will occur. Thus, administrative doctrine must justify and encourage a larger measure of official discretion. How to balance discretion with accountability is a very old administrative problem, but too heavy a burden of accountability inevitably stifles innovation. Incentive systems for administrators operating in areas of development should

be adjusted to foster and reward experimental innovation in implementing public policies and programs.
Accountability must be adjusted to emphasize performance rather than procedures; it must overcome
the goal-displacement effect of the classical interpretation of rule of law, which emphasizes literal
conformity to regulations over substantive performance.

2. Programmatic commitment. The rigid separation of political and administrative roles embodied in Western administrative doctrine, and the
derivative proposition that administrators are
controlled instruments of a political elite who
implement the latter's decisions, does not provide
effective guidance within prevailing conditions in
many developing countries. As we have already observed, the distinctions in roles and even in personalities between politicians and administrators
have become blurred. The doctrine of political
neutrality is meant for situations in which competing political parties or factions alternate in
office. It protects the security of the career
official and guarantees expertise, impartiality,
and continuity in the public services. The price
is often a bland, cautious style of administration.
While democratic governments tolerate this convention — though not without strain — as the price of
orderly administration in a competitive political
system, it is unconvincing to the authoritarian
regimes which populate most developing countries
and are likely to do so for the indefinite future.
These elites demand commitment by administrators
to their regime; the more modernizing ones also
demand commitment to their developmental goals and
programs. If these forms of commitment are to
transcend formal verbalization, they must be tied
to incentive systems which reward and protect developmental effort and performance above caution, time-
serving, and rigid adherence to rules.

3. Flexible, task-oriented structures. Hierarchy, the form of organization implicit in Western

administrative theory, facilitates functional specialization, precise definition and compartmentali-
zation of responsibilities, authoritarian patterns
of supervision and control, and a premium on service to headquarters rather than to clients. It
inhibits the integration of specialized services,
flexibility in the development of staff, and orientation to clientele needs — which are structural
requirements of development administration. Experimentation with new organizational forms which flat-
ten hierarchical controls, integrate services at
the level of clients, increase relative rewards
for service in the field, and organize by project
or multi-professional task force are needed to
loosen the rigidities of the functionally specialized hierarchical structures which dominate administration in developing countries. The risk may
be some loss in consistency, equity, and managerial
control in action programs. The much more important
benefit could be the release of energies for action
and greater responsiveness to clientele needs.
Given the pervasive lack of trust in many poverty
cultures, and the threat of new patterns to existing hierarchical and specialist structures, the
shaping of innovative, flexible forms of organization will not be easy to achieve.

    4. Western administrative theory has regarded
clients as more or less passive recipients of administrative action, the services to be provided
having been determined by law. The duty of administrators is to insure consistency and impartiality
in the allocation of services. This may be satisfactory for services which are readily appreciated
by the public and require little behavioral adaptation on their part. It is not adequate where the
objective is to induce clients to change their behavior. Development administration requires active
flows of information from clients to administrators
and the modification of programmatic content and
procedure in the light of new information. In developing countries, the social distance between

officials and clients must be reduced if services which the regime wishes the public to accept and the behavioral changes which they hope to achieve are to be effective. Clients must be consulted and even brought into administrative roles, a shift on the part of clients from passive to more active roles in their relations with government and administration.

It is not sufficient that administrators be trained to improve their performance or that management systems be strengthened — important as these are. The various publics must be helped to use public services more productively. This includes the development of capacities to identify problems, provide feedback, and pressure administrators: in sum, to develop the confidence that enables them to interact more effectively with officials. This emphasis on the activation of clients will be a major concern of development administration in the 1970's. It will require a breakaway from the authoritarian posture of traditional administration. The new administrative role will be tutelary, an effort to persuade or induce clients to adopt new ways of behavior, in exchange for which the administration has public benefits to confer or sanctions to impose. But this form of persuasion requires the give-and-take of dialogue and bargaining discussed above, and thus revision in the relative status of administrators and clients. Moreover, much development administration deals with areas of great uncertainty where clients' responses to new technologies, policy instruments, or public services are unpredictable. In such major problem areas administrators must experiment, frequently by organizing clients and by involving them directly in the experiments, thus achieving the informational feedbacks, program adjustments, and even forms of self-help that previously were not forthcoming. How to develop these new patterns of relationship between administrators and clients is one of the most urgent research problems confronting developmental social science.

5. The primacy of programmatic outputs. The emphasis on instrumental efficiency in Western administrative doctrine is misplaced in the context of development administration. Clearly, the emphasis must shift from process to product, from efficiency to effectiveness, from staff services to line operations, and from the internal problems of the organization to the needs of clients. Administrative means are instruments to achieve policy ends, not ends in themselves; and efficiency in the use of means is but one of many values associated with public policy. Preoccupation with efficiency, like preoccupation with rules and precedents, is a form of goal displacement which effectively subordinates what should be the primary concern of public administrators: the outputs of governmental action. Development administration shifts its focus decisively toward outputs.

Outputs, however, must be conceived as more than the autonomous products of specialized, professionalized departments. They should be the combined and synchronized contributions of several specialized agencies — public and private, national and local, as the situation requires — on behalf of the needs of client groups as defined by public policy. This is the meaning of "systems programming".[5] It would imply, in the case of farmers, the coordinated delivery of extension, fertilizer, credit, irrigation, marketing, and transportation services to implement a policy of rural development. It might require innovation in the organization and activation of clients as well as in administrative structures and procedures. In this systems context, a new emphasis on outputs can have a genuinely developmental meaning.

The Intelligent
Statesman's Guide to
Development
Administration

How can these new norms of development administration be applied in modernizing countries? Bear
in mind the diversity and complexity of problems
that make generalized prescriptions hazardous, as
well as the tenacious institutionalization of many
conservative behavior patterns among administrators
in all countries. One thing is clear: it is nonsense to denigrate public administration and administrative instrumentalities because of the purported dysfunctions of bureaucracy, its alleged
tendency to frustrate democratic development, or
the impossibility of improving administrative performance in the absence of fundamental cultural
change. As guides to statesmen and men of action,
these prescriptions are inoperable and, in my
judgment, as false as they are futile. Developmental changes of the scope required must be guided,
resources must be allocated and managed, services
must be "delivered" to clients on a large scale.
Public administrative agencies are a major resource
available to governments for the performance of
these indispensable tasks. But because problems
are many, while resources, knowledge, and capabilities of all kinds are few, and demands nearly inexhaustible, the prudent statesman will do the
following:
  1. Attempt to utilize a variety of instrumentalities in the pursuit of public objectives — meaning that structures in addition to national public
bureaucracy should be mobilized to carry out public
developmental programs, even when government must
pay some price in reduced control or in operational
efficiency to secure this participation. Because
bureaucracy has plural features, the statesman can
often choose among alternatives for the management
of new action programs, selecting those that seem
most amenable to the innovations required.

2. Keep administrative procedures simple and
enhance discretion at the operating level in order
to facilitate action — at some risk that fewer detailed regulations may weaken the control of seniors
over operating personnel and even compromise formal
equity among clients. But increased administrative
discretion, if accompanied by better informational
reporting systems oriented to performance rather
than to procedures, could actually provide more
effective control as well as more expeditious responsive action.

3. Invest heavily in the continuing education
and training of public administrators, both gener-
alists and program specialists and at all levels
of service. Such training should include the following elements:

a. The substantive programmatic as well as the
managerial elements of public administration; the
neglect of substantive content — fiscal policy,
regional development, agriculture, education — has
clearly been one of the critical deficiencies in
Western-inspired education and training in public
administration,

b. The political, conflict-management, social
change, and program experimentation roles and skills
of development administrators,

c. Explicit concern with values and public
goals, since strong consensus and commitment to common values, in this case developmental values, can
effectively substitute for formal bureaucratic discipline and thus permit substantial discretion for
program administrators with little loss of effective
control.

Administrators should be brought into training
situations frequently. Especially for senior officials, these experiences should involve in joint experiences not only bureaucrats but also politicians
and other influentials as well as representatives of
client groups.

4. Facilitate the integration of the activities
of specialist personnel at all government levels —
headquarters, the project, and the field. Senior

22

administrators should be explicitly responsible for this. Interprofessional teams of functional specialists should modify, and in some cases supersede, the specialist hierarchies in order to counteract the professional parochialism and control-mindedness of the latter and to focus on the specific needs of developmental projects, communities, regions, or clientele groups. New structures — ad hoc teams, special agencies for specific developmental purposes, coordinating councils focused on the needs of particular clients or areas — should be improvised freely but in all cases should be invested with sufficient financial, technical, and leadership resources to insure their independence of the established specialist hierarchies. These structures should explicitly facilitate "system programming," the mobilization in appropriate sequences of all the specialist contributions required to achieve substantive programmatic outcomes.

5. Reinforce these nonhierarchical structures, especially at the project and field levels, and encourage programmatic experimentation and innovation by co-opting public representatives in consultative roles. In some cases such representatives might even participate directly in allocative decisions. Two cautions are in order here. First, the romance of "participation" should not lead administrators to expect that the results will be painless either to themselves or to citizens. Participation will generate conflict. It will make more work for officials, but hopefully it will improve the relevance and the effectiveness of developmental public services. Second, clientele participation does *not* mean that governments or their administrative agents lose control of action programs or that they merely respond to clientele pressure. Often administrators themselves must promote new services, induce new patterns of clientele response, and even restrain and discipline public demands. Participation does imply shifts in administration from an authoritarian to a more

tutelary role that involves continuous interaction
between administrators and better-organized, more
active clients. Both parties also must willingly
learn, from experience and experimentation, which
combinations of public resources and clientele action are likely to achieve mutually desired developmental results.

6. Improve information management with emphasis
on (a) generating new information through pilot
projects and programmatic experimentation, (b) short-
ening channels of information and speeding its flow
by removing hierarchic organizational structures,
and (c) strengthening the capacity of administration to analyze new information and feed it back
into action programs through policy and programmatic modification. The development of this capability, which should go far toward reducing the
vacuum of information which so frequently confounds
elites in their well-meaning attempts to promote
developmental objectives, will require major reform
and institution-building effort. For the latter,
new structures must be built, qualified social
scientists developed, and a major innovation — the
use of social science research to influence government policy and action programs — must be accepted
by administrators and politicians. The benefits of
program-oriented, applied social research institutions can be very great in informing programmatic
action where rapid change and great uncertainty prevail. Earlier technical assistance sponsored impressive efforts to build administrative training,
developmental planning, and higher educational institutions. The complementary need to build policy
research and program evaluation capabilities linked
directly to operating programs should be high on
any list of new priorities for the 1970's.

Individually, any one of these proposals would
have limited impact on the administrative capabilities and the performance of governments in modernizing countries. Together they produce a pattern,
a gestalt, which departs sharply from the spirit of

24

classical Western administrative doctrine as transmitted to less industrialized nations by colonial experience and foreign aid. I suspect that the administrative doctrines that emerge from the developmental experience of countries now modernizing will incorporate such concepts as these because they respond, more than do inherited Western doctrines, to actual needs.

NOTES

1. For the meaning of "development administration" see Irving Swerdlow, ed., *Development Administration: Concepts and Problems* (Syracuse: Syracuse University Press, 1963); John D. Montgomery and William Siffin, eds., *Approaches to Development: Politics, Administration and Change* (New York: McGraw-Hill, 1966); Edward W. Weidner, Washington, D.C.: American Society for Public Administration "The Scope and Tasks of Development Administration: Recapitulation of Variations on a Theme," in *Meeting the Administrative Needs of Developing Countries* (American Society for Public Administration, 1967).

2. There is a large body of literature which treats the classical doctrine of European and North American public administration. An excellent summary, with a good selected bibliography, is Fritz Morstein Marx, *The Administrative State: An Introduction to Bureaucracy* (Chicago: University of Chicago Press, 1957), pp. 188-193.

3. For a good compendium of social science contributions to administrative thought, see Bertram Gross, *The Managing of Organizations* (New York: Free Press, 1965). Many influential lines of ad-

25

ministrative thought since World War II, including the human relations — e.g., Warren Bennis, *Changing Organizations* (New York: McGraw-Hill, 1966)— and decision-making — e.g., Herbert Simon, *Administrative Behavior: A Study of Decision Making Processes in Administrative Organizations* (New York: Macmillan, 1957) — schools, still focus on the organization and its internal functioning rather than on its outputs and environmental relations; thus they contribute little to development administration. The writings of Max Weber, which have exerted so strong an influence on academic organization theory, had little effect on "classical" public administration doctrine, though his rational-legal model was fully consistent with that stream of doctrine.

4. For a brief statement of institution-building doctrine, see Milton J. Esman and Hans C. Blaise, "Institution Building Research, the Guiding Concepts" (Interuniversity Research Program in Institution Building, University of Pittsburgh, 1966). (Mimeographed.)

5. See Milton J. Esman and John D. Montgomery, "Systems Approaches to Technical Cooperation: The Role of Development Administration," *Public Administration Review* (Sept.-Oct., 1969), pp. 507-539.

Development Administration
and Structures of
Vulnerability

by Denis A. Goulet

Vulnerability: The Key
to Understanding
Development

Underdevelopment is not simply the lack of "development" or a lag in achieving industrial strength,
productive agriculture, or general literacy. Historically, it is the by-product of development itself. Inequalities have always existed among national or regional economic units, but a radical
cleavage was introduced when "the Industrial Revolution of Western capitalist economies not only
accentuated the spread and aggravated the lag, but
actually propelled industrial economies, on the
one hand, and non-industrialized economies on the
other, into divergent paths."[1] The very logic of
the Industrial Revolution led dynamic societies to
establish new kinds of economic relations with non-
industrial nations. Although powerful nations in
the past had imposed unequal exchange systems on
weaker neighbors, or even engaged in outright pil-
lage, their impact on the internal economic structures of dominated countries had been slight.

Pioneer industrial powers, on the contrary, created "partners" whom they needed as suppliers of raw materials and as outlets for finished products. The dominant economy altered the structure of the weaker partner so that the latter might play the dual role of supplier and demander now required for the progress of the stronger partner. As a modern sector was created and traditional economies were disrupted, indigenous "development" was blocked. Not that development would necessarily have taken place had the stronger economy not been present, or that industrial powers deliberately thwarted development plans formulated by the weaker partners. Such plans obviously never existed. Rather, historical forces operated of their own accord to perpetuate the "backwardness" of one partner in the very process of contributing to the "progress" of the other.

Moreover, the modern sector has not served, in non-industrialized countries, to diffuse progress throughout the economic matrix. Instead, it has acted primarily as a way station for flows originating and terminating in other economic centers.[2] Normally, an economy develops under the dynamic influence of leading sectors. But in underdeveloped economies the modern nucleus does not propagate innovations;[3] it simply protects the favored position of interests lying outside native economic circuits. In non-industrialized nations, industrial gains are associated with economic exploitation, political domination, or military intervention. Mechanical inventions may evoke images of forced labor, mechanized agriculture, or the expropriation of native lands by foreigners.[4] Not surprisingly, therefore, psychological or behavioral resistance to "modernization" appears.

Mass demonstration effects, the diffusion of new "myths" (such as a better life for all), and the breakdown of old colonial hegemonies all contribute to growth in consciousness. A new generation of nationalists mobilizes people from former

colonies to regard "normal" economic situations as
abnormal and exploitative. And within underdeveloped countries, opinion is alerted to the "internal
colonialism" governing relations between privileged
and deprived classes or regions.[5] Improved communication assures universal diffusion of the objects,
symbols, and images of a "better life." Gradually,
the awareness of the masses is transformed. They
now perceive their state as one of "underdevelopment"; this perception quickly leads to reaction,
at times to aggressiveness. Occasionally, the
dynamism goes to the limits and produces rebellion.[6]
The imagery used by revolutionary mobilizers is a
sharply honed expression of sentiments shared by
the Third World as a whole. Once they become conscious of the meaning of their deprived situation,
masses throughout the world start thinking in explicitly political terms. This happens even when
cultural mobilization does not aim at awakening a
violent "revolutionary" consciousness.

One example of such effort is the "pedagogy of
the oppressed" employed by Paulo Freire, first in
Northeast Brazil and, after 1964, in rural Chile.[7]
Through adult literacy programs or community projects,
Freire helps pre-conscious groups become aware of
who they are and what their situation is. In so
doing he leads them to discover their human dignity.
Soon the people themselves conclude that their situation is an affront to their humanity. They begin
to understand that their condition is not dictated
by gods, by fate, or by natural laws. On the contrary, it is the product of reversible human arrangements. As they discover who they are, peasants,
urban slum dwellers, simple fishermen, artisans,
housewives, and other "little" folk reflect, often
with a sense of awe, on their own "cultural" achievements. They know how to make tools to tame nature,
and instruments to exercise mastery over animals:
slingshots and arrows for hunting or nets for fishing. Gradually, it "dawns upon them" (in a strict
literal sense, for a new sun appears on the horizon

of their consciousness) that (1) they are themselves cultural agents, (2) that cultural tools
can be used to harness living beings to serve the
needs of others, and (3) that men in society are
also capable of forging cultural instruments to
control other men.

It is but a small step to discovering that
mastery over language (especially in its written
form), over technology and administrative practices are instruments which some men can use to
control other men.[8] As they reason from their
own experience, which Freire illustrates with
slides and film strips, peasants conclude that
inequalities of wealth, status, and power are
not a natural or a divine, but merely a human
phenomenon. They can be examined, criticized, or
opposed without sacrilege. This awakening to the
universality of culture and to its human origins
is the crucial ingredient in the capacity for
change. Before reaching this point, men who live
in conditions of material underdevelopment are
aware of their poverty, of the misery and hope-
lessness in their lives. They may even be conscious of the wealth of others, of rich men's
greater range of choices in life and lesser fragility in the face of disease, natural catastrophe,
or social struggle. But only after critical consciousness emerges do the poor clearly grasp that:
    1. Their own state is one of underdevelopment,
below what it ought to be and what it can be,
    2. Their relative condition vis-à-vis others
can be changed,
    3. They can themselves become agents of that
change.
    They now experience their condition as vulner-
ability in the face of death, disease, hunger, and
the quest for dignity and freedom. Nor is this
awareness confined to localities where outside catalysts elicit new perceptions. On the contrary, the
"shock of underdevelopment" is experienced throughout the Third World.

At Bandung, Third World spokesmen asserted their right to make history and to share in the technological mastery over the universe. But the Bandung Declaration must be interpreted in the light of the U.N.C.T.A.D. conferences held in Geneva (1964) and New Delhi (1968).[9] Here Third World nations bear public witness to their vulnerability. For them, underdevelopment is not mainly poverty, unsatisfied wants, or lack of opportunities. Above all else, it is powerlessness in the face of destiny, of nature, of a machine age, of scientific technology, of more advanced countries, of far-reaching changes they cannot control, of processes they do not even understand. Whereas developed countries possess the knowledge, wealth, and experience which enable them to face problems with confidence, underdeveloped societies feel exposed to forces they cannot understand or control. This impotence is due to six convergent facts:

1. No society is safe from disruptive demonstration effects: old systems are challenged by an image of the good life which tampers with mechanisms of desire and urges people to desire more goods,

2. Only advanced societies possess the knowledge and wealth needed by "backward" ones to meet their own new material aspirations,

3. In the process of gaining new aspirations, nondeveloped societies also create for themselves proud desires for cultural identity,

4. This search for cultural identity is frustrated by the paternalistic structures within which knowledge and wealth are transferred from developed to nondeveloped groups,

5. Hence, the Third World's efforts to develop face a contradiction. The fastest and most efficient way to achieve material progress and technological organization is to pursue development on the rich world's terms. To do so, however, is to betray one's newly discovered social identity. In effect, it is to cooperate in the restoration, in

31

a new mode, of the demeaning relationships characteristic of colonialism. Were the Third World to
accept financial or technical assistance without
imposing its conditions, and were it to model its
cultural patterns on the dominant images, it would
repeat the gestures of native upper classes in
colonies. These classes felt or simulated shame
of their own culture; by aping the values of the
colonizers, they gained entry into the "respectable"
world of those with money, power, and "culture."
Culture, of course, was defined ethnocentrically
in accord with the dominant whims and styles of the
occupiers.

6. At present, however, authentic leaders in
poor countries will not consent to having the rich
world "domesticate" their own development efforts.

To illustrate, Kenya's development planners
formally insist on the "need to avoid making development in Kenya dependent on a satellite relationship with any country or group of countries. Such
a relationship is abhorrent and a violation of the
political and economic independence so close to the
hearts of the people."[10]

Africans have grown wary of gifts and show no
enthusiasm for receiving even "development" on a
platter. They want to achieve it by their own efforts. But this may be impossible so long as richer
nations set the ground rules governing the transfer of wealth and technology. The rich enjoy excessive bargaining strength and will not allow
underdeveloped nations to achieve development on
terms which challenge their technological dominance.
In the final analysis, it is not development which
the rich world wants to keep to itself; on the contrary, it is quite eager to share — in an orderly
way — the fruits of economic advancement. But it
is unwilling to relinquish control over the world's
major social forces. Therefore, Third World nations
are increasingly frustrated by their vulnerability
in the face of strong partners. In simple terms,
their quest for development is symbolized by two

objectives: bread plus dignity. At present, however,
they are largely prevented from gaining dignity as
they search for bread.

The degree of leverage held by governments within underdeveloped countries is narrowed by the political interests of the great powers — and sometimes by the not-so-great powers.[11] Native development efforts will be approved only if they do not
threaten the investments or ideological interests
of rich countries which hold effective veto powers
over internal policies. Economic weakness compounds
the political fragility of such countries. Whatever its wishes, for instance, Senegal is so dependent on French purchases of its peanut crop that it
must sacrifice some measure of economic independence
to economic development. Doubtless it is possible
for a country to walk resolutely along the path of
self-reliance (Tanzania) or refuse proffered aid
(as did Sukarno while President of Indonesia) from
rich countries in order to pursue other goals. But
such attitudes are difficult to maintain over long
periods, and they exact a high price.

Culturally, no less than politically and economically, underdevelopment is an experience of vulnerability. The values of many societies are being
destroyed because they are judged incompatible with
"modern" demands such as productivity, efficiency,
and impersonal merit systems. But a group without
a past is a group without a future. Every society
needs to have its values and its history respected
if it is to face an uncertain future with confidence
in its own ability to control that future. The
effort to make people "modern" is destructive if it
uncritically assumes that efficiency and technological sophistication are superior to the values they
supplant. This is not to plead for maintaining
poor hygiene or superstition on grounds that it is
picturesque, much less that it is ancient or "traditional". Any "folkloric" viewpoint on values is
worthless. On the other hand, poor societies are
now subjected to the domination of a technoculture

which brands their cherished self-images as puerile
and obsolete. The resulting vulnerability in the
face of "contemporary" cultures becomes traumatic
for elites quite as much as for the general populace. It often induces in leaders a deep schizophrenic tension between proud self-affirmation of
their own values and rejection of the old culture,
seen as an obstacle to technological progress.
More pervasively than in eras of overt colonialism,
when metropolitan educational systems were deemed
superior to native ones, today's cultural media
cast doubt on the worth of all cultural values
other than those exported en masse by the purveyors
of progress. It is because the fruits of progress —
lower death rates, better food and housing — are
genuine goods that the problem exists at all. The
solution, therefore, is not to reject modernization
or its authentic benefits. What is needed is dis-
cernment in the choice of impact strategies for inducing change. Strategies now in vogue cause
severe cultural trauma; to correct this blindness
one must begin to view underdevelopment as cultural,
economic, and political vulnerability. Vulnerability is not felt merely at local levels, as when
change impinges on individuals or primary groups.
Rather, the total structures of societies, through
changes going on in their component parts and in
relations among them, are affected.

On all fronts — economic, political, psychological — choices made by underdeveloped countries
become comprehensible only if seen as attempts to
minimize their vulnerable positions vis-a-vis more
powerful antagonists. Policies which seem irration-
al can be explained by the need societies feel to
protect a fragile cultural or political identity.

Vulnerability, in short, is not a purely individual category applicable only at the interpersonal psychological level and not to wider societal
levels. On the contrary, spokesmen from underdeveloped nations testify to their sense of vulnerability before the pressures of the world's powerful

military, trade, and cultural partners. This is
why change strategies must minimize vulnerability.[12]
Administrative agencies in particular must eliminate
coercion and elitism in their dealings with underdeveloped populations.

Two Administrative
Problems: Coercion
and Elitism

   A former World Bank official writes that in
rural Africa it is "difficult to provide administration that will give the farmer adequate incentive."[13] Incentives are indeed directly linked to
the vulnerability structures just discussed and
raise questions about coercion and elitism in
administrative behavior.

Problem No. 1: Are
Administrative Contacts
Coercive?

   African bureaucracies are, to a large extent,
premodern, non-traditional legacies imposed on
native social structures. Whether a specific
bureaucracy is itself ancient, a mere vestige of
colonial days, or something completely new, it is
now expected, qua bureaucracy, to serve as a channel through which flow the stimuli which governments use to provoke development. Consequently,
how a populace views its dealings with bureaucracies
matters greatly. What must be avoided is the perception of relationships as coercive or arbitrary.
Of course, the best way to change the perception
is to alter the reality upon which it is based.
And in real life, administrations are often coercive
or incomprehensible. Even in ideal circumstances,
administrators do not share the vulnerability of
the administered. And their logic is sharply at
odds with the rationality their subjects adopt for
purposes of survival.

Oscar Lewis has observed among the poor "a hostility to the basic institutions of what are regarded as the dominant classes. There is hatred of the police, mistrust of government and of those in high positions."[14] According to another writer, "For most of us the government of city or province or nation is represented by the policeman and the tax-collector. It is the means of repressing the individuality of the citizen."[15] Underdeveloped individuals and entire communities enter into contact with modern sectors of life largely through institutions which operate on them coercively: compulsory military service, mandatory school attendance, police controls, documentary requirements, and tax impositions. Not all administrative agencies, it is true, wear coercive garb; yet even those which do not, behave in ways incomprehensible to marginal underdeveloped people. Punctuality and impersonality, for instance, conflict with the subjects' own attitudes toward time and with their rules of social interaction. But just as "the Sabbath was made for man, not man for the Sabbath," so administrations exist to serve the administered, not the reverse. If this be so, we may do well to redefine desirable standards of administrative efficiency. We might also, with Albert Waterston, ask "Public Administration for what?"[16] or modify the question to read: Administration for Whom?

The answer is administration for vulnerable people. Accordingly, the operating procedures of administrations must reduce rather than reinforce vulnerability if reciprocity is to become possible. The yardstick of legitimacy is not the ability to impose from above but the commitment to elicit consent from below.

There is no way of reversing the coercive or arbitrary images displayed by administrations to their underdeveloped subjects unless theorists take seriously the analysis of vulnerability just outlined. What is discouraging in this regard is that many scholars simply assume the inevitability of superordinate/subordinate relationships between agencies and subjects. Eldersveld's remarks are typical: "The requirement is an aspiration pattern and action pattern which is utilitarian, pragmatic, and consistent with elite aspirations and actions."[17] Vulnerability, we must insist, is not confined to interpersonal relations or small-group interaction; its importance for development lies in institutional realms. In 1968 a six-week conference was held under the joint auspices of M.I.T.'s Center for International Studies and the U.S. Agency for International Development to explore the implications of Title IX of the Foreign Assistance Act of 1966, which recommends "maximum participation in the task of economic development on the part of the people of the developing countries" (Section 281a). The assembled experts reported that although the United States had little success in solving its own urban problems, this fact "should not lead Americans to stay out of this area in the Third World. Quite the contrary, for it offers a unique opportunity. In most fields of endeavor, the undoubted technological superiority of Americans has a stifling and discouraging effect on their host country counterparts. In the area of urban problems, however, we have a rare chance to share ideas and information on a basis of equality."[18] I find it commendable that developers should aspire after mutuality, but why do they assume that mutuality is possible only when technological superiority is absent? It is my contention that all technological superiority is purely relative and that all exchange relationships must be redesigned to foster reciprocity. Mutual vulnerability should prevail universally, especially for administrations in underdeveloped lands.

Clearly, administrators possess more "modern" knowledge than their subjects. In many specialized fields, their superiority can stifle and discourage subjects. So as to offset this, administrations must make themselves institutionally vulnerable. Otherwise, there can be no reciprocity with subjects and administrations will continue to be perceived as coercive, because in large measure they will be coercive.

What does it mean, however, for an institution to be vulnerable? At the very least, it means that professionalization cannot be absolutized or hermetic walls erected between administrators and the populace. China's success in mobilizing rural cadres in 1955-56 suggests that even large-scale organization can be subjected to the control of the interested masses.[19] Likewise, strong reaction has set in within the United States against administrative "efficiency" as a criterion for handling poverty programs, urban renewal, or Model City programs. Therefore, it seems wise for underdeveloped countries to seek models of bureaucracy/populace relations not based on impersonal norms of efficiency. Old "ascriptive" patterns have a way of surviving by reasserting themselves in modern dress. Why not make a virtue of necessity and redefine administrative behavior in less developed areas to include many premodern traits to which mainstream theory has assigned bad repute by calling them ascriptive?

The more modern and efficient a bureaucracy is in an underdeveloped area, the more coercive and arbitrary it is likely to be from the vantage point of the administered population. Nevertheless, administrations could become institutionally vulnerable by adapting their operating norms to the survival strategies of the surrounding community. Such creative adaptation is more difficult than simple invention. But it is precisely in such adaptation that true innovation resides. To the extent that the logic of modernity enhances a community's ability to sustain life, to optimize esteem and freedom, it need not be viewed as inimical to traditional logic, which, given the constraints of information processing and technology under which it operates, also seeks to optimize life sustenance, esteem, and freedom. The argument, in summary, is the following:

38

1. Administration contacts with a populace
ought to be based on reciprocity,
2. But reciprocity is impossible if the superior power is viewed as absolute or decisive in the
relationship.
3. Therefore, such differential power must be
treated as purely relative and not decisive.
4. Accordingly, the administrators' image of
their power role vis-à-vis the administered must be
altered and adapted to premodern norms operative
in the popular value system.
5. In practical terms, this may mean subordi-
nating efficiency and impersonal professionalism
to norms usually regarded as incompatible with
them.

This leads us to our second question: How can
administrations foster change in a nonelitist
manner?

Problem No. 2:
Administration —
Elitist or Nonelitist?

Bureaucracies must serve as dynamic change agents
if innovation is to be generalized. Although bureaucracies rarely initiate, they can help diffuse
change. We must, therefore, ask how propagation is
to take place. Indeed, how development is achieved
is no less important that what benefits it brings.
I shall discuss here a single facet of this question,
the desirability of nonelitist modes of diffusion.
Realists cannot ignore the secular debate between
advocates of elitism and populism. At certain
scales and levels of complexity, it seems impossible
to avoid elitism and to make populism work. Although populists of varying shades have always sought
to mitigate elitism in diverse ways, even Bakunin,
an extreme anarchist, concedes:

. . . that a certain kind of discipline, not
automatic but voluntary and thoughtful dis-

cipline, which harmonizes perfectly with the
freedom of individuals, is, and ever will be,
necessary when a great number of individuals,
freely united, undertake any kind of collective work or action.

At this moment of action, in the midst of a
struggle, the roles are naturally distributed
in accordance with everyone's attitudes, evaluated and judged by the whole collective;
some direct and command, while others execute
commands. But no function remains fixed and
petrified, nothing is irrevocably attached to
one person. Hierarchic order and advancement
do not exist, so that the executive of yester-
day may become the subordinate of today. No
one is raised above the others, or, if he does
rise for some time, it is only to drop back at
a later time into his former position, like
the sea wave ever dropping back to the salutary
level of equality.[20]

We find it inconceivable that peasants, taking
their cue from Switzerland's National Ministers, who
take turns in assuming the Presidency of the Con-
federation and each ministerial portfolio, could
run a credit bank or a community development program in rotation. But are there no intermediate
models between elitist administration and Bakunin's
proposal? Certain precautions are doubtless necessary in any effort to optimize popular decision-
making. In an essay, Everett Hagen discusses the
aversion of most men to assume responsibilities.
Most individuals, he writes, wish to participate in
decisions only within the narrow sphere of activity
in which they have had experience or feel competent.
Outside these realms, the need to make decisions
breeds anxiety. In many cases, anxiety is avoided
by transferring responsibility to officials further
up in the hierarchy. If this happens within structures of institutional legitimacy, decisions taken

by leaders are right, not by any operational test but simply because the leader has made them. Consequently, according to Hagen:

> If within any society, say five per cent of the adults of the society find it stimulating and satisfying to exercise their judgment concerning the broader economic, social and political affairs of the country, then there will be individuals scattered throughout the villages, towns, and cities of the country who like to be leaders. They express viewpoints, other voters turn to them, and democracy will work well, and be satisfying even though facing decisions in broad areas makes nineteen persons out of twenty anxious. But if the number of persons who feel stimulus and satisfaction in facing the use of their judgment in broader areas is only, say one-fourth of one per cent rather than five per cent, then an authoritarian social order will seem preferable and right.[21]

Available evidence suggests that no majorities in any society want an active role in decision-making, even when they are informed of possible options. Moreover, by the very nature of his marginal condition, underdeveloped man is powerless to affect his own lot. Yet he does not wish to be a mere consumer of civilization. How does one reconcile this antinomy? Although most people flee responsibility, they want more control over their own destinies. How can we set some optimum level of participation in development decisions? Where does this optimum lie? There are no easy answers to such questions. It helps, however, to reflect that total participation is impossible and that some social settings favor the emergence of genuinely popular elites more than others do. That total participation is impossible is the chief lesson learned from the history of communitar-

ian movements. The difficulties now faced by the
Fokonolona movement in the Malagasy Republic illustrate this point. Fokonolona's concept of vil-
lage-council democracy is based on three principles:
1. All decisions affecting a group must be
taken unanimously,
2. No one can be presumed to agree with a decision unless he signifies his acceptance positively,
3. All abstentions have to be justified or
excused.[22]

Must we conclude, however, from the scant success Fokonolona has had that the only alternative
is administrative decision-making in the elitist
mode? More pertinently, is "optimum" participation merely the identical level dictated by an
elitist division of labor? Must professional bureaucrats inevitably be socially distant from the populace?

Before reaching any conclusion, we must ask the
larger question: What kind of society is desired?
Often the most efficient solution to a problem is
least acceptable on broader social grounds. Thus,
common experience teaches that foreign technicians
can often "get the job done" more quickly than
native personnel if the latter lack required skills.
But this does not lead us to conclude that the best
procedure lies elsewhere, rather than in training
counterparts to assume responsibility for the long-
term success or failure of the enterprise. Wartime
mobilization can no doubt "make the trains run on
time" and lead to a more "efficient" use of scarce
resources. Yet societies rightly shrink from per-
petuating such discipline because values more precious than efficiency are thereby sacrificed. Similarly, excessive reliance on professional elites
thrusts popular commitment below an acceptable
threshold. Too little professionalism, in turn,
breeds indecision, inefficiency, and failure. The
optimum, therefore, will strive to avoid technocratic elitism no less than unproductive populism.

Seymour Merlman's studies in Israel on the relative productivity of industrial plants operated by management experts and of similar plants directed by cooperatives embracing all workers and staff warn us not to conclude prematurely that elitism is inevitable or that alternative strategies are doomed to fail.[23] Rather, it must be insisted that change pedagogies portray development as the multiplication of agents of progress no less than as the mere production of the benefits of progress. Over the long term, anything less than optimum association of a populace with crucial decisions breeds a form of development which thwarts men's pursuit of esteem and freedom from manipulation. Thus, the answer is not to turn administrations over to the people but to restructure them so that many functions usually filled by bureaucratic professionals are placed under the control of their intended beneficiaries. Let me now add a word about so-called "popular" elites.

To assert that "development ought to optimize participation in decision-making" is to imply that the populace at large is the matrix whence the elite emerges. Leaders are not to be "recruited," a term which connotes external rules or outside agents charged with finding and selecting leaders. Any population can "secrete" its elite if properly challenged by change agents who respect its cultural identity. Students of development throughout the world have noted that most groups contain individuals able to grasp the totality of problems affecting their community and to lead their peers in group responses to that challenge. Such "natural" elites are often distinct from formal hierarchical leaders, chieftains or their sons, members of respected classes, elders, and the like. Natural elites are those individuals who understand the social forces which impinge upon them and have some comprehensive synthesis of the deep meaning of proposed changes in terms of the group's values. They are not necessarily technical, political,

social, or entrepreneurial elites, but people who
can discern what is acceptable in the new values
offered; what elements in the old values may enhance their society's quest for better life sustenance, esteem, and freedom; and what practical
margins of decision are open to the group. Such
leaders innovate at the outer boundaries of their
group's existence rationality while remaining
faithful in essentials to the inner limits of that
strategy. Lasswell and Kaplan, when describing
types of rule, speak of democracy as a system wherein popular trust and affection are vested in leaders, and of ethocracy as related to the moral competence people recognize in their leaders.[24] In
the present context, these terms refer not to a
system of rule but to a position of influence over
the motives and responses of a populace. This influence may or may not operate outside frameworks
of formal authority.

Those who emerge in this fashion personify the
deep aspirations, values, interests, and life styles
of their fellows. The group can trust them and
identify with them. For a society, they become the
pedagogues of its change experience. Any impact
strategy of induced change must therefore facilitate
the kinds of encounter with the populace best suit-
ed to generating such leaders. No assumption is
made that national leaders are always present;
nevertheless, the chances of finding them and allowing them to surface must be optimized. Certain
structures are required if these chances are to
exist. A particular model of the relationships between summit planners, regional and sectoral agencies, and local groups is necessary.

In any such model great importance is attached
to the practice of what the French call "animation,"
a coherent set of pedagogical devices calculated
to identify leaders, help them emerge as leaders,
and guide their community on the latter's terms
toward a degree and rate of change which have been
critically examined. If such "animation" is to

44

succeed, suitable administrative structures must be
implanted at every level: national, regional,
local.[25] Unless such a system exists, it may be
impossible to establish reciprocal exchange of information and influence between small groups and
larger units, all the way up to the national society.
Rural "animators" and "stimulus agents" ought to be
trained in settings not too different from their
native habitat. Experience reveals that even two
or three months spent in modern settings can seriously weaken the psychic capacity of potential
village leaders to return to their original sites
with enthusiasm. What must be safeguarded is the
allegiance of an upward-mobile elite to the values
of the popular groups from which they emerge, so
that they do not identify themselves simply with
privileged-class interests after they become influential. It is manifestly impossible to achieve
such an end unless an administrative organization
is based on communitarian conceptions of responsibility.

Democratic theorists have always been ambivalent
about the relationship between the quantitative
criterion employed to choose elite and the qualitative content of their performance once chosen.
The voice of the majority, Sartori explains, has
no meaning apart from the end toward which choice
is ordained: the quality of leadership exercised
by those chosen.[26] Consequently, in the situation
we are describing, the mode of selection may have
less importance than the degree to which the elite,
after emerging, incarnate popular wishes (even unconscious, unstated wishes).

Although natural elites who thus emerge do not
always enjoy ruling positions, it is desirable that
such positions be made accessible to them. This
is one basic dimension of optimum participation in
decision-making. That administrative practices
may well profit from experiments in this direction
is the burden of these pages. As Eisenstadt has
remarked, "Need to foster change often extended the

scope of the activities of bureaucrats beyond their
specific goals, and made them reach into the realm
of family, kinship, and community life of wide stra-
ta of the population."[27]

One model of associating the populace with administrative agencies so as to develop in a nonelitist mode is provided by Robert Caillot, whose
efforts I shall now describe.

A Nonelitist Model for Administrators

French social planner Robert Caillot has devised
a form of "participation survey" which links administrative, political, and voluntary agencies to a
general population in pursuit of local development
goals.[28] The populace helps define the rules governing the very research being made on its needs
and serves as the principal judge of development
actions taken in its behalf. The operation is designed to reduce elitism. To Caillot, it is axiom-
atic:

1. That development problems are not reducible
to any intellectual perception one has of them,

2. That the possession of specialized knowledge
does not confer on planners or technical experts
the right to decide on behalf of allegedly less
knowledgeable men,

3. That, regardless of how expert he is, no
man can possess more than a partial view of reality.

Caillot is never content simply to study or to
measure attitudes and behavior. He conceives of
research on social change as necessarily leading
to action. Hence, the survey of a population's development needs becomes an instrument for providing
culture. The groups studied are stimulated to examine their problems in broad contexts of their
national and regional development. They are, in
the process, initiated into the character of their
civic relationships to other men across the web of

46

multiple affiliations with them. Finally, they are progressively taught how to assume greater responsibility in implementing for themselves all solutions proposed.

A detailed description of the phases of this participation process lies beyond the scope of the present paper. Nonetheless, it is pertinent to list these five phases:[28]

1. The first step is to give a qualitative description of the component structures of development,

2. Next, the geographic dispersion of these structures is presented,

3. Then the structures are analyzed, to a large extent by those who live within them,

4. Fourth, a synthesis of all these elements is made. This effort is undertaken in the presence of all participants,

5. A final phase consists in transforming study groups into action teams.

Several features of this procedure are worth noting. First, this complex enterprise combines study and action. The agenda for study is the whole spectrum of developmental actions which ought to be taken in a village, a region, or a nation. People affected by summit decisions share in drafting action measures. They are given data on demography, economic structures, employment, and investment, lacking which their aspirations remain unrealistic or parochial. Although advanced statistical techniques are utilized at later stages of the process, in the beginning the populace is required to analyze data manually. This constraint occurs because mechanical or electronic treatment may lead the uninitiated into deep pits of undue abstraction..

Another interesting feature is the mutual relationship between formation and information. Information is not sought for its own sake, and action is recommended only when it flows organically from prior studies. A systematic effort is made to wed the experience of those who face problems to the analytical skills of those who conceptualize them. The development adviser's role is to supply broad information to the populace, pose problems, elicit critical reflection and accurate observation, and coordinate numerous multi-disciplinary teams. Besides fostering direct cooperation between experts and people, the method stimulates collaboration among diverse groups within the population. The main objective is to transform study groups into action groups. Yet these action groups are brought into existence through the catalyst of group study conducted by permanent teams of varied composition. Caillot hopes thereby to produce what he calls "organic cells of authentic democracy."

Specific actions contemplated must always contribute to regional development in all spheres of life: the economic, cultural, physical, and political. Summit decisions are controlled by lower-echelon administrators, pedagogues, entrepreneurs, and "little people" who would otherwise be mere "beneficiaries" of development. When successful, the method creates a rich mosaic of dovetailing actions aiming at constant synthesis each time a new sector, a new level, or a new problem is faced. For its author, this form of participant observation survey is a "laboratory *in vivo* for the elaboration and especially for the control of the principles of a humane economy, as well as the privileged instrument of the implementation of those same principles."[29]

The first two phases of the operation are conducted by Caillot's team (trained social scientists or field researchers) with the influential men of the locality. The latter include elected officials, administrative personnel at all levels, and members of voluntary associations ranging from labor unions and credit cooperatives to Boy Scouts, religious organizations, and women's leagues. Only in the third phase is the public associated with the common tasks. To do otherwise, Caillot explains, makes participation lack direction and become unmanageable.

48

Caillot launches discussion in a public debate on the structures latent in specific problems to be faced. Typical problems are land reform, new farm practices, and the implantation of an occupationally or ecologically disruptive industrial unit in the region. Structural characteristics are relevant national (or international, if need by) conjunctures bearing on the issue. To illustrate, a debate about fish prices necessarily entails discussion of wholesale and retail market structures, pertinent legislation and agreements, investment patterns in the fishing industry, the state of research on fish detection, fish processing, substitute foods, new uses, and so on. Local administrators are challenged by the team to justify their organizational practices to the public, in the light of these broad "structural characteristics." Political leaders must do likewise. The populace is urged to reflect critically on all that it hears. Although structural topics are always posed at the outset of discussion periods, specific agendas vary from one situation to another. Nonetheless, they always include basic demographic, ecological, and macro-economic information.

The public responds to the presentation in terms of this focus: What can be done to improve its present condition? After they have debated extensively, they are recruited to draft precise questionnaires and conduct a survey whose aim is to reveal problems and solutions in greater detail and in quantifiable form. By degrees the populace is sensitized to the issues, contraints, and costs involved in alternative solutions to its own problems. As stated earlier, the final goal is to mobilize a populace in the process of studying it. Such a transformation is to be wrought, however, on a populace's own terms. This is why the team never enters a locality, even if it has been invited by government officials or some nongovernmental contracting organization, until a representative cross section of the population has approved the invitation.

Behavioral scientists and developers have long known that any attempt to study or organize a population has profound effects on it.[30] Caillot's originality lies in his formal incorporation of this fact into a strategy for producing social change in a populist mode. His effort interests administrative theorists because it suggests a way of institutionalizing organization responsibility for larger constituencies.

His surveys have been conducted mainly at local and regional levels. Nevertheless, on the basis of experiments in larger regions, such as Swiss cantons, Caillot believes that in principle there is no reason why participation surveys cannot work nationwide. The course taken by the Chinese Cultural Revolution is most instructive in this regard. Quite apart from its ideological or political significance, the Chinese Cultural Revolution casts serious doubt on the widespread assumption that only small numbers of people inhabiting small regions can successfully take part in development decisions.[31]

To underestimate the difficulties involved is obviously foolish and self-defeating. Nevertheless, broad popular participation in administrative activities remains a valid objective, if only because the wishes of the masses are essential inputs into good development choices. Success will remain localized, however, unless national planners pay special attention to two crucial strategies: a coherent regional strategy of poles and zones of influence and what Closon calls a viable "theory of administrative space."[32]

Since it is an instrument of mobilization, Caillot's formula risks being viewed by administrators as marginal to their central concerns. Nothing is further from the truth; Caillot's importance is not peripheral. His work in research needs doing, by imaginative administrative specialists, in the domain of day-to-day administration. His formula is a possible model of new ad-

ministrative behavior. What would the behavior of
development administrators be like if they adopted
nonelitist modes of collaboration, such as those
outlined by Caillot? To this question I can supply
no answer. Answers can come only from innovations
in various field settings by imaginative administrators working jointly with their subjects.

What is relevant for our purpose is to locate
such forward looking praxis in the larger context
that will optimize its chances for success. In
my view, an overall approach should be derived from
development pole theory and be sensitive to the demands of viable administrative space. A word about
the first may cast some light on the questions at
hand.

Development Poles

The most articulate theorist of development
poles is the French economist François Perroux.
Fruitful work has also been done by Lebret, Gerschenk-
ron, and Higgins. Several clarifications are in order before we can understand Perroux's notion of
development poles.

The first is that progressivity of the economy
and economic progress are not equivalent terms. For
Perroux, *"development is the combination of mental
and social changes in a population which render it
apt to cause its real global product to increase in
cumulative and durable fashion."*[33] Hence, it is
possible for global product to increase in aggregate
or even in per capita terms even though a population
and its economy are not thereby placed in "conditions of development." As Perroux puts it, the
"construction of men by men"[34] is decisive. Nevertheless, growth and the transformation of mental-
ities and societies must start at some given point.
At this point, innovations are concentrated; and
from it both progress and progressivity spread.
A development pole is the geographical point or

51

locale at which developmental innovations are concentrated so as to transmit effects which accelerate progressive change and remove impediments to
the "construction of men by men."[35] This is not
the place to describe in concrete terms how a pole
functions.[36] But important to our purposes is that
pole theory provides an exceptionally congenial
larger setting for nonelitist models of development action such as Caillot's.[37] But pole theory
is incomplete apart from a detailed examination of
the geographical zones of influence affected by
poles, as well as of the networks by which scattered poles are best linked to one another. At the
heart of this strategy lies the desire to rationalize structural imbalances resulting from innovations so as to capitalize on the creative tensions
generated by those innovations.

The pole approach supplies the elements needed
for integrating the geographical with the economic
dimensions of a plan. Accordingly, it is the necessary complement to the participatory and consultative strategy described above. Whereas the latter
is designed primarily to meet the psychological,
pedagogical, and political needs of sound planning,
the pole approach tries to link project-making
spatially with these more "humane" intangible goals.

But integral planning is indissociable from
decisions regarding the distribution of responsibility for integration. This raises complex questions,
not only about optimal planning organization but
also about overall administrative schemes; but I
leave it to administrative experts to settle these
monumental questions. My aim has been simply to
evoke one highly suggestive procedure, Robert Caillot's
participation survey.

Conclusion

I have analyzed underdevelopment as structural
vulnerability and have argued that the key to under-

standing development is the powerlessness felt by societies in the face of massive social forces impinging upon them. My main conclusion is that development strategies must aim at assisting a populace to gain rational control over the processes of change that affect its destiny. Such control is more important than obtaining development benefits: economic well-being, institutional modernity, social mobility, or technical efficiency.

After discussing vulnerability, our attention turned to two administrative problems. The first arises because underdeveloped communities are marginal to society's modern sectors. Most contacts between marginals and modern sectors involve administrations. These contacts are usually perceived by marginals themselves to be coercive, incomprehensible, or both. The problem is how to reverse this perception. The solution lies in asking administrative agencies to assume a posture of institutional vulnerability so as to make possible reciprocity with administered subjects. A second problem flows from the role which administrations are destined to play as change agents in transitional societies. The argument was made that administration ought to foster developmental change in a nonelitist mode.

Solutions will come only if new models of administrative behavior are created. An illustration of what such behavior might be was drawn from the strategy employed by French social planner, Robert Caillot, who utilizes the mass participation survey as an instrument of populist mobilization to induce change. Demands made upon local and regional administrators in this method suggest desired patterns of contacts with a populace on a broader front.

NOTES

1. Jacques Freyssinet, *Le Concept du Sous-Développement* (Paris: Mouton, 1966), p. 334.

2. On the workings of the modern nucleus in a nonindustrialized economy, see J. M. Albertini, *Les Mécanismes du Sous-Développement* (Paris: Editions Ouvrieres, 1967), pp. 47-149..

3. The conditions under which progress is diffused have long been studied by François Perroux. A summary of his position may be found in *L'Economie du XX Siècle* (Paris: Presses Universitaires de France, 1964), pp. 123-295, 585-647.

4. See Freyssinet, *loc. cit.*

5. On "internal colonialism," see Pablo Gonzales-Casanova, "Internal Colonialism and National Development," in Irving Louis Horowitz, Josue de Castro, and John Gerassi, eds., *Latin American Radicalism* (New York: Vintage Books, 1969), pp. 118-139.

6. See L. J. Lebret, *Suicide ou Survie de L'Occident* (Paris: Editions Ouvrières, 1958), pp. 141-157.

7. See Paulo Freire, *Educación como Práctica de Libertad* (Caracas: Ediciones Nuevo Orden, 1967), and *The Pedagogy of the Oppressed* (New York: Herder and Herder, 1970).

8. Obviously these are not the only social functions of cultural implements.

9. On this, see Henri Bazin, "De Bandoung à New Delhi, l'Evolution des Rapports entre les Pays

du Tiers-Monde," *Développement et Civilisations*, No. 33 (March, 1968), pp. 13-26.

10. Republic of Kenya, *African Socialism and Its Application to Planning in Kenya* (Nairobi: Government Printer, 1965), p. 8.

11. Witness France's military interference in Gabon in 1966 to protect its interests there by restoring President M'Ba to power after he had been overthrown by a military coup.

12. For a more extensive treatment of the theory of vulnerability, see Denis A. Goulet, *The Cruel Choice, Normative Theory of Development* (New York: Atheneum, 1971).

13. Peter F. M. McLoughlin, "Studying African Agriculture," *Finance and Development,* 1 (June, 1968), 13.

14. Oscar Lewis, "The Culture of Poverty," *Scientific American,* CCXV, 4 (October, 1966), 23.

15. J. H. Hofmeyr, "Civil Service in Ancient Times: The Story of Its Evolution," in Nimrod Raphaeli, ed., *Readings in Comparative Public Administration* (Boston: Allyn & Bacon, 1967), p. 75.

16. Albert Waterston, "Public Administration for What?," *Finance and Development,* IV, 3 (September, 1967), 175-180.

17. S. J. Eldersveld, "Bureaucratic Contact with the Public in India," *Indian Journal of Public Administration,* II, 2 (1965), 217.

18. *The Role of Popular Participation in Development,* David Hapgood, ed., **M.I.T.** Report **No.** 17 (Cambridge, Mass.: M.I.T. Press, 1969), pp. 10, 117.

19. See Thomas P. Bernstein, "Leadership and Mass Mobilization in the Soviet and Chinese Collectivisation Campaigns of 1929-30 and 1955-56; a Comparison," *The China Quarterly* (July-September, 1967), 1-47.

20. G. P. Maximoff, ed., *The Political Philosophy of Bakunin: Scientific Anarchism* (Glencoe, Ill.: The Free Press, 1953), pp. 259-260.

21. Everett E. Hagen, "Are Some Things Valued by all Men?," *Cross Currents*, XVIII, 4 (Fall, 1968), 408.

22. Remarks based on conversations held in November 1967 with Georges Allo, who had recently returned from a visit to the Malagasy Republic. At that time Professor Allo was director of the section on "Values and Civilization" at I.R.F.E.D. (Institut de Recherche et de Formation en Vue du Développement) in Paris.

23. On this, see Seymour Merlman, "Industrial Efficiency Under Managerial vs. Cooperative Decision-Making: A Comparative Study of Manufacturing Enterprises in Israel." The manuscript I have in my possession is undated.

24. Harold D. Lasswell and Abraham Kaplan, *Power and Society* (New Haven: Yale University Press, 1965), p. 210.

25. On this, see L. J. Lebret, *Dynamique Concrète du Développement* (Paris: Editions Ouvrières, 1961), pp. 389-421. See also Roland Colin, "L'Animation, Clef de Voute du Développement," *Développement and Civilisations*, No. 21 (March, 1965), pp. 5-10.

26. Giovanni Sartori, *Democratic Theory* (2nd ed.; New York: Frederick A. Praeger, 1967), p. 104. Also Ernest Gellner, "Democracy and Industrialization," *European Journal of Sociology*, VIII, 1 (1967), 47-50.

27. S. N. Eisenstadt, "Problems of Emerging Bureaucracies in Developing Areas and New States," in Nimrod Raphaeli, ed., *Readings in Comparative Public Administration* (Boston: Allyn and Bacon, 1967), p. 227.

28. See Robert Caillot, "L'Enquête-Participation à Economie et Humanisme," written in 1963 and reprinted in *Cahiers de l'Institut Canadien Education des Adultes*, No. 3 (February, 1967), pp. 121-144. See also his "Une Connaissance Engagée: L'Enquête-Participation," in *Options Humanistes* (Paris: Editions Ouvrières, 1968), pp. 55-80.

29. Caillot, "Une Connaissance Engagée," p. 56.

30. On this, see William L. Kolb, "The Impingement of Moral Values on Sociology," *Social Problems*, II (1954), 66-70.

31. See "Comments by Michael Oksenberg," in *China in Crisis*, Ping-Ti Ho and Tang Tsou, eds., I, Book 2, (Chicago: University of Chicago Press, 1968), pp. 496 ff.

32. An allusion to Closon and a description of what "viable administrative space" would mean in the specific case of France may be found in Jean Labasse, "Vers une Nouvelle Géographie Administrative," *Le Monde* (Paris, September 18, 1958). Professor Labasse has presented his synthesis of human geography, planning, and administrative science in *L'Organisation de l'Espace* (Paris: Hermann, 1966), pp. 16-17.

57

33. François Perroux, *L'Economie du XX Siècle*, p. 155. Italics in Perroux.

34. *Ibid.*, p. 157. Perroux italics.

35. For a more complete exposition of the general theory of development based on the triad "innovation, propagation, and signification," see Perroux, *Cahiers de l'I.S.E.A.* (Institut des Sciences Economiques Appliquées), Series I, Nos. 1, 2, 3 (1957) and Series F, No. 12 (1959); also "La Methode de l'Economie Generalisée et l'Economie de l'Homme," in *Economie et Civilisation*, II (Paris: Editions Ouvrières, 1958); and *La Coexistence Pacifique*, 3 vols. (Paris: Presses Universitaires de France, 1958).

36. Benjamin Higgins has done this in an essay communicated to the author in 1965, "Poles de Croissance, Regional Interactions and National Development." To the best of my knowledge, this essay is unpublished.

37. This congeniality is emphasized by Professor M. Hentgan, a United Nations official, in his mimeographed course entitled "Administration Publique et Développement." This course was presented in the academic year 1962-63 at I.R.F.E.D. (Institut de Recherche et de Formation en Vue du Développement) in Paris. On p. 29 we read, regarding Perroux's theory: "Cette théorie fondée sur les trois facterus d'innovation, de propagation et de signification peut parfaitement, d'une part, appuyer les arguments en faveur de la décentralisation, et, d'autre part, fournir des données de principe de nature à nous éclairer sur les niveaux q'il est opportun ou necessaire de prévoir en vue de l'action la plus efficace." Hentgen expands the point in considerable detail in the pages following this passage.

The Administration of
Economic Growth

by Irving Swerdlow

This paper attempts to integrate three ways of
thinking about development: institution-building,
public administration, and economic growth. These
are not in the same "universe of discourse," in
the sense that they represent three arbitrarily
selected segments of differing levels of general-
ity. They are abstracted from three different
ways of looking at society. If we merely add
them together, we get unrhythmic chaos. It is
as if someone tried to add a mathematical formula,
a modern novel, and a piano concerto. The result
might be interesting, but difficult to understand.[1]
Yet it may be useful to integrate three different
views in examining some of the basic operational
problems of economic growth.

Economic Growth

It is no longer necessary to protest that economic growth is only a part of development. Even
the most casual observer and the most narrow economist have discovered ample evidence of this. Every

aspect of a society becomes heavily involved in development; and the usual litany of political, social, cultural and psychological changes are added to economic changes in describing the development process. The questionable procedure of dividing the study of human behavior into separate "disciplines" is nowhere more clearly demonstrated than in the discussion of the development process. But it has been so divided; and economists have studied one strand or segment, economic growth. Economists have identified many determinants of economic growth, some probably fairly close to reality, and many so abstracted from reality as to be only intellectual curiosities. The ease with which economists simplify some of the problems that their discipline examines by sweeping the difficult problems "under the rug" is recognized even by economists. However, the generalizations about economic growth are useful because they can provide some operating guidelines and necessary constraints on analyzing social processes, as long as they are treated as only part of the total system.

Economic growth, as defined in the context of the development process, is an increase in production and productivity. One of the elements in goals of the development process is the achievement of a more rapid rate of economic growth than has been experienced. How much more rapid, of course, varies from country to country; and the shape of the increase, in terms of its "mix" and distribution, also varies from country to country. But, in this context, economic growth must increase both production and productivity.

Some useful generalizations can be made about economic growth:

a. The production process consists of using scarce resources to create the goods and services that a society wants. In an improvement of this process, technology, the way the scarce factor inputs are combined, is the chief cause of increasing production and productivity.

b. While improved technology can be abstracted
for analysis as an analytical construct, it is in
reality embodied in the labor and capital factor inputs of the production process. Technology is a
real input only as it is incorporated in the human
and physical inputs.

c. There can be no rapid increase in production
and productivity of a society without the improvement of the labor input, which means an improvement
in knowledge, skill, management, and organization,
including public administration.

d. Also required in the overwhelming majority
of situations is an increase in the amount, and an
"improvement" in the type, of physical capital as
an input. This increase in capital is far easier
to observe, measure, and manage than either the increase in technology, as an abstract construct, or
the improvement in the labor input. While the three
— labor input, capital input, and technology — are
functionally related, this relation is neither fixed
nor linear, and varies over time.

e. The increased specialization and differentiation that higher productivity necessarily involves, requires and results in many new ways to
allocate resources, collect the factor inputs, and
distribute the outputs. A longer time is necessarily required between the initiation of production
and final consumption, and more planning and organizational activity is involved.

Institution-Building

Development in a society requires many new institutions and substantial modifications in existing institutions. This premise implies that institutions are behavior patterns, an organized way of
doing something that society wants. The institutions
that are important for development will thus initiate, maintain, and protect those innovations that
are needed for development. The economic institu-

tions, as defined here, are those organizations or
enterprises that are producing the goods and services that a society wants, the so-called economic
activities; and they are also engaged in establishing norms. There are many other definitions of
institutions, and it is appreciated that this is
a somewhat narrow concept. It is meant to be operational, to focus on behavior rather than on the
pre-behavior or post-behavior aspects of social
processes. It is based on the assumption that
most of what is generally included under development
comes from or through organizations and that organizations can be initiated or changed in a way that
will make possible or will speed up the process of
development.[2]

Looking at development as a process of initiating
or modifying institutions is admittedly a special,
partial view. It chips up the whole process, which
is a "seamless web," into arbitrarily selected chunks
and attempts to analyze how the pieces operate.
While there is some opportunity to take into account
such broad categories as individual motivation, value
systems, social psychology, ideology, and similar
individual and group aspects of human emotions,
thinking, and behavior, the institution-building
view of social change is clearly partial and somewhat
mechanical, and tends to emphasize formal structure
and overt behavior. What it is presumed to bring
to the problem of understanding development is an
operational facility, a way of looking at the complex process of development that can provide some
operational guidance. The institution-building
model accepts and urges the feasibility of social
engineering and examines the structure of a changing society with the purpose of manipulating it.
If it has merit, it helps support a "strategy" for
development. The institution-building approach is
based on the feeling that some useful guidance can
be given to those responsible for creating and operating the institutions that make up much of the
development process. The social engineering and administrative bias of this point of view is obvious.

The research program in institution-building has developed some "guiding principles" that researchers have tried to use in studying specific institutions in less developed countries. Two groups of variables or elements that determine the operation of an institution have been identified: institutional variables, which are internal to the institution; and linkage variables, which relate the institution to its environment.

Institutional Variables

1. Leadership — both formal and informal guidance for the institutions, policies and activities.
2. Doctrine — the values, objectives, and operational methods of the institution.
3. Program — the performance of functions, the production of outputs.
4. Resources — the inputs of the institution: human, physical, financial.
5. Internal Structure — the structure and procedures established for the operation and maintenance of the institution.

Linkage Variables

1. Enabling linkages — provide the authority to operate.
2. Functional linkages — indicate the relationship to other institutions whose product and services are needed.
3. Normative linkages — identify the relationship between values and norms which are relevant to the institution.
4. Diffused linkages — describe general relations of impact and image.
The institution-building approach to studying the process of economic growth is useful but limited. The five internal variables and the four environmental linkages form a sort of map that can be used to guide the scrutiny of economic institution-build-

ing. The emphasis on behavior patterns rather than on formal structure is an operational emphasis, helping focus on operations as they are or can be, rather than on some other kinds of models that abstract in a confusing way from reality. The emphasis on operations-within-an-environment-test is ever present and ever influential as a useful corrective to the usual kind of economic analysis, which tends to include environmental influences only as they are reflected in market transactions.

Yet the classifications of internal and external variables seem less than adequate. The internal variables are so functionally related that it is difficult to consider one without considering all. This is expected, but the question becomes one of degree in descriptive and analytical terms at operational levels. Far less useful are the classifications of linkages. It would seem better if the linkages were combined with the institutional variables because, operationally, this is the nature of the relationship.

The viewpoint that social change can be viewed and manipulated through organizations, through patterns of behavior, requires a concept of successful institutionalization. At some point, an institution must be able to achieve acceptance or sufficient operating momentum to be considered as in existence. This is, of course, difficult to measure and to establish by objective criteria. The measurement is not against the objectives of the specific institution but against what general criteria successful establishment involves. Yet some success in attaining its objectives must necessarily be part of the successful establishment of an institution. Such criteria as use of product, survival, support, respect and approval, spread of normative ideas of the institution, and the persistence of innovation have been approved as appropriate measures of institutionalization. While these help define different facets of successful establishment or operation of an institution, they

64

are quite difficult to measure. This difficulty
should be noted, because it forms a part of one
of the major themes advanced by this paper.

Economists, although they differ in their analysis of what makes rapid economic growth (however
defined) possible, unanimously agree that an essential concomitant (either result or cause or both)
is the increasing complexity of economic institutions.
Increasing productivity necessarily requires better
ways of acquiring improved factor inputs. It also
requires more skillful, more complex organization
and management. This means larger economic institutions, whatever the ideology and type of economic
system. This is not to say that economic institutions, particularly their management, are not strongly determined by ideology and by a country's type
of economic system. It merely means that as economic institutions achieve greater production and
productivity, the objective of any rational economic system, they will become larger, more difficult
to administer, and more involved with governmental
controls or influences and environmental setting —
regardless of the national economic system.

Public Administration

The study of the management of organizations,
particularly that of the state, is of ancient vintage. Almost from the beginning, scholars have argued whether there is any substantial difference
between managing public organizations, now called
public administration, and managing simply any organization, now called "management" or "administrative science." As is usual in intellectual
disputes of this type and duration, both sides
are right — depending upon the assumptions or pos-
tulates accepted. This paper need not take a position in this debate, but its emphasis on "public"
administration will be quite evident. However, the
administration, rather than the public, part of the

phrase is emphasized; and the major source of the systematic presentation of current administration concepts is a scholar who believes that public administration is only a special facet of the broad process of the administration of organizations.[3]

Modern studies of administration are said to begin with this century. Frederick Taylor, Henri Fayal, Max Weber, Luther Gulick, and Lyndall Urwick generally head the list of thinkers who viewed administration as a process for which rules and operating principles could be developed. Here was the beginning of "scientific management" and "administrative science," the principles that ultimately led to the famous P.O.S.D.C.O.R.B., the analysis of administrative activities advanced by Gulick: planning, organizing, staffing, directing, coordinating, reporting, and budgeting. During this period of thinking, there evolved the principles of unitary supervision, span of control, functional departmental organization, and delegation of responsibility and authority. These early efforts to develop a series of principles that would help achieve administrative efficiency have been increasingly questioned by scholars in the field. Today, most writers on administration, while generally describing these principles, suggest they are based on untenable themes of human behavior and are operationally wrong, or at least misleading. Modern administrative theories tend to emphasize the human relations elements of organizations, the importance of informal as well as formal structures, communication systems, the importance of understanding the way decisions are made, and the way administrators function in an organization.

The particular analysis used here as representing modern administrative analysis is an attempt to develop an action-theory approach to the administration of organizations.[4] It leads to a three-tiered schema:

First tier — broad processes: There are two broad processes that permeate and are the substance

of all management, both public and private. These
are decision-making and communication. These can
be examined in terms of their use, guidance, obstacles, and achievements.

Second tier — general functions: There are
three general functions that administrators perform: planning, activating, and evaluating. These,
too, can be examined as processes within any organization.

Third tier — technical functions: These include the technical activities that an organization
must perform, such as budgeting, accounting, marketing, staffing, and research.

An understanding of these kinds of administrative
activities requires an examination of how people are
motivated, the purposes of the organization and how
the organization relates to its environment, how it
secures resources, the conflicts that are part of
every organization, and the distribution of outputs
of the organization. Performance — how the institution operates and concentrates on the achievement
of purposes — which is always defined as a multi-
dimensional "matrix of purposes," consists of six
overlapping, interrelated clusters:

a. Satisfaction of interests, both inside and
outside the organization,
b. Output of services or goods,
c. Efficiency or profitability,
d. Investment in organizational viability,
e. Observance of codes, both formal and informal,
f. Rationality, the use of "best" methods.

The purpose of administration is to achieve the
purposes of the organization being administered.
But the purposes are multiple, of varying intensity,
often contradictory or conflicting. Thus, the administration of development is, operationally, the
management of all organizations, at varying levels
including the all-encompassing state, in order to
achieve whatever combination of the above purposes
creates development.

Thus administration, as conceived by modern scholars, is not a set of rules or principles to be studied and applied. Neither is it a discipline, in the sense of a more or less systematic scheme of concepts and relationships that have been empirically determined and logically deduced. Rather, it is an attempt to develop currently useful generalizations about a complex process; more a way of examining the process than of prescribing rules for its improvement, however defined. Clearly, administration is scarcely a science, in the more precise sense of the term. Public administration, as one writer stated, is a subject matter in search of a discipline.

The Concept of Economic Institutions

Accepting the definition of an institution as a behavior pattern of a group of people organized to achieve some more or less understood purpose, it is possible to designate as "economic" those institutions that produce goods or services that a society wants, in which transactions and market prices form a significant aspect of the output. Presumably all institutions, as defined here, result in an output that is valued; if not, the institutions would disappear over time. Economic institutions, as defined here, are those patterns of behavior that utilize scarce inputs to produce and distribute valued outputs that are generally involved in transactions or trade for other goods and services. Another way of saying this is to include all the institutions whose output can be substantially included in the gross national product at market prices, rather than by some surrogate measure of market-priced output, such as costs of input. This would presumably include all farms, mines, and factories, and the transportation, communication, and power system, the commodity and money markets, banks, and insurance systems. It would not include schools, hospitals, government agencies, and welfare agencies. Of course, a "gray zone" exists; certain kinds of construction (e.g., roads, water, sanitary systems) and productive operations often yield outputs that cannot be measured, even partially, by the usual market operations. Although the gray zone is both large and troublesome, it does not invalidate the process of identifying the economic institutions, whose output makes up an overwhelming majority of the increased production and productivity that is economic growth.

It should be emphasized again that economic growth depends on far more than these economic institutions. While their output makes up most of the measurable product in economic growth, they increase their production and productivity only because other, noneconomic institutions (and many noninstitutional elements and forces) either permit or encourage them to do so. Indeed, the ideas involved in new technologies often stem from noneconomic institutions, and clearly, innovation is far broader in origin and impetus than economic institutions. To "raise" the level of technology, the major element in increased productivity, improved factor inputs of all kinds are required. While some of these improved inputs do come through economic institutions, most come from noneconomic institutions.

For example, a new, highly productive technique for processing vegetable oil may be developed in a university laboratory. This will require some new pressing and refining machinery and some chemicals, as well as the skilled labor and management to set up and operate the mill. Securing improved capital inputs, the machinery, may require the use of such economic institutions as development banks; but the availability of credit and the policies that determine its allocation for specific purposes will be determined by many noneconomic institutions and other aspects of society — including the propensity to save, the ability and willingness of the government to borrow resources from abroad, the availability of skilled labor, and the method of allocating savings. In other words, though one can identify "economic institutions" with some reasonable degree of precision, it is clearly erroneous and misleading to imply that they are the major cause in the creation of the increased GNP. They are some of the many parts necessary for the increase in productivity.

It would be futile to attempt to evaluate which are more important to economic growth, the economic or the noneconomic institutions. Both are "complementarities," necessary adjuncts to each other without which economic growth is impossible. But this paper's central thesis maintains that economic institutions have somewhat different operating characteristics that make their administration different, to an important degree, from noneconomic institutions. Some of these insights are available through the institution-building view of development and from the examination of public administration.

Public administration is an important part of the initiation and operation of nearly all economic institutions. Indeed, one cannot too emphatically insist that it is often the most critical element, critical in the sense of being the dominant constraining element. Government actions and policies are of increasing importance to economic institutions. Not only do the new economic institutions usually require government sanction; they generally require massive amounts of capital, for which government is generally the only conceivable source. Similarly, new or increased production ventures generally require access to inputs which government allocates and controls. The basic economic overhead investments of a country — the transportation, power, and communication systems — require large investments with long-term payoffs, which only government can afford. Also, because many of these ventures tend to be monopolies, most people want them firmly under the control of government rather than private interests, either domestic or foreign. As economic production becomes more specialized, more "roundabout," more market-determined, the policies and practices of government become more and more important to economic institutions.

Some Currently Useful
Generalizations

Only the most fragmentary assertions can now be advanced as currently useful generalizations. An orderly presentation of these generalizations, i.e., one theoretically derived and based, is not possible. An interpretative framework (not important enough to be called a hypothesis, not to say a theory) has not been consciously developed and may not even be possible. Yet some generalizations seem to arise logically from the tentative findings of the institution-building approach to social change and from current public administration theory.

Almost all studies of institution-building emphasize the importance of leadership: ". . . at the early stages of institution-building there appears to be no substitute, no effective way of circumventing inadequate leadership, and the likelihood is that the venture will stall, be reduced to ineffectiveness, or even fail unless adequate leadership is forthcoming."[5] The correlation between success and adequate leadership is fairly obvious; it is intuitively true. However, the successful institutionalization of any innovative organization needs far more careful examination before it can be used as the operational criterion of successful leadership. There may be cases where "the operation was successful but the patient died." But in economic institutions the cluster of criteria that can measure success must be clearly associated with the objectives of the institution: the increased production and productivity of economic goods.

Government policies and practices are developed
and carried out largely by public administrators.
The increasing role of government in economic institutions makes the public administrator's role
more prominent and more critical. It would not be
an exaggeration to assert that today the inability
of governments to perform adequately the necessary
functions in economic institutions represents the
largest single proximate bottleneck to achieving
rapid economic growth. Scarcity of capital and
labor and inadequate management and organization
are the basic difficulties at a high level of generalization; but at an operational level, the inadequacy of governmental actions seems most important.

The analysis of decision-making and communication confirms this emphasis on leadership as a critical variable in economic institution-building and
makes more evident the basic interdependence of all
the institution-building variables. In the administration of economic institutions, decision-makers
must define problems, choose courses of action, and
defend their choices. The information on which they
make their decisions is not abstracted from reality;
it must be based on the situation for the specific
institution at the specific time under consideration.
The information must be related to the objectives
of the institution, the environment in which it is
operating, and the resources it can command. The
flow of information to the decision-makers must be
related to the flow of information from the decision-
makers, also related to the same obstacles, objectives, and desired outputs of the institution.

Thus, the point that adequate leadership is
necessary for the successful establishment and operation of any economic institution quickly leads
to all the other institution-building variables and
to the broad administrative processes of decision-
making and communication. The analysts who proposed these two different ways of looking at administration accept, even emphasize, this relationship.

72

In no way do they wish to imply that operationally the task of administration can be successfully separated into discrete kinds of administrative processes.

Recognizing this tremendous interdependence at operational levels, the analysts have stressed a major point, that clarity and acceptance of the same pattern of objectives simplifies the task of examining all the other variables and processes. In the variables suggested by the institution-building approach, doctrine ("the specification of values, objectives, and operational methods underlying social action") is admittedly the most elusive of the variables to be examined. The core importance of doctrine to most of the other variables and to the administrative processes of planning, activating, and evaluating is obvious. Planning for what? Evaluating with what criteria in mind? How can appropriate communication be stressed without in some way taking into account what the communication is supposed to achieve? The doctrine of an institution clearly affects that institution's priorities and preferences, its program for achieving output, its marshalling of resources, and its choice of processes.

The danger of simplistic formulation of doctrine, of the values and objectives of an institution, is obvious. As administrative analysis has constantly pointed out, objectives are usually multiple and often contradictory; and one objective serves as a constraint or parameter of other objectives. Thus, simplistic statements of the ultimate objectives of institutions, such as "well-being" or "less poverty and more freedom," are inadequate operationally. They may be useful for broad purposes of polemics and education, but at operational levels they provide little guidance and few reference points. What is needed are objectives and values that can help establish priorities and criteria of good performance of the institution and of, and for, administrators.

73

Most analysts have stressed the need for construing the objectives of an institution as a pattern, an interrelated complex that has many time dimensions as well as functional relationships. Thus, the six clusters of objectives advanced by Gross form a time-tied pattern, each cluster with numerous dimensions, different rates of change, and different criteria for measuring achievement. The understanding and acceptance of a common pattern of objectives is one of the essential elements of the successful administration of an institution. Leadership is one of the most important tasks in the establishment of this accepted pattern. One of the major roles of leadership is to ensure the flow of communications upward and downward, through both the formal and the informal aspects of the institution, to make possible the knowledge and acceptance of this common pattern of objectives.

The need for commitment to the objectives of an institution also emphasizes the key role of leadership and doctrine among the institutional variables. A pattern of objectives that is clearly understood and commonly accepted within an institution makes it easier to develop a commitment to the successful operations of the institution. There is much less value in objectives that are operationally vague, that are only of ultimate guidance rather than guidance that is recognizable by most of the administrators within an institution and by the other institutions to which they must relate. Within the codes of behavior that an institution requires, and forming as essential part of the behavior of all administrations, is commitment to the pattern of objectives against which successful operation is measured.

The thrust of this kind of reasoning should be obvious. Economic institutions are of a peculiar kind. They deal, for the most part, with measurable inputs and outputs, where other institutions, almost by definition, have inputs and outputs that are far more difficult, even impossible, to measure. It seems reasonable to assert that advantage should be taken of this fact in administering these institutions, in order to simplify the process of decision-making and communication by the relative ease with which much of the information can be quantified. For both the program variable and the resource variable can be quite easily reduced to costs and sales, to measurable inputs and outputs, in order to ease the process of decision-making and communication. In terms of the administrative analysis, the objectives of output, efficiency, and rationality in economic institutions can, to a large extent, be quantified in ways that most administrators recognize and use.

Thus efficiency, in terms of the objectives of economic institutions, can be given a clearly dominant role. Generalizations about the importance of leadership, the relationships of adequate leadership to a common acceptance of objectives, the improvement of decision-making through reasonable quantification, the need for single, understandable objectives for commitment and for adequate communication — these and many other generalizations about institution-building and administrative processes point to the operating usefulness of choosing efficiency as the dominant objective of economic institutions.

Several additional points must hastily be made, in order to avoid the social disapproval usually aroused by the foregoing suggestion. "Man does not live by bread alone" — more effective production of more goods and services does not automatically create a satisfactory society except by the standards of some extremists who can arbitrarily be dismissed as clearly undesirable. If choosing increasing production and productivity as the prime, overriding objective of economic institutions inevitably condemns a government to ineffective action in molding and changing distribution of income and of noneconomic institutions, then the primacy of production and efficiency for economic institutions is not tenable. But this is not true. Emphasis on production and productivity for economic institutions permits a better distribution of income, better in any way a society wishes to define that term. The cliche "It is easier to be equitable in dividing a larger pie" clearly holds, so long as the efforts to enlarge the pie do not bind the cutting of the pie to the status quo. And governments have learned many ways to redistribute income, to tax income so as to permit the establishment of social priorities in final consumption.

Administration analysts warn against accepting one objective as a criterion for an institution, and they warn specifically against the wiles of "efficiency" as administration's basic objective. For several decades in this century efficiency was advanced as the basic good, the central theme upon which all other doctrines and principles were based. Upon the ability to accept efficiency as the best of administration was built the concept of "neutrality" of administration, the belief that administrators could be committed to efficiency regardless of what they were administering. The separation of policies from their implementation is no longer an acceptable myth, and the effort to make efficiency the core of administration has been firmly rejected. Yet this proposal for making increased production and efficiency a dominant objective of economic institutions does not exclude other objectives and their importance. The need for increased production and productivity in the less developed countries is so great that this primacy can be accepted where it would not be acceptable in the more developed countries. The danger of accepting the dominance of a single objective for economic institutions, one that has so many social dangers as efficiency, must be faced and overcome. It need not spread to other institutions where efficiency of operation is difficult to measure or even to conceive analytically because of the intertwined nature of many important objectives.

Whether or not increased production or efficiency becomes the dominant objective of economic institutions, some other considerations about the relationship of public administration and economic institutions enter. Public administration is an input of critical importance to the initiation and successful operation of most economic institutions. As an input it is difficult to quantify, since its costs cannot be determined through market mechanisms. Equally difficult to assess are the benefits and diseconomies arising from inadequate or improper public administration. Even in economic institutions, with their relative facility for measuring costs of inputs and value of outputs, the cost of public administration is difficult to measure. Yet administrative cost, as one of the more scarce inputs, is significant; in many cases it becomes a more limiting constraint on production and productivity than capital, which seems to receive most attention in the less developed countries.

If direct measurement is difficult, some useful observations may still be made about the application of public administration influence and controls to economic institutions. Some methods of application are more costly than others, using up more of that scarce input, public administration. Thus, public administration in control of economic institutions can be classified into the following kinds of multidimensional continua:

a. Direct and indirect controls — this is a continuum that attempts to assess the degree to which the government is directly involved in operating economic institutions. The extreme of most direct operations would be complete participation in all detailed operations, government ownership, and direct control, as in economic institutions owned and operated as parts of government ministries, an arms plant run by the Defense Ministry or an airline operated as a section of the Ministry of Transportation. "Indirect controls" refers to involvement that changes the environment of economic institutions, with these changes expected to affect the operating decisions of the managers of the economic

institutions. Such aspects as affect the prices
and availabilities of factor inputs, the taxes
assessed by government, the cost and availability
of necessary services of transportation and communication: these are indirect controls. This
is not a simple continuum from one linear ex-
tremity to another, but a complex surface that
defies geometric presentation although its existence and conformity to reality are demonstrable.

b. Discretionary and non-discretionary controls — This continuum attempts to represent the
degree to which government officials are given
discretion in applying government rules. At one
end of the continuum would be a rule that applies
to everybody without exception, applied automatically. At the other extreme of the continuum
would be those kinds of government controls that
lie entirely within the discretion of the public
administrator; each application exists as a separate decision by the administrator, based entirely
on his judgment. While these two extremes would
be difficult to find in pure form, there is no
doubt that the public administration input in economic institutions may be variously measured along
this complex continuum.

c. Specific and general controls — Some government controls of economic institutions are very
specific, relating to detailed operations; others
are very broad and relate to a whole family of operations. This way of looking at public administration inputs into economic institutions is closely
related to the first classification of administrative
inputs, the direct and indirect controls. Specific
controls tend to be direct, while general controls
tend to be indirect. Yet a specific control can
relate to one economic institution even though it
affects the environment of that institution and
therefore is indirect, by this definition.

d. Positive and negative controls — The term
"positive" has been applied to a public administration control that is a stimulus or authorization

78

for action or decision, while negative controls are designed to prohibit certain operating decisions. Subsidies are examples of positive controls, while the prohibition to import certain luxury goods is an example of negative control.

These are not "exclusive" categories; they overlap both in concept and in practice. A specific control by government may be classified in several contradictory categories, depending upon the viewpoint of the classifier. An importer may consider a decision by the government to be most discretionary, negative, and specific, while an entrepreneur wishing to open a new factory may consider that same decision non-discretionary, positive, and general. The inability to develop a more "exclusive" classification system reflects the complexity of public administration as it relates to economic institutions and the existence of many overlapping variables in classifying activities.

There are no easy ways to measure either cost or effectiveness of these different classifications of government participation in the administration of economic institutions. Yet judgments on types of controls are being made constantly. When no consideration is given to the scarcity of administrative capacity, it is being treated as a free good, a costless input. It is asserted here, with appropriate cautions about fuzzy definitions and non-objective judgments, that in terms of the use of that scarce input, controls should deliberately be selected on the basis of minimizing the use of administrative capacity.

More Costly Use of Public Administration	Less Costly Use of Public Administration
Direct	Indirect
Discretionary	Non-discretionary
Specific	General

There appears no way to judge, in terms of the use of public administration capacity, the continuum along positive and negative categories, although negative controls seem easier to apply and often are both general and non-discretionary.

If these assertions do reflect reality, then economic institutions will benefit from emphasis on production and efficiency and the participation of public administrations in the most indirect, non-discretionary, and general controls possible. Even where economic institutions are owned and operated by government, these generalizations hold. The economic institutions should be considered separate entities and not part of the usual public administration machinery. Their management should be given increased production and productivity as the dominant, but not sole, objective; and they should be instructed to operate as if they were not owned and operated by government. Such a style of operation may be impossible in some cases, but these are surprisingly few in number. Even in the most single-minded, ideology-bound country, the separation of general government from the administration of specific economic institutions is possible and generally acceptable. Emphasis on production and productivity and efforts to minimize public administration inputs are not a push toward private enterprise and away from public ownership and control. The need for emphasizing efficiency in production and for minimizing the use of a scarce input, public administration, is present in the less developed countries regardless of their ideology. Perhaps, were it possible to conceive of a situation where public administration is a free good, an input with no opportunity costs, then a different kind of evaluation would be necessary. But so long as public administration is a serious limiting constraint on the efficiency of economic institutions, we must seek devices and arrangements to reduce the inputs required and to increase their effectiveness. This does not eliminate the need for evaluating what type of public administration may be most efficient in each type of economic institution in each specific country. In some cases, direct, discretionary, and specific controls may be the only option. It is important to realize, however, that the usual public administrator — with his limited view of economic growth, his history of a developing fear of market institutions, and his confidence in direct government operation and control — has helped make public administration the chief proximate bottleneck to economic growth.

NOTES

1.   I must be careful not to push the mataphor too far, because this may be the formula for modern music.

2.   This is only a slight modification of the definition used by the Inter-University Research Program on Institution Building. If social analysts object to this preemption of a term that often means much more than a pattern of behavior, such as role system or value system, we can substitute the word "organization" without too much loss in meaning.

3.   Bertram M. Gross, *The Managing of Organizations* (New York: The Free Press of Glencoe, 1964).

4.   This is based on the eclectic and innovative study of Bertram M. Gross, *The Managing of Organizations*.

5.   Milton J. Esman, "The Institution-Building Concepts — An Interim Appraisal" (Pittsburgh: Inter-

University Research Program on Institution Building,
University of Pittsburgh, 1968), (Mimeographed.)

PART II

The African Context of
Change

Some Aspects of Development Planning and Administration in Africa

Note: This paper was not cleared with
United Nations headquarters or the Economic Commission for Africa; these organizations do not, therefore, necessarily share the views expressed by the
author.

Introduction

The main purpose of this paper is to identify some
of the major administrative obstacles to development in African countries during the last decade.
These are dealt with under the broad headings of
administrative machinery and development planning,
machinery for consultation and popularization, resource and project management, development research,
personnel management and training, and administrative and supporting services. Some concluding suggestions are made regarding the areas in which urgent reforms are required so that the existing administrative machinery in African countries can
cope effectively with the task of development.

Although in recent years national development planning has assumed an important place in the machinery of most governments, it is erroneous to assume that it is a completely new art, foreign to and distinct from public administration. One should not lose sight of the fact that the annual budgets which African governments have been using for decades are annual plans combining both their operational and their development programs. A more recent innovation is the national plans of more than one-year duration; these plans have attempted (especially during the post-independence era) to provide infrastructural and social services on an expanded scale while encouraging and promoting agricultural and industrial development as a means of improving the economic and social well-being of the people. This is in contrast with the annual plans of the colonial era, which were instruments to provide the minimum infrastructural services necessary for the maintenance of law and order and technical advisory services, mainly for the production of cash crops for export to the metropolitan countries.

Because of the complex nature of the variable factors which must be taken into consideration in planning for the development of a modern economy (e.g., savings, investment, population, trained manpower, technological innovations, infrastructural development), the services of experts in the various social sciences and technological fields are required to ensure that political leaders and their advisers (including administrators) take full account of the nature and effects of these factors in making their development plans or programs. In performing this task, planning experts must use econometric models in order to develop a systematic approach to the preparation not only of the national plan but also of annual budgets. This has become necessary because of the use of the annual budget as an instrument of the national plan.

Administrative strategies should also be developed as integral parts of development planning.

The achievement of desired results depends to a
large extent on the success of administration and
management of individual development functions and
of the plan's various constituent projects. To
that end,

> Administrative policies, measures and pro-
> cesses to carry out programs and projects
> envisaged in the plan, should be essential
> parts of the basic planning documents. Or-
> ganizational responsibilities, administra-
> tive arrangements, operating procedures,
> and resource utilization should be defined
> for each sector. This applies to such func-
> tions as agriculture, education and public
> works; to local government functions; to
> urban and rural development; and to the sum-
> total of policy and administrative actions
> necessary to promote entrepreneurism in the
> private sector.[1]

Indeed, administrative planning should be a sector
of the national plan, not sacrificed in favor of
purely socioeconomic planning.

The role of the planners and other specialists
in the central planning organization does not end
with the preparation of the plan. After the plan
is launched, they must watch the trends in their
own and allied fields in order to advise political
leaders and administrators as to what steps should
be taken to alter the mix of the variables and to
deal with bottlenecks and constraints so as to
achieve the plan's objectives. If necessary, they
can suggest modifying some of the objectives in the
light of circumstances beyond the country's control.
For instance, a cocoa marketing specialist in the
planning office of a cocoa-growing country which
intends to double the production of this crop during
the plan period would be in a position to advise the
government that in the light of, say, a possible
glut in the world cocoa bean market, it might be

necessary to establish cocoa processing factories
(if such a project would be profitable) in order
to be able to dispose of the planned increased production. If during the same period the cocoa tech-
nologist and the market specialist should foresee
that, owing to the competition of synthetic products, increased production might find no profitable
market, they can advise the government to modify
its policy of expanded production and to divert
part of the resources earmarked for this program
to the increased production of other agricultural
commodities with better market prospects. It is
also the planners' responsibility, particularly in
a mixed economy, to induce various groups in the
private sector to carry out their activities, as
far as possible, in accordance with national plan
objectives. This may involve providing them with
advisory services on such subjects as investment,
supply of plant and equipment, management, accounting, and storage and marketing arrangements.

If this important role of the expert is accepted,
it is easy to appreciate that it is an integral part
of the general administration connected with the
preparation and implementation of a plan. It is
the lack of appreciation for these integral, complementary functions which has led in the past to
insufficient attention to the role of public administration in development planning. It is not that
the existence of administrative inadequacies in
African governments is not recognized (especially
by experts); rather, the problem is that of implementing the numerous expert reports on administrative reforms.[2] The lack of enthusiasm for acting
upon these reports is perhaps due to some policy-
makers' inadequate appreciation of the impact of
the necessary administrative reforms on the successful implementation of development plans in particular, and on the effectiveness of government machinery
in general.

It is encouraging, however, to note that in recent years a number of countries have begun to re-

gard administrative reform as a prerequisite to effective plan implementation. For instance, early in 1969, the Tanzanian Government preceded consideration of its 1969/74 Development Plan with the appointment of a commission under the chairmanship of Professor Pratt, former Principal of the University College, Dar es Salaam, to study the country's administrative machinery with a view to making recommendations which would render it more effective for development. In March, 1969, one of the major subjects considered by the Conference on National Reconstruction and Development in Nigeria was the country's Development Plan Administration.[3] Expressly admitting that success or failure of the national plan will depend more upon the country's administrative capability than upon any other single factor, Ethiopia's Third Five-Year Plan (1968-72) envisages the establishment of an Administrative Reform Committee at ministerial level and the strengthening and revitalization of the Imperial Ethiopian Institute of Public Administration (where the central organization and management unit is). The Institute thus should further improve its effectiveness in providing organization and management services to the government machinery, training for civil servants, and thereby make an effective contribution to the achievement of the administrative capability required for national development.

On the international scene, the United Nations General Assembly passed resolutions on public administration recommending to member states that due attention be given to the public administration in their plans and programs for international cooperation requirements of developing countries.[4] This was in accordance with the United Nations Economic and Social Council resolution that public administration should be accorded an appropriate place in planning for the period following the United Nations Development Decade. In that resolution the Secretary-General was requested to elaborate more specific objectives and programs in this field, in close collaboration with the specialized agencies and non-governmental organizations concerned.[5]

Administrative Machinery and Development Planning

While it has been recognized that social and economic development will not take place without the development of human resources, it is also now widely accepted that, especially in developing countries, development will take place only if the government can produce sound and efficient administration to effectively implement its decisions. In this connection we should note that administration is composed of men, organizations, and methods. Men need training; organizations need reviewing and adapting; in a changing world, new methods are constantly designed to speed up administrative procedures and to respond to the challenges of growing, transforming needs.

The increasing scope, size, and complexity of government activities, on the one hand, and the need to make the most effective use of available resources, on the other, make it desirable to explore the ways and means of developing administrative capability commensurate with the tasks of development.[6] The transformation of "traditional administration" in African countries into development-oriented administrative machinery and management could be a means to that end, bridging the gap between planning and plan implementation.

Traditional administration, also called "executive" administration, was designed largely to fulfill the legal requirements of government operations competently and efficiently. It was process-and technique-oriented, approaching the administrative activity in terms of narrow task components (e.g., personnel, budgeting, finance), as if the purpose of administration was solely the performance of staff services and ministerial functions. In contrast, the new conception, designated as "managerial" administration, is essentially program- and development-oriented. Its focus is on carrying out the decisions and directives of the government system, and on the crucial element of securing prescribed programmatic values.

This brings to mind a very apt observation on the status of administration in most African countries:

In most African countries, the organization and structure of the system within which the Administrator functions are out-dated and incompatible with the dynamics of the new situation which faces us. Systems which applied to the colonial era have been adapted incongruously to the requirements of an age of modern economic and technological development. To continue with the old systems of administrative organization and structure would be like fitting old vintage motor car engines into the latest design of modern carriages required for use on modern highways. The situation, therefore, calls for a drastic re-appraisal of the organization and structure of the public services, of the institutions for training and orientation within them, and for the application of research to policies of reform and modernization. The object of any reformation in this regard would be to ensure that a modern machinery for the exercise of public administrative functions is established which is capable of matching the requirements of modern government. It should also have within it the means by which development can take place to match change in the political, economic and social situations of the country which the machinery serves.[7]

Complementary to such a reform, there should be a continuing review, adaptation, and improvement of

the machinery of government (i.e., the distribution
to ministries and agencies of the major functions
necessary to carry out national objectives), the
internal organization of ministries and agencies,
work procedures, and management practices in order
to attain the administrative capability required
for successful national development. It is equally
essential that adequate qualified and trained staff
be continually developed to enable the government
to produce commodities and services in the desired
quantity and quality as needed; otherwise, the
capability sought will remain a myth.

In view of the leadership and coordinating role
which the central planning organization is now
playing in economic development, it is generally
agreed that the planning agency should be placed in
a senior ministry. This view is supported by a
United Nations meeting of experts which concluded:

> Where planning functions are entrusted to a
> central planning organ, it is desirable that
> the organ should be located as closely to
> the Chief Executive as possible, in order
> to secure for it the high degree of status
> necessary for the performance of its duties,
> especially those of consultation and co-or-
> dination with other branches of the admin-
> istration, political and government circles,
> social and professional organizations and
> agencies of foreign assistance.[8]

Many African countries have adopted this principle, according the planning organization an effective status in the government machinery. In
Ethiopia, Swaziland, and Lesotho it is in the Prime
Minister's office; Botswana placed it in the Vice-
President's office; and in Tanzania and Kenya it
is under the charge of a senior minister. In
Libya, the UAR, and Sudan, planning has a separate
ministry. On the other hand, Ghana and Gambia combine finance and planning in one ministry. The

arguments for placing planning in the Ministry of
Finance include the ease with which financial proposals can be examined according to normal budget
procedure by the experts in the Ministry of Finance,
and better liaison and coordination between the
Treasury and the planning organization.[9] Arguments
against this arrangement include conflict between
the traditional control role of the Ministry of
Finance and the expansionist and resource allocation role of the planning organ, and the fact that
the location of the planning organ in the Ministry
of Finance may overburden the minister with the
additional task of adjudicating between financial
and planning divisions of his department.

Apart from a few countries like the U.A.R.,
many African countries appear to rely heavily on
the services of foreign experts for the preparation
of their development plans. Although this may be
attributed partly to a local shortage of personnel
experienced in planning techniques, it is due mainly to the fact that when some governments attempt
to get foreign aid for development, they are asked
by potential donor countries to present their development plans. This is usually followed by the
donor countries' offering the services of their
experts to prepare the plans.

This creates at least two serious problems.
One is that such foreign experts often know very
little of the administrative system of the country.
Even more important, they are not able to assess
accurately the possible reactions of the population
to whom the proposals are to be presented, or to
interpret the work and consumption habits and other
motivations of the people for whom they are planning.

There is also the problem of periodic reviews,
which ought to be based on accurate reports about
plan implementation. Trained project specialists
are too often unavailable to man planning units in
the main executive ministries which could report
regularly on problems of project implementation.
A few countries, such as the U.A.R., have made some

progress in this direction, and countries such as Botswana and Nigeria have made a start. Even so, it is reported that in Nigeria, because of limited staff, the planning cells in large ministries have not been very effective.[10]

The absence of regular reviews of project implementation has hampered the discovery of timely solutions to urgent implementation problems through the coordinated efforts of the agencies concerned. This was why, during the former civilian administration in Ghana, steps were not promptly taken to erect complete or partial tariff walls to protect the products of newly established government-sponsored industries against cheaply priced competing imports. The result was that large stocks of locally manufactured goods were left without buyers while many similar products were being imported by private firms.[11]

This underlines a need to reorganize the administration of foreign exchange control. Foreign exchange permits should not be issued to importers of commodities which are produced in the country in sufficient quantities to meet local demand. When industrial projects are being planned or constructed, they can be achieved only if adequate consultation and coordination exists between the Ministries of Commerce and Industry and of Finance (including the Board of Customs and Excise) and the industrial and commercial interests concerned.

There is also the allied problem of controlling the quality of locally manufactured goods. While it may be true to some extent that, owing to what is usually referred to as the "colonial" mentality, some consumers prefer "made in Europe" commodities to locally manufactured goods, it is equally true that without the necessary quality control, the consumers have in some cases not been provided with local products of reasonable quality. Some countries have for some years proposed the establishemnt of national bureaus of standards but have not taken definite steps to implement their proposals. In fact,

very little has been done to train nationals as
quality control specialists.

Machinery for
Consultation and
Popularization of
the Plan

In numerous African countries, the limited time
available for the preparation of the first post-
independence national development plans meant that ·
much planning was done "from above" with data collected from the headquarters of the ministries and
of such large government agencies as the development
corporations. Apart from a few countries such as
the U.A.R., which had properly established provincial and district development organizations, most
African countries had no such institutions for consultation and for the provision of planning data.
In recent years Kenya and Botswana have established
these local development institutions. Even in
countries with well-established local government
councils, such as Gambia, Ghana, and Nigeria, these
councils were not consulted, nor did they participate in the formulation of the national plan.[12]
In some African countries the lack of appreciation of the important role of the private sector
in the implementation of a national plan has led
to the absence of any well-established machinery
for consulting or involving the private sector in
the plan formulation and implementation. It is
heartening that countries like Botswana and Lesotho
are taking the lead in the establishment of National Planning Consultative Committees on which the
private sector is adequately represented and which
are consulted in the formulation of the national
plan. Perhaps other countries' lack of enthusiasm
for these consultative committees is influenced by
their attitude toward foreign enterprises, which
still play an important role in the industrial and
commercial sectors of their economies.

A few adverse effects of inadequate consultation with the various sectoral and local interests on plan implementation may be stated briefly here. One is that owing to the paucity of planning date, the plan projections are outside the realm of reality. For instance, it has been said that one of the administrative problems faced by the Somali Government in the implementation of its first Five-Year Plan was that "it was working just on guesswork because of lack of supportive statistical data and preliminary studies of projects."[13]

Another adverse effect is that implementation does not get mass support because the plan is not regarded as the people's, in spite of great publicity after it has been prepared. Even where projects implemented include social services for a particular area, the people sometimes do not fully appreciate the value of the government's investment. For instance, in 1959 the people in a certain West African town refused to pay a tax for the maintenance of a water plant constructed by the government because they claimed that they were not consulted on its financial implications before the project was built. In sharp contrast, the former Eastern Nigeria Government was receiving wide support for its water supply program. There each rural community initiated the proposal for its water scheme, which was eventually included in the regional government's development program, and backed its request to the government by contributing a substantial proportion of the project's capital cost.

One of the difficulties of getting local authorities in most of these countries to prepare medium-term development plans is that they lack the financial and technical resources to formulate and execute projects. This phenomenon is exemplified in Kenya, where, despite the upsurge of development through self-help groups, capital programs in County Council areas have been very low, often because insufficient revenues were available to meet the associated annual recurrent costs; the councils also have not developed the administrative capacity to prepare a long-term development program.[14] In another West African state, the central government — after calling for the development plan proposals of its local authorities and discovering that most of the councils had planned without resources — decided to abandon the arrangement to include local government proposals in the state plan.

While it could be said that some local government councils found themselves in their financial straits because of poor internal resource management, it is equally true that the central governments are partly responsible for this state of affairs. In an attempt to maintain stability in their own revenues from certain traditional sources, such as personal taxes, the central governments "froze" the level of local government revenues that can be drawn from the same sources. This happened in Western and Midwestern Nigeria, where the level of flat-rate tax from the lowest income earners had been fixed at £3 per capita from 1960 to 1969/70; in 1969 it was reduced to £2 in the West and in 1970 to £2.15 in the Midwest. The "freezing" and reduction have been carried out by the state governments even though during the same 10-year period the basic salary and wage rates which the local authorities were required to pay rose by at least 25 percent. Some governments, like those of Ghana and Western and Midwestern Nigeria, also have not maintained very steady payment of grants-in-aid to their local authorities. This has to some extent affected the recurrent revenues of these councils and has made it difficult for them to prepare sound annual budgets, let alone compose medium-term plans.

A number of these governments are trying to solve the problem of the weak finances of local authorities by taking over major local services. In Kenya, for example, the government decided, as of 1970, to assume direct responsibility for the three principal services of the County Councils — primary education, health, and roads — to which the councils had allocated some 80 percent of their total expenditures.[15] In Western and Midwestern Nigeria, water projects and the general administration of primary education have also been taken over by the state governments.

While these steps may alleviate problems of local government finance in these countries, further review is needed of the financial relationship between the central and local governments if the councils are to play their proper role in the formulation and execution of development plans. Such an exercise should seek to define clearly the sources of local government revenue, in a manner which would not make local government overdependent on the current financial position of the central government and on its ad hoc decisions.

Finally, lack of collaboration with the private sector in planning leads business and other private institutions to plan their operations independently of national plan objectives. For instance, in Ghana a government-sponsored factory manufacturing oil drums was experiencing difficulty in disposing of its products and had to shut down temporarily — at a time when the oil companies were importing the same commodity. Later, under the military administration, after negotiations with these companies the factory was able to reopen under a reorganized supply program.[16]

Resource and Project
Management

African countries are beginning to realize that foreign aid as the source of funds for their development budgets is most unreliable. In Nigeria, as against the estimate of 50 percent of its (1962-68 plan) development budget anticipated from external sources, only 12.3 percent of the development expenditure in the plan's first two years (1962-64) came from this source.[17] In the same manner the

Sierra Leone Ten-Year Plan (1962-72) estimated that
as much as 70 percent of the development budget
revenue would come from external sources.[18] The
nonrealization of this hope during the first five
years of the plan led the government to declare in
1967 that hitherto

> The Development Estimates of expenditure
> were drawn up without any real knowledge
> of available funds to finance expenditure.
> In the end, the Development Estimates turned
> out to be either merely expectations, or,
> more seriously, were financed from in-
> flationary sources or on expensive pre-
> finance terms.[19]

The Sierra Leone Governemnt decided, as of 1967/68,
to take a realistic approach to budgeting, with the
result that the plan has now been abandoned. In
Somalia, only 10 out of 28 agricultural projects
included in its First Five-Year Plan (1963-67)
were started by the fifth year; none of them had
been completed because of overreliance on foreign
capital and assistance.[20]
  Although Tanzania originally estimated that 78
percent of the development budget of its Second
Five-Year Plan (1964-69) would come from external
sources, it is encouraging that she was quick to
realize the overoptimism and revised the plan in
this respect. Tanzania was thus able to close the
plan's fourth year by financing 60-65 percent of
the development budget from local sources, as
against 22 percent local funding originally planned.[21]
  Although the uncertainty of the political cli-
mate might have rendered some countries unattractive
to foreign capital in the magnitude estimated by
the plans, there is another major reason: there
are rarely any feasibility study reports of selected
projects in the plan which might attract foreign
capital. Feasibility studies have proved difficult
to accomplish because of the absence in many African
countries of project formulation and appraisal units.

The result is that more projects are presented for government participation by foreign machine peddlers who have little or no financial stake in the projects, and before acceptance these proposals are not properly evaluated by representatives of the government. The failure of a number of industrial projects in Sierra Leone, Nigeria, and Somalia can be traced partly to this casual factor.[22] Although nearly all the governments believe in industrialization as one solution to their development problems, it is ironic that, apart from a few countries like the U.A.R. and the Federal Government of Nigeria (not the state governments), many nations have only a Chief Industrial Officer and one or two assistants in their Ministry of Industry. It is these officers, some of whom have never managed any industrial undertaking, who are expected to examine complex industrial project proposals and advise the government on participation which may involve millions of dollars in public funds.

African countries appear to be slow to realize that big businessmen have attractive offers for investment in many European, American, and other countries with large, settled European populations. In such circumstances, businessmen cannot afford to invest large sums of money and time in making preliminary feasibility studies of projects in African countries. It is left to the governments of these countries to attract investors by selling ready-made feasibility study reports on selected projects. Interested entrepreneurs can then use these as a base for further detailed studies pursuant to possible investment. The example of Pakistan in this connection may be worth quoting:

In Pakistan, over 100 project and programme feasibility studies, besides a number of important sector surveys, were carried through at the same time in a specially organized 'crash programme.' The programme was inaugurated early in the Second Plan period to

build up *a stock of projects* for the latter
part of the Second and, especially, for the
Third Plan period. The availability of a
large number of projects 'ready to go' has
not only made it possible for Pakistan to
obtain increased foreign aid, but also helped to account for its success in fulfilling
and exceeding its plan targets.[23]

While it is true that development in Africa has
been slow because of shortage of capital, it is
equally true that inadequate administration of
these countries' internal resources has been a major obstacle to development. A few examples will
illustrate this point. The administration of direct
taxation, supposedly a major source of public revenue, is very weak in many African countries; evasion still occurs on a large scale. For example,
a study of this problem a few years ago in the former Western Region of Nigeria revealed evasion as
high as 45-50 percent in some urban centers.[24] In
many countries, commissions of inquiry are appointed to review the tax administration, but very little
is done to follow up their recommendations by reorganizing the field tax administration. For instance, while thousands of small taxpayers are arrested and prosecuted every year for nonpayment,
one rarely reads in the press of the conviction of
a wealthy tax evader.

The systems of budgetary control and auditing
which are still in vogue in many African countries
are those inherited from the colonial era. With
the large sums of money being handled by government departments under their expanded development
programs, very little is being done to establish
well-staffed prepayment internal audit units in
large departments. The facts that one country recorded a high of 16 percent of its total public
disbursement in the form of irregular expenditure
in 1967/68, combined with large-scale irregularities in public spending revealed by recent commissions of inquiry in some African countries,

show that postpayment audit systems are not adequate sanctions against irregularities at the prepayment stage.

This emphasizes the need for qualified accountants and auditors in the public service to man the Accountant-General's and the Auditor-General's departments, and thus enable these departments to offer effective supervision of the internal audit units which are established to make prepayment audits. It is regrettable that except in Nigeria (Federal), the U.A.R., and one or two other countries, professionally qualified accountants or auditors are still rare specimens in government accounting and auditing cadres. One major reason for this is that, owing to the dearth of qualified accountants and auditors, government in these countries cannot compete with the private sector in offering salaries to attract and retain accountants. Ghana has tried to solve this problem by the establishment of the State Enterprises Audit Corporation to handle the audit of public enterprises. However, the Corporation is still experiencing difficulty in retaining professionally qualified staff because of competition from the private sector.[25]

Whereas African governments have quite rightly decided on active participation in industrial and agro-industrial projects as a means of increasing the pace of development, very little has been done to protect their major investment interests in these projects. Governments are satisfied with appointing part-time directors to protect their interests; they rely almost entirely on the annual reports of private auditors for the assessment of these enterprises' performances. Since most of these large projects are managed by foreign management agents with little or no shares in them, one would have expected the governments to have had management service units for inspecting the general and financial administration of the projects to ensure that they were managed efficiently and in the public interest. Zambia and, more recently,

Ghana, are among the very few countries to have established such an arrangement.

Development Research

Agricultural Research

Insufficient resources are allocated to such research as is directed to the utilization and processing of local raw materials. It is strange that in Africa, where over 80 percent of the population lives in rural areas and the majority are engaged in peasant agriculture and animal husbandry, in 1964 only 3 and 5 percent, respectively, of agricultural research scientists were engaged in research in food technology and pastoral improvement.[26]

This situation can be traced to the history of agricultural research in many former African colonies. Agricultural research started seriously during World War II, when the metropolitan powers saw it as a means of increasing the production and improving the quality of such cash crops as cocoa, palm oil, cotton, and groundnuts, which were all required in large quantities for the war effort. To a great extent the research institutions established for these commodities have managed to achieve their objectives. Their efforts have continued to be sustained by the national governments mainly because their financing has been tied to the organizations responsible for marketing particular export crops. For instance, the Cocoa Research Institute of Nigeria and the Nigerian Institute for Palm Oil Research are financed from funds obtained by the marketing boards for cocoa and palm-produce marketing. Other examples are cotton research in Egypt and Sudan, and groundnut research in Senegal and the Ivory Coast.

Even in export crop research, much still remains to be done. For example, although rubber is a big earner of foreign exchange in two West African countries, in one of them no national institute exists for rubber research and development. In the other, the Rubber Research Institute has been left virtually as a department of the State Ministry of Agriculture, and there are no signs that it is being given the development priority it deserves.

Research into food crops and animal production has lagged. The only notable exception is in East Africa, where the colonial government was anxious to encourage dairy production for export and for local consumption.[27] Research into breeding and acclimatization became a necessity for this purpose; hence East Africa has one of the best veterinary research organizations on the continent.

Research into food crops (especially those consumed locally) and animal production did not attract the attention of the governments until after independence, when they decided to draw up national development plans. Seeking ways of conserving their foreign exchange earnings for financing development projects, they discovered that much of these earnings was spent on the importation of food items which could be produced by local farmers in larger quantities. The governments therefore decided to intensify the campaign for local production of these items by importing improved seeds and breeds and subsidizing the cost of seeds, fertilizers, and animal feeds distributed to farmers, as well as by increased advisory services.

In Tanzania this effort resulted in self-sufficiency in corn production and wheat production growth from 17,300 tons in 1962 to 32,800 tons in 1966.[28] In Kenya it resulted in an increase from 86,900 tons to 235,100 tons of corn produced and marketed between 1964 and 1967.[29] A similar effort in rice production in Sierra Leone reduced its import of this commodity from 28,000 tons in 1966/67 to about 10,000 tons in 1968/69.[30] In the same manner, Ghana was able to increase its domestic fish catch from 57,970 tons in 1962 to 92,016 tons in 1968.[31] Nigeria, which used to spend thousands of pounds on imported eggs, has now become virtually self-sufficient in egg production.

All these are evidence that, with better planning of investment and mass participation in agricultural development backed by institutional arrangements for extension advisory services and marketing, many African countries can become self-sufficient in producing a variety of food and could thus save reasonable sums of foreign currency (now spent on imports of these products) for investment in other productive sectors.

Much remains to be done in research into food crops and animal health and production, however. For instance, in soil research much of the available but limited data were collected by a few staff of the export crop research centers. In many African countries south of the Sahara, a start is only being made in soil research and water conservation geared to the increased production of food crops and livestock. Until a reasonable achievement has been made in this field and the results have been made available to prospective large-scale farmers, they would be difficult to attract to this sphere of investment.

Other fields in which intensive research for development is urgently needed include land-use classification, selective plant and animal breeding, improvement and control of pasture land, use of balanced mineral fertilizers, pest and disease control, the scope and application of power-assisted farming (including bullock farming), and the preservation of crops, foodstuffs, and animal products. For example, in Ethiopia it is proposed that a Water Resources Council be created to advise the government on all aspects of water resources development and administration.[32] In Mid-Western Nigeria a soil laboratory has been established by the Ministry of Agriculture, mainly for soil research.

A number of factors impose constraints on development research in food and animal production in many African countries. As mentioned earlier, one

such factor is the inadequate allocation of resources
for this purpose in the countries' development plans
and annual budgets. A few research institutions
which exist in a few countries depend too heavily
on foreign assistance or are owned by private expatriate organizations. Consequently, they are
incapable of being easily used to achieve objectives
in the national plans.

According to a recent study, in 14 West African
countries the ratio of foreign to national research
workers is approximately 1:1.5, although the figure
is heavily weighted by Ghana and Nigeria, whose
proportion of the total number of nationals accounts
for approximately 42 percent. In 11 East African
countries, the provisional ratio of foreign to
national research workers appears to be of the order
of approximately 2:1. On the other hand, in four
North African countries 80-99 percent of these
workers appear to be nationals of the countries
concerned.[33] Since some of these expatriate staff
are usually working on research for higher degrees,
it is not surprising that what is spent on research
in such fields as soil and water conservation is
not yielding commensurate results for the countries
concerned.

The third problem is that of coordinating the
activities of existing organizations. While it may
be true that some research duplication is necessary
in order to cross-check the results of different
units, a multiplicity of institutions without a
coordinating body, such as exists in some East and
West African countries, is likely to lead to more
human and financial resources being devoted to research with relatively insignificant results. One
obstacle here is that those heading some of the
existing research organizations are not keen to
give up their independent status. It is encouraging, however, that countries like Ethiopia, Nigeria,
and those of the East African Community are trying
to set up national or multinational scientific and
technical research councils (including agricultural

research councils), consisting largely of scientists, technologists, and government officials, to coordinate and promote various aspects of scientific research.[34]

In conclusion, while it can be said that some progress has been made in government encouragement of increased production of a few import-substituting agricultural products, except in a few countries like the U.A.R. not much has been done to establish comprehensive research policies and programs for the development of a wide range of import-substituting products. Such policies should cover research on extension services, storage, and marketing facilities, as well as the economic utilization of manpower to produce these commodities.

Industrial Research

Industrial Research is usually based on the industries concerned, including their development and improvement of designs and of production processes. Because most countries in Africa south of the Sahara had traditionally agricultural economies, the people had developed skills only for the production of very elementary handicrafts for household use. Beyond these, little attempt was made to embark on large-scale production of manufactured goods for markets beyond the areas of the traditional kingdoms and city-states. It is therefore not surprising that no serious industrial research had been considered necessary before or immediately after the advent of the metropolitan powers — although the future need for such research will be mentioned later in this section.

It can also be said that the few industries which existed in most of these countries when they attained independence were mainly those promoted or established by foreign firms, usually as subsidiaries of "parent" factories in Europe or America. Factories were few because a principal aim of colonization was to promote the production of agricultural commodities and mineral ores to feed the industries in the metropolitan countries.[35] In fact, only after World War II were some half-hearted attempts made by the foreign firms to establish local industries, usually for the production of beverages, textiles, and cement.

Since these local factories were subsidiaries of those in foreign countries, the companies concerned chose to use the industrial research facilities of their "home" laboratories to meet local production problems, such as those arising from machine design or use of raw materials. This was done mainly for economy, since it was cheaper to staff, equip, and maintain one central laboratory. Since independence, Africans have made more serious attempts, with government encouragement, to participate intensely in the commercial activities of their countries. The technical know-how and capital required for industrial ventures are such that there are still very few large industrial concerns owned by African businessmen in the mixed economies.

Obviously it is not difficult to appreciate why, apart from a few government industrial research centers for the development of local products, very little industrial research has so far been done in most African countries. It would appear that if any significant progress is to be made in this respect, each government must take the initiative. Until a number of industrial research laboratories are set up locally, the technology for industries will not be properly established in these countries. One way of doing this could be for the government to urge foreign firms to set up these duplicate laboratories locally by offering them such incentives as capital allowances for tax purposes, and insisting that the laboratories be established as a condition for giving them licenses to manufacture and sell prescribed quantities of the commodities they propose to produce in local factories.

A second method for enhancing industrial research locally is for the government to set up laboratories mainly to examine the possibilities and problems of utilizing local raw materials in new industries or as replacements for materials being imported by existing local factories — e.g., vegetable fibers, rubber, timber, and food processing. One problem which has been encountered in this experiment is that sometimes there is difficulty in applying the research results to production on a commercial basis, i.e., in designing plants which can utilize the local materials concerned at competitive rates of investment return. Here the government might find use for a national science and technical research council, with a subsidiary industrial research council for coordinating the activities of government-sponsored research laboratories with the program of the industrial sector. This would ensure that the latter take a sufficient interest in following up the research results of the laboratories.

The government could also, in partnership with private companies, promote research in the utilization of the country's mineral resources. For if this is left entirely in the hands of expatriate companies, the latter can be placed in a strong position to dictate to the government the conditions under which they can utilize the resources — according to their research results. If the studies are carried out jointly, the government can decide under what terms it will issue the necessary extraction and utilization licenses.

Under the conditions of a mixed economy which prevail in most African countries, except countries like the U.A.R. and Tanzania, and owing to the limited resources at its disposal, government alone clearly cannot undertake all the necessary industrial research; it may perhaps be best to undertake this in partnership with private industrialists. It seems necessary that the government encourage and offer financial assistance to businessmen and technologists (particularly native ones) to establish industrial research services.

One aspect of such services is consulting engineering, which is lacking in many African countries, particularly for small-scale industries. As mentioned earlier, the big firms have their own research laboratories, usually in their home countries. The industrial research laboratories suggested here should provide local factories, on request and at reasonable prices, such services as identifying and solving problems connected with plant operation and breakdown.

These research service organizations could also provide testing and control services to industrial firms for periodic evaluation of their raw materials and finished products. This would be particularly useful for the food processing and beverage manufacturing plants. Certificates issued by the research organizations would both reduce the chances of the manufacturing firms purchasing raw materials of poor quality and ensure that consumers are getting finished products of good quality. It has been suggested that quality control should be a government function. It is doubtful, however, whether in a mixed economy the government should place itself between producers and consumers. Its position as a final arbiter might be compromised should matters come to a head as a result of, say, a public outcry against the quality and price of a particular product which is offered government protection against competing imports. Moreover, it is desirable that if the testing and control services are to be efficient, they should be commercially organized, instead of simply providing jobs for civil servants and the public.

Personnel Management
and Training

The structure of the public services inherited
from the colonial administration has not been properly reoriented toward meeting the development
needs of African governments. For instance, because of the lack of coordination between the technical ministries and the Ministry of Establishments
and the Public Service Commission, steps are not
taken in advance to introduce new posts into the
public service structure for such specialists as
petroleum engineers and professional cost accountants _ until the candidate applies for a job. Is
it therefore any surprise that a state with vast
mineral oil resources did not have a post for a
petroleum engineer to oversee its interest during
the first three years of oil production in that
state? Even when the specialist post is provided,
steps are not taken to create adequate career prospects for the incumbent; after a year or two, he
becomes frustrated and leaves for the private sector or the university. This situation has made it
difficult for governments to retain the services
of professional accountants and auditors.
    There is also the problem of civil service pro-
cedure which unduly emphasized seniority as a basis
for promotion; and in fact the alleged seniority
is often only longevity in the service. A professional accountant who finds the posts in the accounting
department manned only by unqualified but experienced
accountants might feel that, under seniority, he has
very little chance of getting to the top merely on
the basis of merit and professional competence.
    The other factor which limits promotion pros-
pects for those in the professional cadres of the
public service, as compared with their generalist
administrator counterparts, is that whereas the
latter belong to a large administrative class and
can be posted to any ministry, the former, by virtue of their specialties, belong to small cadres.

Each of these is restricted to a ministry, e.g., civil engineers to the Ministry of Works and Transport and agriculturists to the Ministry of Agriculture.

The problem of these small cadres of professionals has become more obvious in recent years, as the need has grown to employ new groups of professionals, such as industrial engineers, industrial economists, and planners for development project evaluation. In a country the size of Nigeria one way of creating a larger class of such professionals (thus improving their career prospects) is to have a single cadre serving all the governments in the Federation.[36] Even if this solution is satisfactory for the fairly large countries, the problem remains a difficult one for smaller countries.

Apart from the restrictions on promotion which the public service structure imposes on professionals and which reduces the number of competent candidates seeking government employment, a major factor which dampens the enthusiasm of those already in the service is the lack of incentive for innovating scientists and technologists. The inherited colonial-oriented regulations provide for long procedures to obtain the approval of heads of departments — even for scientific publications by civil servants. The absence of any provisions in these regulations for the award of incremental credits and other incentives for innovations also does not encourage innovation. Countries like Somalia have realized that the absence of incentives for the hard-working, and disincentives for the lazy, civil servants is a major administrative obstacle to development. "The efficient and dedicated are not rewarded and the dishonest and lazy prosper."[37]

Some of the discussions in this section point to weak links in the planning chain — the absence of effective manpower planning. It is strange that up to now a number of African countries have not established manpower planning units, although some propose to set up such units. Is it therefore any surprise that some countries approaching a stage of surplus arts graduates are still experiencing serious shortages of technologists and middle-grade technical personnel? The existence of a Manpower Board in Nigeria has enabled the local universities to be influenced in their policy on the mix of the undergraduates admitted, giving preference to students taking science and technical courses. Consequently there appears to be a swing from a 60:40 arts/science mix toward a 50:50 ratio, with the ultimate goal a 40:60 mix. In the same manner the Liberian Manpower Commission, established in 1966, was able in its first survey in 1966/67 to identify the severe shortages in the system of training middle- and high-level personnel. Manpower planning and utilization policy actively encouraged and supported by the President and Cabinet seems to have enabled Tanzania to redirect the education and training of its citizens, particularly youth, toward occupations required by the economy and objectives of national development.

The identification of these imbalances is one thing. Correcting them is a Herculean task which requires proper planning and good leadership at the executive (political) level. Some of the instruments which could be used for this purpose are training of science teachers and instructors, relating the training of unskilled manpower to development needs, reorientation of the primary and secondary school curricula and of the attitudes of their products to nonclerical jobs, and the provision of financial and technical facilities which would increase the productivity and income of peasant farming and improve infrastructural facilities to make rural life more attractive. For it is distressing to observe that a feature reported as early as 1902, that "some of the barely literate products of primary schools in South-Western Nigeria found manual work degrading,"[38] has since assumed much larger proportions not only in Nigeria but in practically all African countries.

Since independence most African governments
have devoted considerable resources to preservice
and in-service training. The main problem with
in-service training is that more serious efforts
must be made to gear it to the development needs
of the government. For instance, because of the
anxiety to utilize fellowships offered by donor
countries and organizations, many officers who
are anxious to have a "holiday" abroad are sponsored for courses from which they are not basically
qualified to benefit, or which have no bearing on
their post-training assignments, and/or are not
geared to the requirements of the economy. Both
the external and "local" contributions to the
training are thus virtually wasted in terms of
their potential contribution to the country's development.

Another example of poor planning of training
programs is that the institutions for middle-grade
training (such as the agricultural colleges in
most English-speaking African countries) have not
introduced into their curricula such subjects as
district and local development plan formulation and
implementation, farm management, and accounting.
The result is that the graduates are as good as
their pre-independence forerunners in modern methods of growing specific crops (mainly cash crops),
but they cannot advise peasant farmers how to control their production expenditures and how to keep
simple farm accounts. How, then, can the activities
of these extension staff seriously affect the peasants' farming methods if the farmers cannot, through
better management and the maintenance of records,
achieve and assess the increased productivity and
income possible under the new techniques? Is it
surprising that all political appeals and platitudes
encouraging school leavers to return to the land
have achieved insignificant results, since they
cannot see — because their parents have no farm
records — that farming is a paying proposition compared with the employment of wage earners in the

towns, whose monthly take-home pay, no matter how
small, they can easily assess?

The training of middle-grade personnel such as
agricultural, cooperative, and rural development
assistants has little or no interdisciplinary approach. They are still trained in their different
"cells" without taking account of the fact that in
the field these officers must assist local people
in formulating development programs which embrace
several ministries. They must be trained to work
as a team with officials of other departments and
agencies. An attempt is being made to fill this
training gap by the establishment of subregional
Pan-African Institute-sponsored Development Training Colleges in Douala and Buea, Cameroon, for
French and English-speaking countries, respectively.
These schools are also designed to give middle-grade
planning and extension staff an interdisciplinary
training in development.

Administrative and
Supporting Services

Given financial resources and trained manpower
as well as the availability of other factors of production, in order to get things moving, the government's administrative and supporting services and
its development agencies should function efficiently
and their operations should be subject to constant
review, so that they can meet the expanding needs
of functions in the public sector. This essay does
not intend to enumerate all the areas in which the
inefficient operation of public services presents
obstacles to development; only a few will be mentioned.

The two fundamental, related problems which affect the coordination of development programs are
those of confidence and of delegation of authority.
Far too much time is spent "minuting" on minor
subjects. This has been attributed to the legacy

115

of colonial administration. In recent years the
problem has been further aggravated by the question
of confidence. Heads of departments are wary of
delegating responsibility to their subordinates
at headquarters and in the field, while junior
officers, even where they possess delegated responsibilities, fear to exercise them without prior
consultation with their superiors for fear of making
serious mistakes. This not only leads to delays in
the formulation and execution of development programs, but also creates serious problems of coordination among field officers in different departments
who are involved in the execution of multi-depart-
mental projects. For where each officer must obtain approval from his head of department on every
minor issue, nothing ever gets done. For example,
a few years ago in Madagascar "The Ministry charged
with repairing a highway after the Ministry of Telecommunications had placed telephone cables underground,
repaved the highway before the Ministry of Telecommunications had laid the cables."[39]

The frequent changes in government, with the subsequent appointments of commissions of inquiry by
the incoming government to investigate the activities
of its predecessor, have added a new dimension to the
problem of confidence. In some African countries
which have witnessed frequent changes in governments,
civil servants are becoming very wary about policy
advice they tender. They are equally cautious to
record the advice in writing, in order to protect
themselves against unwarranted charges at future in-
quiries. This attitude encourages the exchange of
unnecessary correspondence between departments and
also discourages delegation of functions.

In the administration of technical services,
problems of coordination exist. In the absence of
a central organization with sufficient authority to
coordinate the purchase of vehicles, air-condition-
ing, and office equipment, each department usually
obtains its supplies from whatever source it likes.
The result is that the Ministry of Works and Trans-

116

port experiences serious difficulties in stocking spare parts and in staffing its workshops with technical personnel who can maintain this wide range of vehicles and equipment. Sometimes prototype equipment for which there are inadequate supplies of spare parts in the country are purchased by a department, and they fall into disuse after a short period for lack of maintenance.

In other cases coordination between the agency installing a plant in a new project and the department which is to undertake its maintenance becomes problematic. For instance, in one country the organization responsible for the maintenance of the plant installed in a newly built hospital was not given due notice to arrange with the manufacturers of the plant for the training of the maintenance staff until the hospital was due to be opened.

There is also the question of coordination between the Establishments Ministry and the Technical Ministry as to the nature of the staff required for certain technical jobs. In one country, for example, the posting of experienced senior clerical staff as storekeepers in facilities containing spare parts for vehicles and other agricultural equipment has created a problem. Because these clerk/storekeepers have inadequate technical training, they do not understand the roles of certain vital spare parts in the life of a vehicle or other equipment, or the life expectancy of such spare parts. They therefore do not place replacement orders well in advance; vehicles and mechanical equipment consequently break down and cannot be promptly repaired when they are most urgently needed by farmers.

Furthermore, the absence of effective supervision of junior staff causes trouble in organizations where the existence of good human relations and expeditious dispatch of business are essential, e.g., airports and seaports. For instance, in one African country it takes about a year to get a passport issued or renewed, and sometimes the applicant's file is lost by the Passport Office in

117

the process. In another country the discourtesy
with which the immigration staff treats visitors
is enough to scare off prospective foreign investors and tourists, on whose capital and currency the
country's development could to some extent depend.
If it is realized that foreigners' first impressions
about the attitude of citizens toward nonnationals
are usually formed at ports of entry, one easily
apprehends the need for having carefully selected
supervisory staff at these centers — not only to
ensure that subordinate staff are courteous to
visitors and perform their duties with efficiency
and dispatch, but also to see that supervisors are
available to attend anyone in difficulty.

There are, besides, far too many forms which
the public is required to complete for immigration,
or taxation, or for vehicle and other licenses and
permits. The questions in these forms are too complicated for the semieducated persons who form a
sizable proportion of the population of the African
countries. At one international airport one is
expected to complete in duplicate a form of two
foolscap-size pages, only to declare whether he
is taking away some of the country's currency or
works of art. Because of the length of the form
the immigration staff usually has no time to examine every completed form when there are perhaps
100 passengers queueing to board an international
flight. This has now led to the emergence of an
unauthorized professional class of "form fillers"
who are found around the motor licensing offices
and airports of this country. The function of
these persons is to assist drivers and travelers
in completing their immigration and application
forms — "in consideration" of a fixed charge or
a substantial tip.

The filing registries of many government departments have not been reorganized to cope with the
expansion of their activities. Whereas the system
of submitting incoming mail to all senior officers
in an office before it is filed may function toler-
ably well in a small divisional office with a dis-

118

trict officer and one or two assistants, this is
certainly a slow process which could delay the
handling of urgent mail in a secretariat of a ministry with about 30 to 40 senior staff. The significant adverse effect of this procedure came to
light a few years ago: the members of a health
workers union in one West African state were on
the point of striking before top officials of the
ministry realized that the union had several weeks
earlier sent a petition listing their grievances,
and had followed this up with a strike notice. It
was eventually discovered that all this correspondence
was in the mail jacket on the table of an officer who
was away from station for a long period. This officer had no connection with this particular subject.
Even more significant, the ministry was already taking steps to meet more of the demands in the petition
but had not communicated this fact to the union.

The submissions which young professional, administrative, and executive staff make to their superior
officers and other urgent work are often subject to
considerable delays in being typed. This is a result of understaffing of the typing pools because
many of the stenographers posted to each ministry
are attached to the offices of the senior officers,
where they are underemployed while the officers
are away attending meetings or on tour. Because,
as a matter of prestige, these officers must have
personal secretaries around them, urgent typing
work is often difficult to redistribute when there
is pressure on the typing pool.

Conclusion

It is neither intended (nor is it possible) in
a short essay to propose comprehensive solutions
for the various development administration problems
mentioned above. One can only suggest a number of
areas in which reform appears to be urgent for the
amelioration of existing problems, in order that

African countries can make reasonable progress in
the economic and social fields during the Second
Development Decade.

The system of development planning which each
country will adopt will depend on its political,
economic, and social orientation. Whatever system is adopted, the administrative machinery for
planning should be designed and staffed in such
a manner that, as far as possible, the permanent
top civil servants in the country should bear
major responsibility for formulating and implementing the plan. Foreign experts should only
act as technical advisers to the civil servants.
It is here that the countries which need advisers
can use the services of the Multidisciplinary Advisory Planning Teams which the United Nations
and its Regional Commissions plan to offer to
them.

The planning experts in the planning organization
or in other allied agencies such as the Development
Bank should also descend from the "ivory tower" of
econometric models down to the earth of continuous
dialogue with the so-called generalist administrators during the plan's formulation and implementation. The plan should in this manner be based as
far as possible on the existing and properly estimated future administrative capability of the
country. This of course means that if government
functionaries at the various levels are involved
in the planning process, they will be in a position
to advise on the administrative capacity available
to execute the program. Here we can join Professor
Arthur Lewis in cautioning:

> No administration should be loaded with
> tasks more numerous or more delicate than
> it can handle, the quantity and forms of
> planning should be limited strictly within
> the capacity of the machine.[40]

120

Recognizing that the techniques and procedures of modern national development planning are relatively new and that many top civil servants in ministries have not yet acquired them, it is desirable to establish planning units or cells in the large ministries. Where they exist, they should be strengthened by the posting of planners from the central planning organization, who could assist the staff of the ministries in formulating development programs and reporting on their implementation to the central planning organization.

In the long run, especially for countries of moderate size, in the interest of economy it might be useful to give many administrative officers crash postgraduate training courses in economic development so that some of them could man the planning units of the ministries. This would also help to bridge the mental gap between the "generalist" administrators and the "professional" planners. In this manner the existing "generalist" administrative class would develop into an integrationist administrative class better oriented to appreciate the terminology and the tools which the expert planners use in their reports. In the same vein, these experts and other civil service scientists and technologists involved in development should, by means of staff college and similar short courses, be encouraged to appreciate the political and social factors which the political leaders and their administrative advisers take into consideration in modifying their development proposals.

Particularly for countries without centrally planned socialist economies the cooperation of the private sector in the implementation of the plan is necessary. For instance, as mentioned earlier in this paper, the profitable disposal within the country of the products of public and other enterprises depends on the willingness and ability of commercial interests in the private sector to popularize domestic products and restrict imports of competing commodities. For this and other reasons,

the government, with the support of the central
planning organization, should establish a broadly
based Central Planning Consultative Committee or
Board representing the various major economic,
social, and political interests in the country.
The committee should be consulted by the government on the major policy guidelines for its development plan, and on the draft plan before it is
approved. It should also be consulted for advice
and assistance regarding major bottlenecks in the
implementation of programs. In addition, the major
development ministries, such as Agriculture and
Industry, should be encouraged to have sectoral advisory committees representing official and business interests in these sectors, which can offer
detailed advice on their development programs.

Since no government can expect to provide entirely from its central Treasury the financial resources, or from its own limited civil service the
human resources, to implement a development plan
without the participation and cooperation of the
people, African countries should devote greater
attention to designing the administrative machinery
for "planning from below." To do this successfully,
they should tackle the problem of establishing
local government councils with adequate human and
financial resources to provide reasonable support
to any district and local development committees
for the formulation and implementation of local
development programs. Until this step is taken,
the efforts of these committees tend to be *ad hoc*
for lack of permanently established institutions
with legal powers to raise funds for financing,
partially or fully, local projects included in the
national plan. For unless such financial contributions can be systematically raised and utilized,
the principle of mass participation in the plan
cannot be realized. Provincial, district, and
local development committees without such an institutional base will only degenerate into assemblies.
In turn, the assemblies' principal interest will

be to put up as many development project proposals as possible for inclusion in the national plan — to be financed from the Treasury which is assumed to have inexhaustible reserves. On the other hand, projects which are not included in the national plan are left to be executed *ad hoc* by means of the self-help efforts of the individual local communities; the operational link between the "grass root" organization and the national planning organization virtually breaks.

For any government which is committed to promoting industrialization by active participation in public enterprises, the establishment of a Project Formulation and Appraisal Unit manned by industrial engineers and economists, agricultural economists, and other specialists is a desideratum. While a fairly wealthy or large country can afford to employ a large team permanently, a smaller country might so employ a few experts and supplement their services with those of other experts employed on short-term contracts. Here the services of technical assistance consultants from the United Nations and other organizations can be used effectively. The unit's main task would be to prepare preliminary feasibility studies of selected projects, the execution of which the government could promote as public enterprises by means of a "shopping list" for private participation. The unit should appraise and advise on the feasibility of projects initiated by various government departments and agencies, and by private businessmen for government participation.

Once the government decides, on the basis of the evaluation reports of the unit, to participate substantially in any project, it is desirable that the proposed project be advertised for bidding. On consideration of the various bids, the government can decide whether or not to go into partnership with the firm which made the original proposal, with or without modifications in the proposal, or to make alternative arrangements for the establishment of the project.

The employment of independent consultants to supervise the construction of any large project is necessary to ensure that the work, materials, plant, and equipment meet the specifications in the bid. To avoid collusion, care must be exercised in selecting for each project a consultant who has no connections whatsoever with the contractor and the technical partner.

In order to ensure that the taxpayers' interests are adequately protected in all public enterprises in which the government has a substantial financial stake, the establishment of a central management service unit is desirable. The unit should be staffed by professional accountants, auditors, and management service experts. It should regularly inspect the interprises' administration and suggest to the management, the boards of directors, and the government, ways and means of adjusting their structures and their personnel and financial organizations to achieve greater efficiency.

The effectiveness of the management service unit would depend to a great extent on the cooperation which the managements of the public enterprises are prepared to give to the unit in the form of accurate information about the problems of the organization, rational use of its expertise, and prompt implementation of recommendations they have accepted. For this reason, it is in the country's long-term interest to have its own qualified nationals in strategic management positions in these enterprises. This it can do only by giving sufficient priority to the training of accountants, auditors, public secretaries, and market specialists. The increased government involvement in large-scale development projects implies the need in the accounting and audit departments for professionally qualified accountants and auditors who can advise the government on such matters as modern budgetary control. The recent start made by the Kenya Government in the accelerated training of these personnel for localized professional qualifications is a step in the right direction. Hopefully other African governments will cooperate with the Economic Commission for Africa as it encourages them to establish similar multinational training programs and qualification standards.

Since the pace and the degree of success with which development programs can be executed in the field depend greatly on the amount of coordination between the extension staffs of the different ministries and agencies, the need for an interdisciplinary approach to their training cannot be overemphasized. As mentioned earlier in this paper, so far, apart from a few institutions such as those in Douala and Buea, very little appears to have been done in this field in African countries south of the Sahara. It is left to the governments to follow the examples of the sponsors of the two institutes and decide how multinational institutions may provide adequate interdisciplinary training in the development of middle-grade planning and extension personnel.

In the field of research for the development of agricultural products, it is hoped that when agricultural research councils are established by various African countries, these councils will devote their attention initially to the evolution of an all-embracing national policy on the development of the various facets of production, storage, and marketing of certain key commodities — especially those which have import substitution applications. In addition, various suggestions have been offered in the section on development research of this paper on the ways and means to encourage research into the development of industrial production.

While African governments plan for the large development projects, they should not ignore the need to reorient various routine administrative and supporting services (some of which have been mentioned in this paper) to meet the needs of the growing development functions of these governments.

NOTES

1. C. S. Magat, "Manpower Planning and Administrative Management," a paper presented to the Regional Seminar on Manpower Planning and Utilization Dakar, October, 1969.

2. Albert Waterston, "Administrative Obstacles to Planning," *Economía Latinoamericana*, I, 3 (July, 1964), 349-50.

3. A. Adedji, "Federalism, Economic Planning and Plan Administration," presented at Conference on National Reconstruction and Development in Nigeria, March, 1969.

4. United Nations General Assembly Resolutions 723 (VIII), 1024 (XI), 1256 (XIII), 1530 (XV), and 1710 (XVI), *United Nations Public Administration Newsletter*, No. 28 (November, 1969), p. 1.

5. United Nations Economic and Social Council resolutions, *Official Records*, 42d Session, May 8-June 6, 1967, Supp. No. 1 (E/4393), p. 25.

6. "From the 1960s to the 1970s, a New Year Message," *United Nations Public Administration Newsletter*, No. 29 (January, 1970), p. 7.

7. A. L. Adu, "The Administrator and Change," Working Paper No. 1 for the Sixth Inter-African Public Administration Seminar, Achimota, Ghana, November, 1967.

8. "Administration of National Development Planning," report of a meeting of experts held at Paris, June 8-19, 1964. New York: United Nations Publication No. ST/TAO/M/27, p. 14.

9. *Administrative Organization for Development,* Conference Report, Royal Institute of Public Administration, London: Lawrence Bros. Ltd., 1965, pp. 39-40.

10. Adedeji, *op. cit.,* p. 37.

11. *A Report on the Administration and Operation of State Enterprises Under the Work Schedule of the State Enterprises Secretariat for the Period 1964-65,* Accra: Government Printer, 1969, p. 68.

12. Adedeji, *op. cit.,* p. 32; E.C.A., *Public Administration Mission to The Gambia, August 1969,* document no. M69-3143, p. 6; and *Public Administration Mission to Ghana, July 1969,* document no. M69-3013, pp. 6-7.

13. Report on the S.I.P.A. Special Seminar "What Went Wrong with the Somali First Five Year Economic Plan (1963/67)," Mogadiscio, November, 1967, p. 9.

14. Republic of Kenya, *Development Plan 1970-74,* Nairobi: Government Printer p. 183.

15. *Ibid.,* p. 182.

16. *A Report on the Administration and Operation of State Enterprises Under the Work Schedule of the State Enterprises Secretariat for the Period 1964-65,* pp. 65,66.

17. Federal Republic of Nigeria, *National Development Plan: Progress Report 1964,* pp. 30-33.

18. I. A. Malik, *Harmonization of Fiscal and Budgetary Procedures and Policies with Development Planning,* Economic Commission for Africa, Trade and Economic Co-operation Division, Document no. 69-860/35 (August, 1969), p. 58.

19. *Sierra Leone — Statement on the Budget for
1967/68*, broadcast by Col. A. T. Juxon-Smith, Chairman, National Reformation Council, June 30, 1967
Sierra Leone: Government Printer, 1967), pp. 6-7.

20. Report on the SIPA Special Seminar "What
Went Wrong with the Somali First Five-Year Economic
Plan (1963-67)," p. 11.

21. United Republic of Tanzania, *Background to
the Budget — an Economic Survey, 1968-69* Dar es
Salaam: Government Printer, p. 1; *Second Five-
Year Plan for Economic and Social Development,
1 July 1969 - 30 June 1974*, Vol. I, *General Analysis*
Dar es Salaam: Government Printer, 1969), p. 16.

22. E.C.A., *Public Administration Mission to
Sierra Leone, August 1969*, E.C.A. Document No.
70-31/85), p. 20; P. C. Asiodu, "Plan for Further
Industrial Development in Nigeria," presented at
Conference on National Reconstruction and Development in Nigeria, March, 1969, p. 2, Report on
the S.I.P.A. Special Seminar "What Went Wrong with
the Somali First Five Year Economic Plan (1963-67),"
p. 9.

23. Albert Waterston, *Development Planning,
Lessons of Experience* (Baltimore: John Hopkins
Press, 1966), pp. 354-55.

24. G. Oka Orewa, *Taxation in Western Nigeria —
The Problems of an Emergent State* (London: Oxford
University Press), p. 20.

25. E.C.A., Report of *Public Administration
Mission to Ghana, Economic Commission for Africa,
July, 1969*, Addis Ababa: E.C.A. Document No.
M69-3013, p. 21.

26. *Report on Policy and Manpower Issues in
African Agricultural Research — the Implications for*

Africa, ECA/FAO Joint Division of Agriculture, Addis Ababa, 1966, p. 62.

27.   Kenya, Colony and Protectorate of, *Report of the Committee of Inquiry into the Dairy Industry* (Nairobi: Government Printer, 1956), para. 17.

28.   United Republic of Tanzania, *Second Five-Year Plan for Economic and Social Development, 1 July 1969 - 30 June 1974,* Vol. I, *General Analysis* Dar es Salaam: Government Printer, 1969), p. 48; *Background to the Budget — An Economic Survey, 1968-69* (Dar es Salaam: Government Printer, 1968), p. 45.

29.   Republic of Kenya, *Economic Survey 1968* (Nairobi: Government Printer,   ), pp. 56-60.

30.   E.C.A., *Public Administration Mission to Sierra Leone, August 1969,* E.C.A. Document No. 70-31/85, p. 21.

31.   Republic of Ghana, *Economic Survey 1964* (Accra: State Publishing Corporation, 1965), p. 71; *Economic Survey 1968* (Accra: State Publishing Corporation, 1969), p. 73.

32.   *World Plan of Action: Ethiopia, Survey of Needs and Priorities,* E.C.A. Document No. M 70-581, 1970, p. 23.

33.   St. G. C. Cooper *et al., Agricultural Research in Tropical Africa, an Introduction* (Nairobi: East African Literature Bureau) E.C.A. Document No. M.69-2996, pp. 135-37.

34.   E.C.A., *World Plan of Action: Ethiopia,* p. 21.

35.   Margery Perham, *Lord Lugard: The Dual Mandate in British Tropical Africa* (Frank Cass and Co., Ltd., London) pp. 615, 617.

36. Adedeji, *op. cit.*, p. 37.

37. Report on the S.I.P.A. Special Seminar "What Went Wrong with the Somali First Five Year Economic Plan (1963-67)," Mogadiscio, 1968, p. 19.

38. Margery Perham, *Native Administration in Nigeria* (London: Oxford University Press), p. 16.

39. Albert Waterston, "Administrative Obstacles to Planning," p. 328.

40. W. Arthur Lewis, *The Principles of Economic Planning* (Washington, D.C.: Public Affairs Press, 1949), p. 122.

Complexity and African Development Administration: A Sociological Perspective

by W. Bediako Lamouse-Smith

. . . all scientific descriptions of facts
are highly selective. . . . It is not only
impossible to avoid a selective point of
view, but also wholly undesirable to attempt
to do so; for if we could do so, we should
get not a more "objective" description, but
only a mere heap of entirely unconnected
statements. But, of course, a point of view
is inevitable; and the naive attempt to
avoid it can only lead to self-deception,
and to the uncritical application of an unconscious point of view.

K. R. Popper[1]

The 1960's were called Africa's decade by some observers. It was the decade during which a majority
of African colonies attained political independence
and assumed the full responsibilities of nationhood.
Their assumption of political independence was accompanied by the inheritance of structures which
somehow had served their original creators fairly
well. After independence our leaders saw that a

number of these structures lacked properties essential for public institutions of free nations. Public administrators and their organizations did not escape the criticisms of dysfunction — sometimes expressed in terms such as stooges, colonial agents, or imperialist lackeys — from the new political ruling elites. In fact, African countries inherited a public administration which oriented itself to British or European tastes while not solving British or European problems. This kind of public administration was not fit for politically independent countries, yet there was no immediate substitute. The tasks which administrators faced, and are still facing, are not meant to be coped with through the traditional systems of administration, which has its roots in the Western systems.

It was perhaps in order to make the operation of post-independence public administration acceptable to a world which has not always sympathetically understood, appreciated, and accepted African problems that new tags had to emerge to characterize the kind of administration which exists in Africa today. Hence the term "development administration." Of course, the concept of development administration was not meant only for Africa; it was meant for the "backward" nations, sometimes also called the "underdeveloped" or the "developing" nations. The implication is not that countries which take on the adjective "developed" have hit the ceiling of development. We are told they are also developing, but that relatively they are more advanced technologically and in terms of per capita income. Yet the concept of development administration, for instance, would not be used for the developed countries even though they have by no means come to a halt in improving their public administrations. However, if nothing else, the concept of development administration evokes sympathetic attitudes toward problems of administration in developing countries by drawing attention to the fact that these countries have administrative and political

difficulties as well as interests and aspirations
which do not coincide with those experienced in the
administrative operations of the developed nations.
The goal of this paper is fourfold. First, it
seeks to point out some of the events (not necessarily peculiar to Africa) which affect public administration in Africa and are affected by it.
Second, we shall show why these problems being aspects of development, should be approached with
instruments of development — breaking with the past
and planning for the future. Third, we shall argue that a number of problems, often seen as dysfunctions of the system (in this case, the public
administration) or its environment, could be better
understood if they were seen through a theory of
complexity. Fourth, an attempt will be made to
present tentative suggestions to reduce the complex
relations which hamper planning and administrative
effort in Africa.

The Concept of
Development
Administration

Let us take the second point first, since the
concept of development administration has already
been mentioned. Swerdlow has argued that the concept of development administration is not an empty
one and should not be made to lose its meaning,
since operationally it distinguishes the kind of
public administration which obtains in the developing countries from that of the developed countries.[2]
For him the dividing line between the developing
and the developed countries is the economic differentiation in income; if the developing countries
wish to develop their economies and experience social change. then their administrative structures
and operations would not be identical with public
administration in developed countries. One may
question the basis of Swerdlow's assumption that

developing nations desire or even aspire to be
identical with the developed nations in public administration. Perhaps Swerdlow did not state his
case clearly enough to rid it of this implication.
However, I agree with him that there are administrative problems and functions in developing countries which may not be appreciated by those unac-
customed to bureaucracy other than the Western
type. If Max Weber's ideal type were ever to be
a real type, then public administration in developing countries could be dismissed in one word —
pathological.

The countries designated rather benignly as "developing" are perhaps more aptly and bluntly described as economically primitive countries. They
have to get out of their primitiveness. Hence, for
Merle Fainsod:

> Development administration is a carrier of
> innovating values . . . it embraces the array
> of new functions assumed by developing coun-
> tries embarking on the path of moderniza-
> tion and industrialization . . . (it) or-
> dinarily involves the establishment of mach-
> inery for planning economic growth and mobi-
> lizing and allocating resources to expand
> national income.[3]

If Fainsod had not mentioned "functions assumed by
developing countries embarking on the path of modernization and industrialization" in the quotation above,
his description of development administration might
have been said to be equally true for the developed
nations. Surely they also must innovate, draw up
development programs and operate economically in
such a way that there is no stagnation or retro-
gression in the real national income per capita.
When Max Weber predicted the universal spread of
bureaucracy across nations, he certainly did not
take the differential growth of per capita income
into consideration.

Riggs pointed out in an early work the role of public administration in assisting economic development.[4] And in a later publication, where he introduced the concept "administrative development," he expanded on the previous idea to show that development administration is not just the

> . . . administrative means required to
> achieve developmental goals, i.e., growth
> . . . Rather . . . (it) occurs only if we
> find bureaucracy increasingly responsible
> as agent for the implementation of policies
> formulated by institutions outside the
> bureaucracy.[5]

For African countries, for example, this would mean that the emergence of development administration, its survival, and its successful operation would be a function of the coincidence of goals of the civil servants and the politicians, of the various ministries and the ruling political party, and of trade unions and ministries.

All the definitions which identify the concept of development administration with problems often cited by the developing countries, (e.g., "modernization," industrialization, land reform, raising of per capita incomes) are poignantly summarized by Weidner. He draws attention to the two major meanings implicit in the concept: that development administration is both programmatic and goal-oriented.

> Development administration in government
> refers to the process of guiding an organ-
> ization toward the achievement of progressive
> political, economic and social objectives,
> that are authoritatively determined in one
> manner or another. (Further) if there are
> no development goals, there is no develop-
> ment administration.[6]

If I accept the concept of development administration as apt for understanding public administration in tropical Africa, it is not only because of the various interpretations of the concept as discussed above. Rather, it is because the concept manifestly draws attention to the concrete problems encountered in a number of countries. It also shows how the problems' multivariate characteristics make simple generalizations difficult. At the same time it sheds light on some of the problems which are not immediately visible. Considered from the point of view of the revolutionaries in contemporary Africa, development administration assumes a special meaning and importance. It is that special kind of public administration which has not come to a standstill and may perhaps be contrasted with the "established" mother administrations of the West which gave birth to those in Africa. (Robert Merton, Michel Crozier, and Niklas Luhman have unearthed a number of patho--logies which are associated with the "established" public administration.)[7]

In development administration there is room for trial and error, dynamism, uncertainties, and experimentation. Ideas and method would be adopted from wherever they may be found, but their adaptation should be governed by local conditions and requirements. A recent reminder came from the then President of Uganda, Dr. A. Milton Obote, when he was outlining his government policy (which included a number of new decisions on Uganda's public administration):

> These decisions have been taken in order to promote the policy of Uganda being able to control, manage, and direct the development in our own style, fashion, and standards.[8]

Administrative systems inherited at the time of independence must of necessity go through processes of adaptation and innovation to suit unorthodox situations. These changes are what give public administrations in Africa the quality of development.

The manner in which present-day African development administration has been conceived here is tantamount to the accepting non-predeterminable and non-static ecological factors shaping new role performances and images for the public bureaucracy. For instance, I do not consider problems (concrete or imaginary) in development administration as necessarily dysfunctional in the sense of measuring the empirical administration against some ideal type or a particular goal expectation. I would reject such a polarization and would classify as functional those problems which other scholars might call dysfunctional: development administration is a "process in civilization."[9] Errors in experimentation often constitute an inevitable, and a precious, ingredient in the process of seeking that which will satisfy. (The Apollo 13 mission was in this sense valuable, although the goal of collecting rocks from the moon was not achieved.)

Some African Problems

The approach to the concept of development administration suggested above offers clues to where we should look for problems besetting public administrations in Africa. What I call problems are those events whose appearance disturbs, then concerns, influential individuals or groups as well as large sections of the masses in a nation, who, either overtly or covertly, demand correction of the particular events. The influential groups (usually the educated "high and mighty") may take their corrective reference from administrative models existing in the West. The peasant or worker who has never seen the four walls of a classroom, and who may have no notion of French or British models of public administration, would, through his ordinary common sense, recognize when the administrators and their organizations err in fulfilling the expectations of the masses, the promises of independence.

In discussing development administration in Africa, it would be idle to pretend that traditional African systems of government had any profound impact on the operation of the public bureaucracies set up by the colonial administrations — notwithstanding the institution of indirect rule in the colonies of Britain. In fact, the public administration introduced into African countries during the colonial era was not a voluntary adoption by the "natives" but, rather, an imposition from the outside. Paradoxically, however, development administration in African countries came to exist only after independence. As A. L. Adu succinctly puts it:

> . . . the old colonial administrations and technical departments were concerned with such matters as maintenance of law and order, local administration, the provision of a moderate level of social services, elementary communication networks and the husbanding of natural resources. There were no five or ten year development plans, no major policies on industrialization, no talk of providing economic infrastructure services, nor any full development of the economy, no balance of payment difficulties, no talk of deficit financing policies, no central banking nor the creation of money markets, and no external relations problems whether political, economic or commercial.[10]

Some people think that it is all too common for educated Africans and politicians to beat a dead horse — colonialism. I think eight years of freedom from colonial tutelage, even 13 years, as in the case of Ghana, is, in terms of historical time, too short to allow the mind to forget events which took place prior to independence. Complaints from Africans about systems of ideas, beliefs, values,

and artifacts inherited from the colonial era,
which in one way or another affect the operation
of development administration in their countries
today, should not be brushed aside with a light
wave of the hand. Recently I asked an elderly
administrator why his organization had not changed
certain forms of operation. His answer was, "This
is how we were brought up by them ('them' were his
British administrative predecessors). You expect
us to give it all up and forget it in eight years
of independence?" A number of the problems we shall
enumerate have their origins here.

Let us look, for example, at some of the decisions taken by the Uganda Government for its public service. By inference one can decipher the
shortcomings which these decisions are meant to
correct:

> The first point in the decisions is that
> from now on there shall be one Public Ser-
> vice embracing all public officers in the
> Government, district administration, and
> urban authorities and teaching services.
> Secondly, Government has decided that there
> shall be one uniform salary structure for
> all persons working in any organization
> known as or designated as a Public Body,
> and this will include persons working in
> any company where any Parastatal Body or
> Bodies own at least 51% of the shares.
> . . . This is designed to remove the ex-
> isting anomalies whereby many people with
> the same basic education and the same
> number of years of training are employed
> in different salary scales.[11]

These diverse associations, plus all the parastatel
commercial enterprises, join to form the new public
service. It is unusual that non-civil servants are
grouped with the officials of public bureaucracy
and subjected to common conditions of employment.

Perhaps only under the rubric of development administration can students of public administration encounter the recruiting procedures and organizational rules of a civil service being extended to embrace voluntary organizations: "co-operative unions and societies, the trade unions, and the Uganda People's Congress."

Another decision abolished extra allowances paid to public officers when they were transferred from one part of the country to another:

> . . . no acting, duty or disturbance allowance shall be payable to any officer, except in the case of an officer who may be called upon to perform the duties of a Permanent Secretary, or a Head of Department.

These allowances, which had been paid to civil servants on occasions of transfers, acting in higher offices, or working overtime, "were an important administrative matter which the Government inherited from the colonial days."[12]

Problems associated with one of the vital factors in planning and administration — efficiency — were also decided upon:

> The biggest obstacle to efficiency and raising of standard in the Public Service has been almost rigidly based on seniority determined on length of service. This has frustrated bright young officers who are capable of serving at higher levels, but cannot do so because of short service. . . . Government has therefore decided that no officer who is otherwise capable and meritorious will be deterred from promotion on the grounds of seniority based on length of service. Similarly, officers who have lived their usefulness will be retired in the public interest.[13]

The problems for the development administration of Uganda which are deducible from the "decisions" quoted above are many, but I will highlight only a few. The overtime allowances paid to civil servants, for instance, amount to double payment, since the contracted terms of service state that an official's services can be called upon anytime during the twenty-four hours of the day. These allowances are thus a drain on money which could be directed into development projects. But are not other problems created by enforcing a contractual condition which has been ignored for such a long time? How were these allowances evaluated by those who were accustomed to drawing them and who, perhaps, made sure that they did work overtime? The decision to introduce examinations which public servants would take every five years, as well as the decision to promote young officers who were efficient and hardworking, are meant to raise the standard of work performance. While this problem is being solved, another is simultaneously created by releasing "in the public interest" the old hands who cannot match the bright young officers. How does the public look after those retired for not passing their examinations?

In the pursuit of a public service which is not extravagant and which provides its consumers with the expected services, the Government had to decide on these measures, which may appear unorthodox in nations with "established" public administration. One might further argue that those public servants whose statuses in the administration had been determined solely by length of service (seniority) are less receptive to the new ideas of development. Resistance to new ideas is also a problem in planning. The decision on leveling salaries throughout all organizations which now come under the public service draws our attention to problems hitherto experienced when new hands are being recruited into civil service. Chief among them is the loss of prospective civil servants to the non-governmental sectors of the economy.

In order to put the problems in African development administration into the perspective of these essays, we should bear in mind how these problems relate to organization per se and to development planning. The usual executing machinery for the latter is the public service. As the idea of having or intending to draw up a five-year development plan has come to acquire respectability for its own sake, the world creditor banks will not readily give loans unless sophisticated econometric models, purported to be plans for development, are put on the counter. (The interested observer often wonders how many top public officials and politicians acquire the faintest understanding of the models they are expected to transform into empirically visible results.)

A. L. Adu's *The Civil Service in New African States* has dealt at length with the structure, operation, strengths, and deficiencies mainly of British colonial service in tropical Africa and the problems which would accompany its transition into the post-independence period.[14] René Dumont's *False Start in Africa* has exposed and extensively discussed a variety of problems, drawing mainly from francophone[15] Africa, which plague the African era of development administration and has justified his question whether Africans are not the cause of their own backwardness in social and economic development.[16] In spite of the extensive presentations, neither author could exhaust the problems encountered in Africa's development administration. Much less can I exhaust them here. The problems are variegated; each is multi-dimensional. Taking for granted the existence of real differences in detail when any single problem is isolated and examined within the context of any particular African nation, it can be suggested that regardless of colonial background, all independent countries of tropical Africa encounter identical or similar problems in their efforts at development administration. A few of these problems which abound in the literature on African public administration, economics, politics, and sociology will be mentioned here.

For the sake of analysis the problems will be introduced under the typologies "externally induced," meaning that the weight of the source(s) of the problem lies outside the nation, and "Internally originated," meaning problems whose sources are overwhelmingly traceable to the social structure of a given nation. These are types, not a classification.[17] The choice of a typology is a matter of convenience, for in any empirical situation events may intermesh so finely that no distinction of sources can be made. One could also have taken a continuum along which to differentiate rural, municipal, district, regional, and central administrative problems insofar as each category bears on development.

Externally induced problems

The myth of impartiality

The colonial administration propagated the idea of a civil servant's impartiality to the clientele of the public bureaucracy. This idea was based on a model which has never been wholly realized in the concrete situations met by the bureaucracies of the metropolitan countries. In fact, the idea of impartial public service and servants can be counted among the myths of the Weberian ideal type of bureaucracy. Yet in the post-independence civil services of Africa, one frequently meets complaints especially from top officials, that the impartiality of the civil service is being tampered with by the new political leaders. I would suggest that the real meaning behind this complaint is that when the civil servant feels threatened by the dynamism of the imaginative politician, the concept of impartiality becomes a useful channel of escape.

It is difficult to see how a civil service committed to the idea of undertaking projects hitherto unknown to or ignored by the colonial administration can claim impartiality vis-`a-vis the plans of the government in power. Impartiality to programs is not the same as treating all clients impersonally. When governments have insisted on the introduction of revolutionary ideas and rejected the impartiality myth, a number of African civil servants have left the service, and even their countries, for jobs elsewhere. An identical situation arises with the armies. A number of armies in Africa consider themselves heirs to imperial military traditions and values. The soldiers are more loyal to their officers than to the state, while the armies claim to be "nonpolitical," i. e., impartial, and expect to be accorded "martial freedom," like university teachers propagating academic freedom. There is another myth inherited from colonial service values — "I serve the government of the day" — meaning the civil servant takes no blame for a political decision and action whose origin might in fact be traced back to him. After all, he not only advises his minister but also supplies him with facts and guides the selection of the optimum decision.

The problems deriving from the myths of impartiality, apolitical civil service, and martial freedom reflect the lack of commitment of these very important parts of the public administration to the formulation and/or implementation of the programs planned for development. A letter on intellectual honesty addressed to senior civil servants of Tanzania by the head of that country's civil service stated:

> As citizens we are not prohibited from political activity or interest; on the contrary, it is necessary that we should play an active part in Tanzanian national life. We are inevitably involved in political affairs. . . . Our task demands the full use of our brains, intelligence and energy. We are partners in the great struggle to build our country. . . .[17]

144

While the Tanzanian civil servant accepts full commitment to and participates freely in his country's development goals, we do not observe this trend in many African countries where the legacy of the myth of impartiality provides rationale and cover for the actions of the conservative and of those who sit on the fence.

Foreign aid and trade

A common occurrence in Africa has been the influx of "experts" from developed countries to help the new nations plan their development. Guy Hunter has this to say about experts:

> . . . developed countries advise the creation of a system (to tell the truth, the developing countries also demand it), which reflects their own sophistication and resources. . . . Because most of these are provided on aid terms at present, they are not seen as "a burden on the back" of the developing country. But this is an illusion.[19]

The sophisticated plans of these experts later come to be blamed upon the politicians as prestige projects by the very nations who sent the experts. Since the experts often have the latent obligation of selling the produce of their own countries, it should be no wonder that their plans for a poor country should "reflect their own sophistication and resources." However, the least such plans do is to strain the extremely limited manpower and financial resources available to the development administrator. The plans delivered by experts from the developed nations cannot fail to include built-in obsolescence. The progress of development becomes slower than the politicians and their civil servants expected.

Under the very misleading name of "development aid," loans have come from developed nations to finance projects that supposedly contribute to the economic and social development of the developing nations. Closer scrutiny reveals that loans are given more often to serve the economic interest of the donor countries than the economic development of the African recipient countries. Some donor countries give loans in order to stem their domestic inflation (e.g., West Germany); others give loans in order to monopolize a country's natural resources (e.g., British and American monopolies of Nigerian oil). When the latter occurs, a receiving country has, at best, only a limited range of control over the revenue from its natural resources. Where the resources have not been tied to the markets of a particular developed country, there is still no certainty that the world price of a cash crop, such as cocoa in Ghana, on which a whole development plan depends, will not drop so drastically as to contribute to the fall of a government.

Our African administrators and a number of our politicians are often so careful that if one asks why a raw material should not be developed locally instead of being sold abroad at beggar prices — only for its refined version to come back to Africa at cutthroat prices — the answer is almost always the same: "Yes, we have the raw material but we lack the capital to start exploiting it, and when we get the capital (perhaps in the form of a loan from outside) we do not have the qualified manpower. And even when we have both capital and manpower, we do not have the communication network needed for such an undertaking; and at any rate we are not sure of markets for the finished product." And so it goes; the questioner is made to appear an unimaginative utopian.

Yet even if African countries must rely on trading natural resources for the requisite development revenue, one might have expected a stronger bargain-

ing position for them than they have now. In this
connection one wonders whether organizations like
the O.A.U. and the United Nations' Economic Commission for Africa have not been disappointing
in their concrete contributitons to African economic
development. Much of their work, so far as I can
see, remains on paper. Yet given its resources
and influence, the E.C.A. could have revolutionized
the economies of African nations and thereby left
its impact on the development administration of
each country. Unfavorable trade balances, unfavorable conditions in receiving foreign financial aid,
have left the real control of many African national
economies in the hands of foreigners. Short-term
loans with steep rates of interest and foreign con-
tractor-financing of development projects have played
major roles in weakening the economy of various
African countries. The implication of all these
economic arrangements for development administration
in Africa is that it becomes a precarious adventure
for a government to entrust the long-term pursuit
and achievement of planned goals to its public administration. When resources expected from the
outside — from aid or trade — do not materialize,
the development which the administration is to undertake becomes meaningless. (Hence the wisdom in the
Tanzanian choice of self-reliance as laid down in
the Arusha Declaration.)

Ideologies

In order to sustain the efforts and hopes of
their people when introducing a development plan,
African political leaders are wont to address themselves to one or the other leading world economic
ideology. The ideology most frequently invoked has
been socialism. In many cases, the politicians
have not even understood what socialism means, regardless of the adjective placed before it. (A
minister in Ghana during the Nkrumah era is reported
to have defined socialism as "chop some, make I

chop some," a pidgin English expression implying the existence of a booty of which everyone may at will take a share.) The man on the street can least be expected to comprehend the total implications. To tell him that there is going to be a redistribution of wealth in the country and that he will be part owner in a cooperative enterprise does not always spark his imagination. The civil servant who must implement development plans on socialist principles may have an aversion to a word which is redolent of communism. Further, the success of any sort of socialism might threaten the wealth he has acquired by virtue of his office. His tendency, then, is to put a wrench into the wheel of the administration.

Instead of the new ideology supporting development, its meaning is distorted, often manifestly, even among the political elite. Equally, then, the plan goals are distorted; and difficulties faced in implementation are attributed to the imported foreign idea. It is also common knowledge that various foreign governments manage to work in African countries, for or against ideological views which the political leaders wish to establish.

Socialism having failed, African development administration turns to capitalism. With it comes familiarity through association with former colonial masters. The African administrators revert to Malthus while their former colonial masters pursue Keynes. The lip service paid to ideologies in societies where conditions are not the same as they were in the countries where the ideologies originated has led to a breakdown of development in some African countries. A classic example is Ghana under Nkrumah's government. The leaders of the junta cited the introduction of socialism into that ocuntry as one of their justifications for overthrowing Nkrumah.

Internally originating problems

The responsibility which public administration in independent Africa bears has been widely dis-

cussed. Kenneth Younger has put the argument quite
well:

> The major difficulty arose from the new
> burden imposed on the service by the dyn-
> amism of the new government. . . . A new
> state will naturally wish to signalize
> its independence by accelerating develop-
> ment to the limit of its resources and
> often beyond. Ministerial decisions can
> be taken rapidly and each one sets a
> fresh task for the administration. If
> this period of creative endeavour ends in
> frustration for want of governmental ma-
> chinery to carry the burdern, the new
> state's political stability and its capac-
> ity for democratic development may well
> be endangered.[20]

These tasks which the public administrations of
independent Africa are expected to perform are
interspersed with a multiplicity of problems the
weight of whose origin might lie within the countries themselves. The body of literature on these
problems is growing, and I shall discuss only a
few of them. The pattern noted in the case of
Uganda will be true of many other African nations.

Africanization and Its Costs

One aim of Africanizing the top ranks of the
civil service at independence was to fill the offices hitherto occupied by non-nationals with nationals, who would identify themselves with the
goals and aspirations of the new nation and serve
it faithfully. In many cases the new government recruited replacements for non-nationals from within
the service itself on the criterion of efficiency.
Where the expected efficiency from the nationals
was not forthcoming, strict disciplinary action was
taken. In Tanzania, for instance, five newly ap-

149

pointed African permanent secretaries were fired on the grounds of inability to cope with the responsibilities attached to their offices.[21]

The predecessor non-national civil servant was very expensive. His high salary with its concomitant fringe benefits could not, in my opinion, be justified on any grounds: not on grounds of inducement to work in the malaria-infested part of the world, or of labor market, or of opportunity costs, or of a higher standard of living in the metropolitan country. If non-national civil servants stayed on after independence, their loyalties would be in question and their financial remuneration might far outweigh their output. They would be a drain on the finances required for development. One might have expected the Africans who replaced the colonial officials to be paid salaries enough for their upkeep, but modest in comparison with the incomes of the rest of the population. On the contrary, the African civil servant not only received the salary of his European predecessor, he also drew the expatriation allowance of a colonial officer. In fact, what happened has led René Dumont to call these top civil servants "the elites: a modern version of Louis XVI's Court." Further, he writes:

> The principal "industry" of these countries
> at the moment is administration. It is not
> productive and simply adds to general costs.
> Such costs should be reduced, but, in fact,
> are being swollen to the point where per-
> sonnel expenses alone absorb 60 per cent of
> the internal income in Dahomey. As presently
> conceived, administration will be the ruin
> of these countries.[22]

The effect of this financial drain on resources for development administration and planning will not lead to the accelerated development expected. In addition, while the top offices are manned by efficient Africans, the middle level lacks personnel

150

who could effectively and efficiently carry out
orders from the top. Top administrators are thus
overloaded with work while they hurry to implement
projects whose types and size they have not experienced before.[23]

Nepotism, Tribalism, Corruption

The frequency with which one hears complaints
of favoritism among top officials in African public
bureaucracies is fairly high. Often these complaints
are dismissed by responsible persons in administration as unfounded. But the frequency with which
these complaints come up and the consequences which
they are capable of producing, such as those witnessed in Nigeria, make one hesitate to dismiss the
complaints as untrue. The law courts naturally
always ask for evidence that no favoritism has taken
place. The procedure is simple: the top administrator produces all the personnel files. He says,
"Six people applied for the advertised position
and we looked at their qualifications. At the inter-
view which followed, the panel thought Mr. So-and-so
was the best candidate." A recent leader described
in a Uganda daily how, in order to avoid direct
public criticism, friends in different public bureaucracies employed each other's close relatives.

I have often been appalled by public servants
who see their stagnation in the service as a function of their tribal origins. When they are not
promoted, regardless of their awareness of their
own ability and performance, they lament that they
belong to the wrong tribe. Some become apathetic
to their employer's cause; others sink into frustration and await the day when their tribesman will
head the ministry.

So much has been said about corruption in developing countries and in Africa that I need only
mention it to evoke associations in the reader.

It is beyond the scope of this paper to trace
in any depth the causes of these three problems
and to offer explanations for their continued prac-

tice in any African public administration. My main
concern is to point out some of the areas in administration which they affect. Manpower suffers where
the recruitment of new staff and the promotion of
established members are not based on the achievements
and demonstrated performance of the individuals, or
on some universal system of evaluation. Levels of
production within the administration suffer as much
as descipline enforcement. Efficiency and effectiveness are equally affected. All such consequences
detract from the administration's set goals and are
manifested in financial losses, disrespect to supervisors, blockages in communication channels, and an
atmosphere of tension and unfriendliness toward the
client.

Africa's Armies

African nationalist leaders were surely proud
when on the first day of independence they inspected
starched khaki uniforms, shiny metal buttons, and
bayoneted rifles. The national army was a colonial
product, but not a poor ceremonial inheritance.
Soon after independence, plans were formulated to
expand this most unproductive sector of the economy. Vast sums of money were taken from the
available scarce resources to maintain armies
specializing in skills remotely related to control
of domestic violence. African soldiers made the
French and British armies their models and increasingly demanded "the modernization" of their armies.
It is sad to note that most of these demands were
met. Huge budgets of the defense ministries became a common feature in Africa. While we were
asked to tighten belts for national development,
our soldiers were seen living in conspicuous luxury.

The problems of bribery, corruption, tribalism,
and nepotism which have accompanied Africa's development aspirations have always provided a cogent
pretext for military coups. Some of the governments
toppled had offered very dynamic programs for de-

velopment and social change. For development administration, a coup interrupts, at least temporarily, whatever projects the administration is implementing. Whenever there is a coup, uncertainties are created among public servants, since the effect of the forcible change of government on their offices may not be immediately clear. One regular consequence of a coup is the purging of the public service. Such purges are meant to get the "right boys in the job." But they create problems of succession and legitimacy for the administrators who remain in the service to carry out the policies of the usurper regime.

Some African countries have experienced more than four military coups within six years of independence. It is a paradox that the soldiers' first coup against the civilian politician is undertaken in order to uproot corruption; later coups of soldier against soldier are also to uproot corruption. Coups by the military in African countries have disrupted efforts to get out of backwardness. Invariably, development plans of the predecessor government are discarded and the administrator must start all over again.

Politician versus Civil Servant

A military coup has the side effect of uniting public servants with soldiers, even if this union may not last long. While the soldiers discredit the fallen politicians, the public administrators' prestige is boosted. For many African public servants, the fall of a legal government through military insurgence is a most welcome event; the coup fulfills a suppressed desire: to get rid of the "illiterate politician." David Apter has observed:

> Civil servants are a difficult group for
> political leaders to deal with or assim-
> ilate because they are generally better
> educated than the politicians, with a

subtler awareness of their own position,
and . . . have a greater security of tenure, which creates a totally different
outlook.[24]

The kinds of relationships existing among a number
of African politicians and their civil servants
are not optimal for cooperation and coordination of
efforts. Communication, which should link all
those involved in development, breaks down between
the politician, who suspects that the civil servant
is intentionally sabotaging his plans, and the civil
servant, who does not think much of the intelligence
and capabilities of his political head. The kind
of strain which develops between many African top
civil servants and their political bosses undermines the confidence of the masses in national development projects. The otherwise enthusiastic
support of the masses for these projects no longer
comes voluntarily. I have often heard comments
from top civil servants about their ministers which
have left me wondering whether the African civil
servant lacks the spirit of entrepreneurial risk-
taking, or is just too realistic.

Organization

A number of problems associated with failure
to achieve goals of development planning and administration in Africa can be reduced to organizational deficiencies. What Westcott said generally of
developing countries is not exaggerated for Africa:

. . . inadequate attention to middle and
lower level administrative problems, excessive centralization of authority and
control, insufficient middle level personnel, inadequate contact between managers and subordinate employees, excessive paper processing, need for greater
responsiveness to the citizen's needs,

unnecessary secrecy, superfluous committees and meetings, inconsistencies of
promotions, lack of incentive and initiative, inattention to production standards,
etc.[25]

These are all problems in teamwork, leadership, communication, initiative, personnel management, definition of work, and authority, which are usually
considered dysfunctional in the pursuit of organizational goals. If all these problems are located
within any single organization, one can imagine
their complexity when the task is to coordinate
and evaluate the activities of various parastatel
bodies as well as those of governmental ministries,
private organizations, and rural, district, regional
and central administration, and to direct them to
the fulfillment of development goals.

The Problem of Complexity

     The problems mentioned above are among the most
obvious which have evoked representations for correction. The list is by no means exhaustive. It
appears contradictory when I argue that the problems
earn that designation because observers demand their
correction while insisting that the problems should
not be interpreted as dysfunctions. Dysfunction
as used by sociologists, such as R. K. Merton, means
actions whose consequences do not contribute to the
adaptation and/or survival of a social system. The
implication is that of a social system which is explicitly definable both in structure and in action,
and which thus is able to set limits or standards
for the measurement of what is dysfunctional or
functional. This set of assumptions may be valid
for "industrialized and developed" states/societies
whose historical growth has rested upon a philosophy of liberal economic rationality. Countries
that are said to be developing, however, surely

cannot be said to possess the historically established standards which enable them to determine their trends as the developed nations do.

Another sociological implication of dysfunction which has been consistently belabored is the conception of normative deviance. One may even argue that most of the sociologists who can be associated with structural-functional analysis can also be identified as those who confine themselves to the integration of society per se; they see integration only at normative levels, while neglecting institutional organizations.[26] Max Weber, Emile Durkheim, R. K. Merton, and Talcott Parsons provide examples of overconcern with normative analysis. I appreciate societal analysis on the normative level insofar as the societies under consideration can be shown to be already highly integrated. The scientific benefit of the unqualified application of the concept of integration to developing nations is doubtful. Integration presents, however temporarily, insurmountable empirical experiences to the societies in developing countries, *pari passu*, in Africa.[27]

Sociologists who are wont to evaluate societal problems through normative categories are likely to dismiss the many problems confronting development administration in Africa as consequences of normative deviance. Perhaps they would argue for "pattern-maintenance." I would ask what pattern is to be maintained. I suggest that "the pattern" for development administration in Africa does not yet exist; it is now being developed or evolved.

Faced with the tasks which public administration in Africa must undertake, and in the absence of indigenous administrative patterns which have taken root, planning becomes an empirically "reasonable" means of effecting economic and social development. (If rational planning were not chosen as a means of attaining development in African countries, market rationality of the liberal economic type might possibly evolve. The latter would not be inconsistent with the pre-independence experience of these countries.) Planning is only a means of problem solution; it should be taken neither as an end in itself nor as an explanation of the internally and externally originated problems. On the contrary, planning in Africa seems to accept these problems as existing and incorporates them in its goals. The plans thus compromise with reality, even though this concession may not be spelled out. A way of visualizing the problems faced in African development administration is to consider the plans themselves as formal rules within whose limits the substantive norms may operate. It is the absence of coincidence between the formal rules of the plan and operational norms which draws attention to the problems.

Planning is chosen as a means whereby limited resources can be optimally apportioned and utilized — a means of postponing immediate consumption. The same argument can be telescoped into a formulation that planning is generally undertaken as a means of reducing or managing the complexity of social action. Parsons' analysis of unit action and Homan's analysis of the elementary forms of human behavior demonstrate that a complicated social process takes place between the mental conception of a goal and its concrete realization. Planning is thus a means of reducing the complexity of "human behavior" in the process of pursuing set goals.

If it can be argued that interaction among individual persons, under any system of norms, values, or beliefs which is acceptable to them, takes place consciously or unconsciously in order to reduce the fundamental problems of complexity, then social and economic planning, with their concomitant administrative apparatus, have the same purpose. Complexity may be reduced so that operations can take place, but it can hardly ever be eliminated. It is in a similar sense that Parsons' analysis of

the social system can be evaluated as an attempt
at explicating complexity. Yet no definitive proposition on the reduction of social complexity has
been offered by sociologists. One wonders whether
this failure cannot be attributed to the assumptions
on which most sociological analytical efforts rest.
Assumptions such as equilibrium, self-maintenance,
and interdependence of parts often end in circular
arguments when, for instance, causality enters the
foreground.

A structural-functional analytic approach to
planning would tend to highlight dysfunctions and
even to disregard unintended consequences which
might be functional. System analysis, contrary to
what many scholars argue, makes room for, and to a
large extent is able to accommodate, social change.
The more serious limitation which both forms of
analysis exhibit, when combined, is their inability
to relate systems to their environments. To treat
development planning or its administrative apparatus
as an isolated system would facilitate analysis but
would not offer an accurate view of reality. An
effort to consider the dynamics of planning and its
administration as a process, however, enables us to
be more aware of the complexities present and of
their strategic exploitation to the goals set.

An approach which recognizes the formal rules
of the game (the plan) and its operational norms
(the real-life, day-to-day implementation and accom-
panying problems) as a single process grasps the
interpenetration of a system and its environment.
Such an approach may bring us nearer to tentative
theoretical assertions. As assertion which may
not be out of place, in view of the problems met
in African development planning and administration,
could be stated: Social complexity tends to increase in the process of attempting to progress
from a natural to a money economy. The increase
in complexity is manifested in the kind of problems
whose immediately perceptible effect may be negative but which in the long run contribute posi-

tively by exposing and testing the weaknesses and strengths in the apparatus (i.e., the means) selected for the management and reduction of complexity.

Policy Implementation

I have argued that planning is the means through which public administrations in Africa can meet their development programs and problems. This proposition agrees with the views expressed earlier in the paper on the purpose and justification of maintaining a costly public administration. Development administration, as Riggs and Fainsod noted, is a bearer of modernization, innovation, economic development, and industrialization for developing countries. It has been put forward by Weidner that the major justification of development administration is its ability to pursue goals of national progress which have been authoritatively defined.

At least three schools of thought may reject my insistence on planning, especially since I do not qualify it with an adjective like "indicative." The first rejection may come from those who principally do not believe in or accept planning for African countries; the second, from those who might think that I am proposing a single-factor solution; and the third from those who, looking at the shortcomings of African development plans, think all planning is utopian.

Several factors should be coupled with planning in order to reduce the complexities which obstruct goal achievement. Among these, the most important are not the material or the financial resources. It is the managing of the plan, the scope of authority behind it, and the education of the general public which come to the foreground. Instead of taking each individual problem mentioned above and showing how it can be reduced along these dimensions, I prefer to point to an

empirical case in Africa where the public administration is successfully implementing development
planning: Tanzania. The success of the Tanzanian
self-reliance program lies in planning within realistic goals, and in intensive political socialization
of all nationals; these enable the politician, the
civil servant, and the *Mwanchi* (the masses) to
speak the same language and to accept common obligations. But behind the facade is the party, the
Tanganyika African National Union, whose chief
national role lends authority and legitimacy (through
its grassroots organization and participation) to
actions aimed at reducing or eliminating obstruc-
tions to plan success.

NOTES

1. K. R. Popper, *The Open Society and Its
Enemies* (Princeton: Princeton University Press,
1963), II, 260-61.

2. Irving Swerdlow, ed., *Development Administration: Concepts and Problems* (Syracuse: Syracuse University Press, 1963), p. ix.

3. Merle Fainsod, "The Structure of Development Administration," in Swerdlow, *op. cit.*, p. 2.

4. See Fred W. Riggs, "Public Administration:
A Neglected Factor in Economic Development," in
*Annals of the American Academy of Political and
Social Science* (May, 1956), pp. 70-80. This paper
is reprinted in Riggs's *Administration in Develop-
ing Countries: The Theory of Prismatic Society*
(Boston: Houghton Mifflin, 1964), pp. 243-59.

5. Fred W. Riggs, "Administrative Development: An Elusive Concept," in John D. Montgomery and William J. Siffin, eds., *Approaches to Development Politics, Administration and Change* (New York: McGraw-Hill, 1966), pp. 225, 252-53.

6. Edward W. Weidner, "Development Administration: A New Focus for Research," in Ferrel Heady and Sybil L. Stokes, eds., *Papers in Comparative Public Administration* (Ann Arbor: University of Michigan Press, 1962), p. 98.

7. Robert K. Merton, *Social Theory and Social Structure* (New York: Free Press of Glencoe, 1964); Michel Crozier, *The Bureaucratic Phenomenon* (Chicago: University of Chicago Press, 1964); Niklas Luhman, *Funktionen und Folgen Formaler Organisation* (Berlin: Springer-Verlag, 1964).

8. "President Obote on the New Political Culture," in *The People* (Kampala), No. 407 (April 21, 1970), p. 5.

9. The dynamics of change and societal development have been excellently analyzed by Norbert Elias. If writers on theoretical aspects of development administration had read him, there might have been less emphasis on static models. See Norbert Elias, *Ueber den Prozess der Zivilisation,* Vols. I and II (Basel: Franke Verlag, 1939).

10. A. L. Adu, *The Civil Service in New African States* (London: Allen & Unwin, 1965), p. 226.

11. "President Obote on the New Political Culture."

12. *Ibid.*

13. *Ibid.*

14. Adu, *op. cit.* He discusses the problems further in *The Civil Service in Commonwealth Africa: Development and Transition* (London: Allen & Unwin, 1969).

15. "Francophone" means French-speaking or French legacy. It is now in standard professional usage to distinguish large areas of Africa with a French colonial experience from those with a British colonial experience (Anglophone).

16. René Dumont, *False Start in Africa* (London: André Deutsch, 1968).

17. For the distinction between typology and classification, see Carl G. Hempel and Paul Oppenheim, *Der Typusbegriff in Lichte der neuen Logik* (Leiden, A. W. Sijthoff's Vitgeversmaatschappij, 1936); and Carl G. Hempel, "Problems of Concept and Theory Formation in the Social Sciences," in *Science, Language and Human Rights* (Philadelphia: University of Pennsylvania Press, 1952), pp. 65-86.

18. J. A. Namata, *The Civil Service in Tanzania* (Dar es Salaam: State House, April, 1967), pp. 1-3.

19. Guy Hunter, "Development Administration in East Africa, " *Journal of Administration Overseas* (January, 1967), p. 8.

20. Kenneth Younger, *The Public Service in the New States* (London: Oxford University Press, 1960), pp. 72-73.

21. William Tordoff, *Government and Politics in Tanzania* (Nairobi: East Africa Publishing House, 1967), p. 85.

22. Dumont, *op. cit.,* p. 78.

23. David E. Apter, *The Politics of Modernization* (Chicago: University of Chicago Press, 1965), p. 167.

24. *Ibid.*

25. J. B. Westcott, "Government Organization and Methods in Developing Countries," in Swerdlow, *op. cit.*, pp. 44-65.

26. Rolf Dahrendorf, *Essays in the Theory of Society* (Stanford: Stanford University Press, 1968), p. 9.

27. See, for example, J. S. Coleman and C. Rosburg, *Political Parties and National Integration in Tropical Africa* (Berkeley: University of California Press, 1964).

Planning, Plans, and Planned Economics

by Brian Van Arkadie

Planning Objectives

Planning must be judged either by the achievement of objectives which those who adopt planning intend to achieve, or by some explicit view of the purpose of planning defined by the critic.

This is by no means simple. Economists and political scientists see planning as a process of making and implementing decisions. The process is then judged according to its effectiveness in maximizing a "social welfare function" or resolving potential problems by conciliating political interests. The student of the planning process is neutral as to the objectives being pursued. Development planning, however, is inherently a system whereby the state seeks to achieve mobilization for national economic development. If the political situation is such that those who control the state are not interested in, or hold other objectives prior to, the pursuit of national economic development, development planning may well be irrelevant; what pass for development plans may be but minor tactics in a larger political battle.

Further, the development we are concerned with here is definitely economic development; the societies we are concerned with are underdeveloped in a material sense — in a social or political sense there is no reason to suggest that they are "underdeveloped" or "poor," except insofar as they are weak or dependent as a result of their material poverty.

This having been said, it might appear that a perversely narrow and technocratic stand is being taken — that, for example, the pursuit of a high rate of growth of gross domestic product should take precedence over other objectives. This is not so, because national economic development is itself a multi-faceted objective; its ultimate character and the appropriate strategy for its pursuit are subject both to choice and to dispute.

Dedication to short-term output objectives and evaluation on the basis of short-term output performance are unsatisfactory. Only in the long term, over many decades, do economies develop. Over the short term of three to four years, output performance is inevitably dominated by climatic and external market conditions.

Also, development is not necessarily a stable, continuous process. Periods of apparent confusion and instability, with attendant declines in output, may prove to provide a necessary jolt out of a stagnant situation — to have laid the foundations of longer-term economic progress.

Moreover, even if the primary concern is the advancement of material welfare, this priority does not imply that welfare can be readily measured by a simple aggregate, such as gross domestic product. Surely, the distribution of welfare among regions and classes is as relevant as the size of the aggregate. This is particularly important where extensive foreign ownership exists, where there are economically privileged minority communities, or where urban-rural and regional disparities are great — all true of East Africa.

The pursuit of long-term development in the spirit expressed here implies a number of specific concerns which East African development plans need to reflect.

1. Mobilization. Mobilization for development requires a concentrated national effort to raise the savings and investment rates and to generate external finance on acceptable terms; these objectives may be pursued both through short-term fiscal policies and through the creation of new institutions.

2. Structural change. Inherited comparative advantage does not provide a satisfactory basis for long-term development; a change in the basic conditions which determine international comparative advantage will not occur in response either to market conditions or to sectoral planning decisions taken in a short-term framework.

3. Institutional transformation. Many institutions, either inherited from the colonial period or created immediately after independence, incorporate ideas and standards inappropriate to East African conditions; this is true, for example, of school curricula, university infrastructure standards, hospital development (which has tended to emphasize concentrated curative facilities rather than extensive preventive programs), town planning, and housing policies (which have tended to reflect standards appropriate to countries with per capita incomes many times greater than those to be expected in East Africa in the foreseeable future).

4. Desirable patterns of income distribution and property ownership. In the absence of vigorous countermeasures, classes are likely to become increasingly differentiated, partly as a result of the inherited colonial salary structure and partly as a result of the acquisition by Africans of property rights of displaced minority communities.

5. National control. A feature of the colonial system in much of East Africa (particularly in Kenya and Tanzania) was the dominance of all nonprimary

productive activities by non-Africans, through
either ownership or monopoly of acquired skills;
in Kenya (and to a lesser extent Tanganyika) there
was also substantial alienation of land.

6. African economic integration. A further
objective of policy must be the achievement of expanding regional economic integration — over the
longer term a geographically broader market is a
prerequisite to successful industrialization; however, East African experience indicates that regional
arrangements can survive only if a carefully nego-
tiated balance of interests among the participating
members is reached.

7. Maintenance of a reasonable balance of regional development. This is necessary for the
achievement of national cohesion, which is essential to sustained economic expansion.

At this early stage, planning cannot hope to be
comprehensive in the bureaucratic sense of incorpor-
ating substantial information on all projects, or
even having fully meaningful targets for all sectors;
it should aim to make strategic use of key policy
instruments and major projects, in the pursuit of
a critical set of objectives, rather than combining
theoretical comprehensiveness with the pursuit of
a very limited, short-term growth of output.

Policies which are dominated by supposedly
"neutral" output objectives are combined with enthusiasm for private foreign investment and an acceptance of accelerated social differentiation.
Such policies tend to be perceived as realism by
Western commentators — the sort of realism which
dresses capitalism in "African socialism" clothing.
This is a short-sighted realism which may, it is
true, achieve faster growth in gross domestic product over the shorter term, but it does so at the
expense of eventual stability. Opening with obei-
sance to nationalist and socialist principles, the
plans end up selling the country to the highest
foreign bidder.

The experience of the Tanzanian First Plan illustrates this point. At the time of its formulation Tanganyika was already in principle committed to an independent socialist course. The First Plan, however, placed a heavy emphasis on external public and private finance. Despite some modest Left initiatives, it incorporated a strategy which, if followed over a number of years, would have led to increasing dependence on foreign ownership, the promotion of a domestic capitalist class, and exaggerated earned income differentials — all in the name of the pursuit of growth. Only the sharp change of direction in 1967, with the Arusha Declaration and its implementation, prevented this outcome.

Planning and the Mode of Production

A substantial body of planning experience exists in the three East African countries. In a significant sense, planning efforts began in the colonial period, particularly at the end of the Second World War. Moreover, all three countries now have a substantial experience of post-colonial plan publication and implementation efforts. The Second Tanzanian Five-Year Plan and a new Kenya Plan were published during 1969, and work is now underway on the Ugandan Third Five-Year Plan.

However, this planning experience has been accumulated in a basically transitional period, particularly in relation to the staffing of government services. Nowhere has this been more evident than in the staffing of the planning operation itself, where dependence on expatriate technical assistance has been extreme, although hardly avoidable. The dangers and cost of this dependence were considerable, although it should be recognized that this was but part of a more general problem of dependence on foreign technical manpower. One difficulty in evaluating the planning experience is to judge how far

the styles and difficulties characteristic of this
period are peculiar to this situation of dependence
and manpower shortage, and how far they are likely
to give way to a quite new set of problems in the
coming years. The comments made by Cranford Pratt
in his analysis of the First Five-Year Plan in Tanzania related very much to conditions arising from
the virtually inevitable dependence on a small expatriate planning team.[1]

The period has been transitional in other ways —
particularly in an ideological sense. The evolution
of fundamental political assumptions in all three
countries, in differing ways, has been carried far
in the post-colonial period and has been crucial
for the role and meaning of planning.

Planning is viewed as a rational, systematic
approach to decision-making, applicable to various
situations and problems. Thus, in the market economy the private company plans, and so does the government. To quote Waterston, "It is not limited
to totalitarian or socialist solutions (sic!). It
can be and is used by democratic and capitalistic
countries."[2] The function of planning, according
to this tradition, is to allocate scarce resources
systematically and efficiently, in an orderly institutional environment, through a highly control-
lable sequence of policy decisions in those areas
susceptible to public influence. The Five-Year
Plan is judged, on publication, according to the
degree to which it incorporates a set of planned
policies and investments which will maximize some
fairly straightforward index of economic progress,
and in retrospect according to how far it proves
"realistic," either in the administrative sense
of being implementable in practice or in the economic sense of achieving stated targets.

This approach represents an inspired recovery
by the West to capture for its own purposes a concept which held hope for progress and change in the
Third World, but which carried with it ideologically
dangerous associations. For according to such

169

thinking it becomes possible to plan with any degree
of government control, as much as in the rhetoric
of African socialism it became possible to be socialist with almost any degree of private ownership.
Moreover, the plan becomes, par excellence, the device whereby Western "rationality," backed by the
power of supposedly multilateral agencies and national aid agencies, represented in the Third World
by teams of experts, could act as a suitably cau-
tionary influence. The mechanism whereby this is
achieved is fairly subtle. Plans are written which
are "ambitious" (i.e., they contain arithmetic holding forth the hope of much higher rates of growth
than have been achieved in the past), the achievement of which will require "reasonable" policies
toward private foreign investment and aid donors.

Thus, the plan becomes a shopping list for aid,
not only because this was, in part, an initial intention but also because the logic of Plan-making
itself leads in this direction. The constraints
on mobilizing domestic resources and managing the
balance of payments are severe; the possibilities
of directing economic activity are limited. However, the existing growth momentum is unacceptable —
freedom of maneuver is sought in the planned "mobilization" of external resources. This was, for
example, a key characteristic of the Tanzanian First
Five-Year Plan, which was widely welcomed on publication as an ambitious plan; only later did it
become evident that ambitions depended on external
finance.

The relevance of this sort of planning depends
on the effectiveness of a strategy of dependence.
It is not suggested here that there is some crude
or conspiratorial effort to use the planning apparatus to control the domestic economy; rather, the
aim is to point out the effect, albeit sometimes
unwitting, of such a system in operation.

Technocratic planning, conceived as a professional exercise and located in the bureaucracy, must necessarily take as given the structure of ownership

and, except for marginal adjustments, the power of the State and the nature of the political environment. Those in the bureaucracy take the mode of production as given. The inherited structure is susceptible only to marginal changes brought about by the use of a limited set of policy tools.

Western thinking in relation to such planning is neither inflexible nor monolithic. At the moment, for example, there is a considerable concern over the need to generate greater employment from growth, which is stimulating research and advisory activities on a worldwide scale; in this case, although the motivation is specifically counterrevolutionary, the results may introduce an additional flexibility, which, while leaving strategic interests untouched, may well, within certain limits, generate real benefits for local populations. Similarly, the land settlement program in Kenya, although intended by overseas finance agencies to be counterrevolutionary, generated real benefits for some of Kenya's landless people.

A reaction against planning is now afoot among a school of liberal Western commentators who correctly point out the inadequacy of much planning activity, and who feel secure enough to cast doubt on the possibilities of five-year planning at all, retreating to a conception of piecemeal policy-making better adapted to their liberal image of the State.[3] In practice, the possibilities of acting upon economic reality with available policy tools have not been as great as optimists originally hoped; moreover, their use has often been influenced by existing vested interests rather than by the internal logic of planning.

Some critics have therefore argued that economic planners have been naïve in their neglect of the play of interests in the "real world," in which various forces act in the key political processes. Despite accuracy in this characterization, the full lessons are rarely drawn. Naïveté as to the real interests at work is apparent in relation both to the model of public decision-making implicit in much thinking by economists about planning and to explicit claims regarding the susceptibility of the economy (under the existing mode of production) to influence by public policy.

The initial belief in planning in the Third World came not from any feeling for the virtues of sophisticated models of rational decision-making but, rather, from observation of the successful experience of the planned economies. By introducing the five-year plan, however, in the form in which it has generally been adopted, the developing countries have acquired no more than a vocabulary — and not the most relevant one, at that — from the planned economies. For what is significant in this context about the planned economies is not the superior rationalism of their decision-making process; indeed, many Western commentators have pointed out the ineffectiveness of coordination and the micro-inefficiency of much socialist planning in practice. The crucial characteristic of the planned economies has been the degree to which the state seized central initiatives in entrepreneurship, in the mobilization of resources, and in driving the economy toward a few overriding goals, often at the expense of choice, diversity, and micro-efficiency.

If planning, in this sense, is adopted as a means to achieve the objectives set out above, this has profound implications for the arrangement and control of production and distribution. A society with a capitalist mode of production, where substantial parts of the economy are foreign-owned, can certainly have plans for government activities; in such situations the government has available instruments of policy for influencing the private sector. We should note, however, that the private sector in turn has leverage upon government policy — an elementary fact of which political scientists tend to be more aware than economists. However, it must also be recognized that a capitalist mode of production has a logic of its own. One cause of confusion and disillusion regarding development planning derives from a certain disingenuousness regarding the character of this logic in a period of development mobilization; this leads to an excessive readiness to advocate mixed-economy approaches. If industrial, financial, and commercial sectors are to be dominated by the capitalist mode of production, then very high rates of growth are achievable only if the possibilities of private accumulation are considerable, if the stimulus to private entrepreneurial activity is great, and if an acquisitive ethic is pervasive. The appropriate role of the state in such a situation is to bolster the necessary indigenous capitalist elements in the economy. Efforts to limit the energies of private initiative along the familiar lines of social democratic intervention in advanced capitalist countries are likely to be counterproductive on two grounds:

1. The driving force of the "animal spirits" of indigenous capitalism is likely to require maximum encouragement — premature control is likely to stifle what is, in the African case, a recent growth.

2. If the capitalist ethic is vigorous enough to provide the dynamic for fast growth, then its logic is likely to prevail over the bureaucratic logic of the state: public decisions are likely to be open to corruption of the crudest kind, while through more sophisticated arrangements, rapidly expanding capitalist elements are likely to place themselves in positions where they can use the machinery of the state to further their interest. The use of the term "planning" to describe the systematic organization of state policy both in such a situation and in a planned economy is to attribute a common character to diverse situations and is justifiable only for purposes of esoteric administrative theory.

The Shifting Balance

The transitional nature of planning experience
to date has meant that the fundamental strategic
choices implied by the previous remarks are only
gradually being made. If we look back at the 1960's,
all three East African countries enjoyed considerable success in undertaking certain high priority
tasks. In particular, the massive expansion of the
educational system and the extraordinary effort involved in displacing expatriates in the government
administration may be recognized as major achievements of the period in all three countries. The
task was to take over administration of the state
and to train people to man it. The steps involved
were straightforward and were vigorously pursued.

The agenda for the subsequent operation of the
state was less clear. Balanced, reasonable reports
by World Bank teams provided one prospectus of possibilities. Advisors, expatriate planners, and
academics all added their contributions. The political leadership and local public opinion were
necessarily tentative about grand strategy initially — in some areas pushing insistently for
clearly defined needs, for example, in relation
to education. In other areas the political leadership provided a major impetus for innovation and
experiment. Thus all three countries carried out
experimental initiatives in agriculture.

But in many areas strategic for longer-term
structural change, local thinking was initially
less sure and inventive; this was notably the case
in industrial development and foreign investment
policy. Until the Arusha Declaration, understanding
of these matters throughout East Africa was based
on standard imported conventional wisdom (restated,
with suitably bland platitudes and evasion of all
the important questions, in the Pearson Report).

In terms of power, at independence the economic
position of the state in Kenya and Tanganyika could
be described only as being close to that expected

in a laissez-faire economy (in Uganda the situation
was different because of the peculiarities of her
economic structure and of postwar colonial policy).
In addition, in both countries, industry, commerce,
and finance were dominated by foreign interests or
ethnic minority communities.

At the margin, the role of government can be
extended by the bureaucratic accretion of powers,
and an attempt at systematic planning can become
the occasion for such an expansion. However, it
was highly unlikely in the period in question that
the professional planner would be a major direct
force in a dramatic extension of the state role.
I have argued elsewhere, for example, that the importance of the First Tanzanian Plan was not that
it was in itself the direct instrument for dramatic
changes. Rather, by setting out objectives which
were not achievable in the existing institutional
setting, and under its assumptions, the First Plan
made an indirect contribution precisely by calling
into question that setting and those very assumptions.[4]

It is, of course, no great point that the creation of the conditions in which planned development is possible is too important, difficult, and
strategic a job for planners — and has nowhere been
undertaken by them. In the struggle to place the
state in a position to dominate the economy, a
period of crisis and conflict occurs in which the
tactics are the opportunistic initiatives of the
battlefield. Only after the state has established
its position can planning become effective and convey an image of the sort of bureaucratic rationalistic activity so often visualized as characteristic. The struggle to place the state in a position
where it can shift the direction of the economy is
political rather than professional, ideological
rather than technical. Moreover, it involves sharp
changes in short, critical periods of tension,
rather than the ordered progress of a five-year plan.

In this presentation, there is not space to discuss in any detail the way the balance has been struck so far in the three countries. However, certain simple generalizations seem possible.

Tanzania in many ways benefited from backwardness — the limited development of a privileged elite, the small stake of the imperial powers, the obvious magnitude of the task at hand. The continuing disinterest and neglect from London, combined with the authentic initiative of the local leadership, led to an ambitious extension of the public sector, along with a commitment to a socialist mode of production.

Following the extension of socialist control, it is now both possible and necessary to come to terms with the logic of a socialist mode of production in an African setting. This presents challenges in four areas:

1. In the agricultural sector the dominant form of production remains smallholder agriculture. This ranges from low-productivity farming, in which subsistence production still forms the major part of output, to high-productivity, specialized farming, beginning to employ both labor and capital — emerging as capitalist farming. In this situation the most effective influences for improved output performance have in the past been material incentives and examples of effective innovation provided by individual peasant farmers; probably the most effective short-term policy tool has been agricultural price policy.

The firm commitment, particularly by the top leadership, to the pursuit of a collective form of rural organization (which has survived the evident difficulties of the settlement schemes) does not derive primarily from the spector of the Kilak haunting Tanzania — although there is legitimate concern about the dangers of increasing social differentiation in the rural areas — or from ambitions to expropriate rural surplus. Rather, there is a belief that collective forms of production could provide a means of shortcutting existing laborious paths to rural progress. Although the commitment to Ujamaa Village Development was asserted as a priority of the Second Plan, the tactics defined for pursuing that objective remained voluntary and pragmatic. Many of the problems to be overcome in creating rural socialism were vigorously spelled out in the Dumont Report, which the Tanzanian government published in October, 1969.[5]

2. In urban economic activities, problems of control and initiative in the state sector must be of increasing concern as the dust settles on the events of actual nationalization and day-to-day questions of management increasingly impinge on economic performance and achievements. On the one hand, there is the danger of the bureaucracy itself becoming an exploiting class (spelled out vigorously in the Dumont report, implicit in the report of the cooperative inquiry, and certainly recognized in Nyerere's own thinking). On the other hand, the sheer lack of management expertise is a problem, particularly in a situation in which Tanzania inevitably remains dependent on imported technology and capital goods.

3. In a country which has moved so far in the direction of public ownership, there is a need to impose the logic of a planned economy (with emphasis on mobilization rather than choice). Yet the logic of a capitalist mode of production is still very much alive, and is dominant in neighboring economies with the same common market.

4. There are tricky technical economic problems of achieving structural change in such a small economy. This essay is clearly not the place to air questions of substantive economic policy; but it should be noted that many of the central themes of debate among socialist economic planners about strategy have related to much larger economies, of sufficient size to develop production of a significant range of capital equipment.

177

The Kenyan situation seems much more complex.
The more considerable development of an enclave
economy involving a substantial international stake
meant that there was a considerable external interest in defending the capitalist mode of production,
while the long colonial history of restriction of
the development of African farmers meant that there
were possibilities of dramatic African advance
within a reformist framework. The British were
willing to finance the transfer of a significant —
if minor — part of the European-owned land, thus
partially meeting the need for genuine land reform; and by so doing they "took the steam out of
the kettle" of potential radical pressure in Kenya
while leaving substantial large-scale farming interests intact and at the same time buying off a
particularly vociferous and disgruntled British
lobby. This, combined with the effects of the
crucial changes in policy toward existing African
smallholders from the early 1950's on, led to the
quite remarkable growth of incomes of African smallholders in the 1960's. Now the displacement of
Asian traders is allowing a continued extension of
African income opportunities, in a manner possibly
enbarrassing to the United Kingdom government but
which still leaves intact the most substantial
foreign interests.

One possible interpretation of Kenya's evolution is that under the banner of African socialism,
and alongside an expansion of African smallholder
farming and petty capitalism, the most significant
factor has been the entrenchment of larger-scale
external economic interests. However, this interpretation may prove premature, since there is an
objective need in Kenya, where the rates of illit-
eracy, population growth, and landlessness are the
highest in East Africa, for continuous extension
of African participation in the economy. The underlying dilemma is that this will not be possible
through capitalist development because indigenous
capitalists are unlikely to emerge to lay claim to

the financial and industrial sectors, while a direct move toward outright socialist control is difficult, given the power of external interests and the commitment to a capitalist mode of production of an expanding group of small-scale African businessmen and commercial farmers.

One medium-term development is likely to be the adoption of increasingly sophisticated measures by international firms to preempt radical moves in the direction of public ownership. The joint project, which offers the state the opportunity to participate in the equity, even on a majority basis, but which retains for the international firm its strategic interests by one form of detailed arrangement or other, will be increasingly popular. National and Grindlay's Bank has taken such an initiative recently in Kenya, presumably as insurance against any repetition of its nationalization in Tanzania.

The Uganda government, toward the end of the colonial period, already played a more central role than did governments in the other two countries. Not only did the public sector account for over 60 percent of recorded investment, but through the Uganda Development Corporation it already extended well beyond the traditional concentration on infrastructural activities. Moreover, the structure of private activity was quite different. African smallholders dominated agriculture, and the cooperative movement was already well established.

Without dramatic change the government in Uganda found itself in a position which Tanzania reached only through a process of radical political development. However, while Fabian-style colonial rule had left a legacy of extended state activity, this represented a pragmatic arrangement rather than a commitment to socialism.

The desire expressed in the Common Man's Charter in 1969 to move in an explicitly socialist direction gave rise to the decisions announced in May, 1970, to take a majority interest in a wide range of foreign-owned enterprises. An obvious commitment to

179

an acquisitive ethic among the now considerable elite suggests that there might be a substantial basis for opposition to pushing such developments further in a socialist direction. State interference in foreign enterprise could well, in practice, prove to be a step in the development of indigenous capitalism. Any comment must be highly speculative until the implications of current developments become clearer.

The Role of the
Economic Planner

This paper has so far treated the overall objectives of development planning and raised some questions ragarding the institutional situation in which plans are made. The point has been made that the most important prerequisites of planning are political and institutional rather than economic and professional. What, then, is the role of the professional planner and planning technique? Can the extension of the state prove viable where there is a scarcity of technical expertise?

When the discussion moves from the broader questions of institutional environment to more practical problems of operation, the issues become blurred and the potential conflicts less obviously dramatic. However, the nuts and bolts of planning and implementation become increasingly crucial as the state extends its influence. In thinking about the work of the planner, it is necessary to move from the strategic to the tactical. Naturally, much of the daily business of the working planner is at the mundane, practical level.

It is important to remember that planning expertise can be created only by practice; in some respects experience gained elsewhere is not readily transferable. Moreover, the extension of the role of the state cannot await the development of planning expertise, partly because that capacity will emerge only in response to need in practice and partly because the historical opportunity for such an extension must be seized when it arises.

Given a favorable general institutional situation, the next prerequisite for effective planning is serious commitment. The prevalence of "pseudo planning" in many parts of the world is as much the result of the desire of politicians for pseudo plans (which avoid the discipline and costs of real plans) as it is of the incompetence of planners. Plans can be little different from the platforms touted by British or American political parties at elections.

Even when the political commitment is firm, the task remains difficult. Results must be produced in the short term even if longer-term objectives are kept in sight. The administration is typically overburdened. It is easy to despair and reasonable to be cautious. There has been much bogus planning, and obviously the widespread skepticism regarding macro-planning is not unjustified. Surely the grand design is inappropriate if the detail can be executed only faultily. Although it is reasonable to emphasize the need for improved administration and effective detailed work in planning, there is little merit in the abandonment of macro-planning.

To provide perspective, let us review the reasons why macro-planning is both possible and sensible even in the face of inadequate micro-capacity.

1. An obvious, but sometimes neglected, economic point is that some policy tools and objectives are inevitably macro-economic in character and can be handled without detailed micro-control. Indeed, because of the nature of underdevelopment, effective planning at the project level presupposes strategic macro-planning — few broader considerations of structural change would emerge from a purely "micro-project evaluation" approach.

2. Efforts may often be mobilized in a sector even without detailed programming (this is true both for the prosaic use of price policies and also for

the more adventurous use of the party as mobilizer,
in land reform, etc.).

3. Excessive worship of formal "project evaluation" has its dangers. If there are only 10
economists in each country (a generous estimate in
East Africa of the early 1960's), then the full
evaluation of projects would entail a drastic reduction of investment levels; even then, it would
be necessary to choose projects for evaluation by
some method other that "project evaluation." It
is both worthwhile and possible to raise the rate
of capital formation even if one is not sure that
all projects implemented are feasible. At the margin, under conditions of scarce planning capacity,
the least feasible projects are not necessarily
excluded.

4. It is characteristic of development that
risks must be taken (and therefore a certain degree
of failure expected). An underdeveloped country
may be defined as a country where most projects
are not feasible. Sometimes, working in the field,
one feels that if the World Bank had fully evaluated early 19th-century American development the
United States would probably not have been feasible.

Given scarce capacity, a judgment must be made
as to where economic evaluation can be neglected
(such as traditional public sector activities sat-
isfactorily controlled by public accounting techniques), where only an occasional review would be
valuable to reassess standards required (e.g.,
standard educational building costs), and where
nearly all projects will require fairly sophisticated evaluation. Most industrial projects, for
example, would fall into the last category.

Formal evaluation is particularly important
for industrial projects because they are typically
promoted by foreign firms whose interest cannot,
in general, be expected to coincide with that of
the country concerned. This danger is not avoided
by the existence of state industry. State concerns
in many instances implement projects in response to

foreign private initiatives, and we should all by now be familiar with the dangers of carpetbagging machinery salesmen peddling turnkey projects.

It should be noted that one danger of economic planners is that too often their activities respond exclusively to others' initiatives. For example, the planning ministry sees itself as choosing between projects presented to it. In this situation the productivity of planners is too often the negative (although valuable) one of preventing nonsense, rather than the positive one of promoting sense. This has two disadvantages:

1. It is difficult for planners to play a continuing role if their main activity is "stopping" things, for it is possible to prevent a bad project from eventually entering a budget only if there is a good one to replace it.

2. The appearance of a large number of bad projects is evidence that help is needed at an early stage with project identification. Project identification is, however, a much more difficult art than project evaluation and has been neglected in thinking about the operation of planning.

Waterston has tended to emphasize the importance of the annual budget as a tool of planning.[6] It is useful for planners to control the development budget, if only because it provides a potent weapon in bureaucratic infighting and carries with it substantial status. The budget is important because it is there — it is an administrative device which is familiar to the civil service and which involves a serious, business-like dialogue between the ministries. However, its importance can be exaggerated. Project identification comes well before — possibly years before — the project appears in the budget. Many spending decisions are preempted outside the budget-making arena (e.g., in aid and other external finance negotiations). Also, of course, in important sectors (e.g., agriculture), results are achieved more by policies than by capital projects.

In the planning debate, the pendulum is in danger
of swinging too much in the direction of excessive
emphasis of the short-term, on the piecemeal, and
on immediate implementation efforts.

Many five-year and prospective plans have proved
meaningless, but the need for a sustained commitment
remains. The existence of transitory uncertainties
does not detract from this — with large year-to-year
fluctuations it is possible to carry through major
projects and substantial developments only by focusing attention on the longer-term lending priority
of required development expenditure, even in the
face of fluctuating resource availability. In a
number of sectors a long time horizon for plans
is inescapable — this is the case with education,
major communication links, and tree crop and livestock development, to give a range of examples. In
some cases implementation of a project may take a
number of years. In some areas, such as industrial
policy, a much longer-term perspective than has so
far been attempted would be desirable in all three
East African countries.

Decisions, however, are made at a given point
in time; and the unfolding of the long term is a
series of immediate events — budgets, legislation,
cabinet decisions, decisions about project design,
new departmental and entrepreneurial initiatives,
etc. Planners must insert themselves into the
daily grit of government decision-making in order
to be of any practical use — indeed, often in order to assert the longer-term view.

Role of Five Year Plans

To conclude, some comments on the appropriate
role of five-year plans as such may prove useful.

By now, everyone recognizes that the five-year
plan is but a part of the planning process — there
is little clarity, however, about the nature of
its precise role. The five-year time period is a

184

compromise, but a remarkably useful one. It would
be surprising if the widespread currency of a five-
year period for planning purposes results merely
from a simpleminded plagiarism of the original.
Five years is a time period within which most large
projects can be carried from initial budgeting to
completion; it tends to be long enough to even out
some of the year-to-year uncertainties of the
weather; and it is infrequent enough to avoid a
continuous activity of plan writing. For some
activities — such as educational and manpower planning — the time period is too short. For detailed
project planning the period is too long, in that
it is difficult to prepare and evaluate a comprehensive list of projects when producing the plan;
capacity exists to prepare one year's projects
fully in about one year of plan preparation. Therefore, in a five-year plan, longer-term programs
will be framed in some sectors to detailed project
formulation that is being attempted for a shorter
period, say, two years, which is the detailed project planning horizon for the new Tanzanian plan.

The plan itself serves various functions. It
should set project priorities fairly firmly for
major projects, such as major communications investments. It can be effective in that respect if
accepted by the government, partly because large
projects require effective support at an early
stage if the rather lengthy process of implementation is to be carried out.

The plan also provides a set of objectives and
policies which can be a guide for the future exercise of policy instruments insofar as the plan
document retains any ascendancy during the plan
period. The plan will retain ascendancy as long as
it receives political support and as long as there
is an effective planning agency with access to the
effective instruments of policy. Further, plan
formulation is itself a policy instrument. The
period of systematic work and appraisal which pre-
cedes the production of the plan has been the

occasion for introducing new ideas into departmental thinking and, in the case of the current Tanzanian plan, for significant ministerial reorganization.

Although the plan appears as a fairly homogenous document, in reality the nature of the work in each sector necessarily varies tremendously. In some areas, no capacity, or no need, exists for substantial new analysis, so that the plan is no more than a restatement of existing policies. In other sectors, firm decisions may be made about priorities between major projects, decisions which must be made at the highest political level and can be made rationally only in the context of an overall analysis of resource availability and competing demands over a number of years.

Other sections of the plan will be experimental and exploratory. The plan will be a fitting occasion to initiate new policies and define possible new policy objectives while admittedly leaving gaps in identifying adequate policy instruments. This was true, for example, in the Uganda Second Five-Year Plan in relation to the introduction of an incomes policy. In the Tanzanian Second Five-Year Plan, a first attempt has been made to pose some of the problems which must be faced if a satisfactory pattern of urban development is to emerge. In this case, some of the possible instruments for achieving the desired objectives were identified, though additional instruments will clearly be required. To ensure that this requirement would be met, a new ministry was created in the final stages of plan formulation. Similarly, the Ujama program included an important element of research and experimentation and deliberately left a large element of flexibility regarding the means to be used to pursue the ambitious objectives.

Elements in the five-year plan are undoubtedly didactic. There is a paucity of economic literature available in East Africa (although that situation is changing fast), and one objective of the plan is to present a coherent perspective on the future problems and choices which must be made. The five-year plan in some parts is formulated according to the textbook model of a set of tightly defined decisions. In other parts it will be a probing, experimental exercise.

In an overall, strategic sense, the plan presents a hypothesis regarding the way development will be achieved. Insofar as the plan does involve a systematic hypothesis regarding development strategy, during the plan period the government must not only be concerned with implementation but must also be ready to evaluate the hypothesis in the light of performance.

To argue in this fashion is not to attempt an *ex post* rationalization of actual experience — an apology of a practicing planner — but, rather, to suggest the need for a slightly more elaborate framework within which to understand and evaluate plans than the heuristic plan models found in the economic literature, which so often are used as the focal point for discussing plans.

NOTES

1. R. C. Pratt, "The Administration of Economic Planning in a Newly Independent State: The Tanzanian Experience, 1963-1966," *Journal of Commonwealth Political Studies*, V, 1 (March, 1967), 38-59.

2. Albert Waterston, *Development Planning: Lessons of Experience* (Baltimore: Johns Hopkins Press, 1965), p. 26.

3. This seemed to be a theme running through a number of the sessions of the conference "Crisis in Planning," held at Sussex in 1969, which brought

together many of the leading commentators on development planning. Colin Leys in particular made a
number of perceptive criticisms from the standpoint
of a liberal political scientist. See Mike Faber
and Dudley Seers (eds.), *Crisis in Planning*, (Sussex,
England: University of Sussex Press, 1973), for
contribution by Colin Leys.

4. *Ibid.*

5. René Dumont, *Tanzanian Agriculture after
the Arusha Declaration* (Dar es Salaam: Ministry
of Economic Affairs and Development Planning, 1969).

6. Waterston, *op. cit.*, pp. 201-48.

The Politics of Nation-Building in Kenya: A Study of Bureaucratic Elitism

by Julius Waiguchu

> Politics, at its ephemeral level, concerns
> the rivalries of power; at its deep, secu-
> lar level, it concerns the order of society.
> The deep problem for developing countries
> is the search for an order; the ephemeral,
> but critical, problem is to prevent the
> rivalries of power from ruining the nation.[1]

The problem of nation-building is set within a context of rivalries for power. The search for order
is inherent in nation-building; it exists because
rivalries for power do not always make order possible. The argument presented here revolves around
the premise that the nature, content, and direction
of national development are ultimately determined
by those who wield power. Authority without power
is operationally ineffective; power — legitimate
or illegitimate — builds a nation.[2] Whether it
is the power of the national elite, that of the
army generals, that of a political party, or even

that of the bureaucracy, it is an absolute necessity that someone have power — power to coerce, if necessary. It is beneath this power umbrella that nation-building does, and must, take place.

This paper, therefore, attempts to establish the extent to which rivalries for power among various influential groups in Kenya have influenced the process of national integration, the degree of political participation in the national life, and the development of a national consciousness. Of primary importance in this discussion are two important groups: the ruling party and the administrative bureaucracy. It is argued that the rivalry between these two groups most influences the nature and direction of nation-building and that bureaucratic domination of public life in Kenya has caused party influence to decline, discouraged participation in the political process, and hampered the growth of national awareness.

The Political
Background

Before going further, it should be pointed out that authority and power in Kenya lie in the Presidency. Of any group it can be said that its authority and power over other groups are commensurate with its proximity to the Presidency. Since the Presidency is the embodiment of both authority and power, it seems fair to assume that the most influential group in terms of affecting the input functions of nation-building would be the one with the best access to the Presidency. Although some attention is given to various interest groups operating in Kenya, such as labor, the press, chambers of commerce, and so on, the primary focus remains the behavior and interest articulation of both the party and the bureaucracy and how these two relate to the Presidency, to the conduct of national development programs, and to other groups.

One should start by noting that under the colonial administration, the bureaucratic machinery was
subject to no political control within the territory
of Kenya.[3] In these circumstances, "administrative
institutions proliferated while political structures
remained embryonic and largely extra-legal and hence
unable to relate themselves effectively to the control over bureaucracy."[4] Riggs's point is relevant
particularly in regard to national integration and
political accountability. As it developed in Kenya,
political organization on a country-wide basis was
prohibited from 1953 through 1960, while the colonial bureaucracy grew at an ever-increasing pace.[5]
The period between 1950 and 1960 was one of great
political awakening on the part of the Africans; but
this awakening remained unorganized and undirected
toward any goal, such as the propagation of national
consciousness. Instead, the British Government and
the colonial regime in Kenya encouraged and sanctioned tribal and regional political associations,
whose net effect was to polarize political sentiments by tribal and area bases, thus retarding the
possible development or creation of a national consciousness across tribal and sectional lines.

By the beginning of 1960, 64 political parties
and associations were officially registered as
organized on district or tribal bases. Of these,
42 — the exact number of Kenya's tribal groupings —
were African and the rest were formed by the immigrant communities.[6] With the removal of restrictions over political organization, these tribal-
political groups were affiliated to one or the other
of the two major political parties — the Kenya
African National Union (K.A.N.U.) and the Kenya
African Democratic Union (K.A.D.U.). Until 1960,
when these parties were formed, no forum existed
for encouraging a national consciousness; the only
African unity to speak of was the one produced by
common struggle and emotion against colonial im-
perialists. Creating a nation out of 40 tribes
and overcoming other socioeconomic obstacles was,

191

and still is, a monumental problem that appears to be almost insurmountable. In terms of political organization, a strong, all-inclusive, and mass-embracing movement was thought perhaps the best form of organization to meet those challenges.[7] The premise underlying this theory of organization on a mass basis was that it would facilitate political mobilization of Kenyans of all tribes and political factions, and motivate them to meet the new challenges. It was anticipated that such mass politicization could broaden the lines of communication between elites and the masses.[8]

The two major parties merged into one after the first year of independence, 1964. For quite a while, theories of mass politics were popular in Kenya. This merger of the two opposing parties seemed to be a move in the direction of mass politics and a positive step toward the political integration of the many groups that constitute Kenya's population.[9] Prior to the merger of these two parties, Kenya had been threatened by internal dissension and by tribal and cultural groups who wanted to secede from an independent Kenya.[10]

During the first two or three years of independence, great importance seemed to be attached to the role of the party in both political integration and socioeconomic development. This was underlined by the President himself when he said:

Our national party — KANU — has become the instrument by which the people can be mobilized and through which we can convey to the people our ideals. It is therefore essential that party workers should be trained to understand and implement the national plans for reconstruction and development. Too often in the past, we have tended to forget the party members and officials at locational and district levels. But it is these voluntary servants of the party, locally known and trusted, who are

our link with the people. I have emphasized the importance of unity and national
mobilization. We have already achieved integration within one political party. We
must now strive to promote unity and dedication within every section of our society,
so that everyone may feel that he is a part
of the national effort. . . . National unity,
as a means of expressing and developing our
national personality, must vitally extend
to the trade union movement, to supplement
solidarity in the political field.[11]

Some significant points to be noted from the
above passage are those which relate to national
mobilization for both political and economic reasons, reorienting the party workers to the implementation of national development plans, the notion
that party workers function as the link between the
ruling elite and the masses, and the need to develop a national consciousness. These are important
points not only because they imply a degree of
Kenyan awareness but also because they imply the
future direction of national affairs. For our
purposes, however, two points raised by the President are of interest because they will arise again
and again: (1) training the party workers to understand and implement national plans for reconstruction and development — which really seems to imply
involvement of party workers in the administrative
affairs of nation-building; and (2) the idea that
these party workers are the locally known and
trusted link between the ruling elites and the
masses, and that they too have been often forgotten.
Perhaps a question that we may appropriately deal
with is "Forgotten by whom?"
    Before attempting to answer this question, let
us examine another speech that the President delivered exactly one year later. In this one, the
audience was mixed: party workers and the civil
servants. He said:

In a sense, politicians and civil servants
have always been learning from each other.
Here, perhaps, for the first time in our
country, we have politicians and civil
servants sitting down together to learn.
This is good. It is good for the people
taking part; it is good for the development programme; it is good for the people
we serve. In Kenya, civil servants are not
politicians, and politicians cannot be
appointed to civil service posts. Each
have their proper roles and functions.
But this should not be an obstacle to mutual trust and co-operation.. . . Each
makes an important contribution to the
success of the project. They are jointly
and equally participating in a single national project.

    If we are to bring to fruition our
plans for developing our country, it is
of paramount importance that we establish
without delay, and clearly define, harmonious working arrangements between
politicians and civil servants . . . more
particularly in the field (that is, in the
Provinces) where Ministers cannot be present to provide a bridge. The misunder-
standings which have occurred in the past
arise partly from historical attitudes
which prevent the habit of consultation
and co-operation, and partly from lack of
clear definition of roles.

    The attitude that there is an antagonism
between politicians and civil servants as
natural as the enmity between the leopard
and the goat, is a remnant of colonialism.
It must be eradicated from our thinking.
I have ordered that there shall be established, in each district and province in

the country, development committees where politicians and civil servants will sit together, to discuss on matters affecting the progress of the areas.

It is my sincere hope that from the discussions in these councils there will develop better understanding and respect between these two vital sections of the government machinery. I hope also to learn when I go around the country that the habit of friendly social intercourse between the politicians and the civil servants is being fostered.12

Because the President's comments are so clear, perhaps we should now attempt to answer the question raised earlier: Party workers forgotten by whom? The point is that the "enmity" the President notes between politicians and civil servants is not enmity in the sense of hatred of a foe but, rather, a conflict of interest between two factions. This conflict has continued to breed competition — and thus further conflicts. The nature of conflict is one of struggle for power (influence, if you wish), that is, power to control or influence the course of national development toward one's own perception of goals. In such a contest for power, it is highly unlikely that a lasting détente can exist between the two groups until the competition is resolved.13

A second point that addresses itself to the same question is that these two groups are basically different in background and in general outlook. By and large, bureaucrats are successors to the colonial administrators; and, besides being comparatively conservative, they have their own interests to protect. Most party officials, on the other hand, tend to be more progressive (and usually radical) in both economic and political outlook. That being the case, the two groups do not see eye-to-eye on

195

most issues. It is in this context that the President's remarks should be understood. His appeal for harmonious cooperation between the two groups is also a recognition of the fact that things are not going well. To be more precise, the bureaucracy then had the upper hand in the struggle for power. Let us now further examine the reasons why bureaucracy had the upper hand and was able both to isolate and to neutralize the party.

Policy or
Administration?

British traditions of public service do not permit civil servants to engage in political activities. By virtue of being a British colony, Kenya's colonial service followed similar traditions; colonial civil servants and their successors at independence were theoretically prohibited from taking part in politics. Even after independence Kenya's Africanized bureaucracy preserved nearly all of Britain's public service traditions, including those of political neutrality and anonymity.[14]

This paper takes the position that political neutrality is impractical and that the post-independence functional setup of public service does not permit such neutrality. First, civil servants have many political functions that, however they may be described, remain essentially political — such as resolving departmental conflicts informally, vetting matters for the minister's attention, addressing public meetings on national issues, testifying before parliamentary committees, and coordinating government activities on interdepartmental committees.[15]

Second, if we assume that the new Africanized service is accountable to a government freely elected by the people, it seems logical to concede the possibility that such service is intended, at least under the circumstances of nation-building, to serve those people and be subject to their social, economic, and political pressure. Like anyone else, civil servants have political views. They do not operate in a sociopolitical vacuum. They too are bound to respond to some political stimuli in a manner that befits the norms and mores of the society they come from and in which they operate.

In most emerging societies the bureaucrats are the most intellectually and technically sophisticated segment of the national population. They are without doubt best equipped to conduct the affairs of nation-building in a rational manner; they possess the vital information, know-how, and experience that any society must have to meet its challenges. If that is the case, then one is compelled to agree with President Julius Nyerere of Tanzania that:

> Once you begin to think of a single national movement instead of a number of rival factional parties, it becomes absurd to exclude the whole group of the most intelligent and able members of the community from participation in these (political) discussions of policy simply because they happen to be civil servants. . . .[16]

Besides, "The distinction between policy and administration is only useful in theoretical terms but in practice no such sharp distinction exists."[17] Too often, "In the same actions policy is being formulated as it is administered and it is being administered as it is being formulated. . . ."[18]

The argument that political affiliation on the part of public servants impairs their sense of impartiality and efficiency raises serious questions. For instance, it would seem somewhat contradictory, because in a one-party state presumably only one political line exists; one must assume that the single-party view is reflected in the government's policies.[19] Hence public servants theoretically should experience little loyalty conflict as, by way of illustration, might be the case for a Republican working with a Democratic administration or a Conservative serving a Labour administration. The Kenyan situation is not like that, even if one assumes that the above examples from the United States and Britain are valid. Indeed, Kenya civil servants, particularly those in administration, too often function both in political situations and as party cadres. For instance, they convene public meetings (*baraza*) in their administrative capacities not only to explain government policies but also to explain the meaning of African Socialism to the masses. Similar activities include publicizing government programs, self-help projects, and government progress; welcoming and guiding touring ministers or the President himself; and advertising public rallies or meetings. Now, there is no reason why civil servants cannot or should not do these things. But considering the President's own appeal and call to party workers to be trained to understand and implement national plans for reconstruction and development — and, further, considering the President's own admission that party workers are the more locally known and trusted and that they are the link between the rulers and the masses — one assumes that some of these activities might be undertaken jointly by the two groups. It also raises the question whether the President's desire for training party workers ever produced results. And the question of mobilization of the masses for the purposes of nation-building would be a difficult one if those the President declared "locally known and trusted" were not fully involved in the mobilization.

Relations Between Party
and Bureaucracy

The relations between the party and the bureaucracy in Kenya have been deteriorating for some time.
Since the early years of independence, in many instances party functions and voices have been successfully muzzled by the bureaucrats.[20] That bureaucracy muzzled the voice of the party is indicative
of rising bureaucratic power over the party. In
the first place, the government, through its bureaucracy, has always laid down the ways and means of
party governance; for instance, the holding of political rallies, when and how to conduct elections,
and so on.[21]

More specifically, party workers were arrested.
On July 6, 1965, 27 party workers and officials were
arrested and imprisoned without bail because they
attempted to take over the ruling party headquarters.
The point here is not one of the merits or demerits
of the take-over but, rather, one of an entirely
internal political party dispute being handled by
bureaucrats. Generally, political disagreements
and controversies within a political body should
be sorted out by the politician involved. But
because of the relative power position of the bureaucracy in Kenya, bureaucrats could and did intervene in a political controversy.

In another instance, in 1966, party elections
for the District Branches were held in various places.
Again, because of conflicts among the rank and file
of several party branches, the government saw to it
that a slate of candidates it preferred was put up
for these positions. Perhaps such behavior is expected of all governments, but in this case all the
government-backed candidates "were publicly pro-
claimed as branch officials without elections organized in accordance with the party constitution.
The most glaring examples were: Murang'a, Kisii,
and South Nyanza districts."[22] The Attorney-General,
who arranged for and supervised the conduct of

elections, did not declare these elections null and void. And the only interpretation one can offer is that his silence on the irregularity of the matter implied official approval. As a matter of fact, the General Secretary of the ruling party (the late Tom Mboya), who was also a Cabinet Minister, is said to have publicly stated during the annual conference of the ruling party that "The party constitution was out of date; in fact, so out of date that there was no need even to follow the procedure laid down in the constitution for its own amendment. . . ."[23]

Other instances that indicate the general rise of bureaucratic power and the apparent decline of party influence are manifested by the President's tours of the countryside. The bon voyage and receptions held during his trip are occasions for the Chief Executive and the provincial bureaucracy to get together with as little party business as possible. When Kenya became a republic, celebrations of the occasion were organized largely by party workers and civil servants alike.[24] But the former had to follow the latter's instructions. Soon after the celebrations, the President of the young republic visited the Coast Province. On arrival, he was welcomed by the mayor, the Provincial Commissioner, and other senior civil and administrative officers.[25] When the President returned to the capital (Nairobi), he was welcomed by Cabinet Ministers, Members of Parliament, the diplomatic corps, and senior civil servants.[26] Going through the press releases, one gathers the impression that this association between the President, his Cabinet, and civil servants — with little or no mention of the presence of party officials (that is, officials of the party who are not simultaneously officers or members of the Government) — indeed indicates the rise of bureaucracy.

That bureaucratic power is on the increase while party influence and power are shrinking was further underscored by the National Organizing Secretary of the ruling party (K.A.N.U.) in January, 1966. He wrote a bitter letter to President Kenyatta on the effect of the withering of the party's machinery and functional role:

> His report on the appalling situation of the party noted that the last KANU delegates' conference had been held in October 1962 (another was held in March, 1966), that the last party secretariat meeting had been convened in February 1964, and that the party's executive council last met in January of 1963. Unpaid party debts had reached a total of $56,000 and many of the party staff members and their families had been thrown out of their former houses because salaries had not been paid for seven months. Telephone and postal services were said to have been cut off because the bills for these services remained unpaid.[27]

Echoing the Organizing Secretary-General, the then Minister of Marketing, Cooperatives and Housing, Paul Ngei, remarked similarly that the party was not functioning and that he could not comprehend the party's dying so when it was ruling the country.[28]

So far, two points have emerged clearly: (1) the rise to dominance of the bureaucracy, which, as has been indicated, was really a continuation of a previous situation; and (2) the decline of party influence and effectiveness. All this has occurred in spite of the President's reassuring words. Although the President has often talked about the party and its various roles, and although his political and leadership credentials are unmatched on the Kenyan scene, it cannot be said that his party organizational role has been productive or helpful to the causes that he has championed. Indeed, nowhere can this writer find a single proposal for party reorganization and rejuvenation authored by, or attributed to, the President.[29] He expressed his sorrow in 1962 when President Nyerere resigned from the premiership in order to devote his full time to the party organization.[30] Even the Secretary-General of the party, the late Tom Mboya, seemed to downgrade the importance of party organization. The Nairobi daily, *The Daily Nation*, is said to have quoted Mboya as saying, "The actual Party organization is not so important, perhaps, as the discipline in thought-lines which KANU (Party) must learn."[31] Mboya seemed to alter his views on party reorganization later in an article in the magazine *Pan Africa*, where he stressed the importance of improving means of communication between the Members of Parliament and the masses but still preferred a party dominated by the Government.[32]

Decline of the Party

To repeat the above point, the rise of the bureaucracy and the decline of the party tends to indicate that something is basically awry in both structure and function of the party. Structurally, the party is anachronistic. It was built to fight colonialism — to fight for independence — not to build a nation (which is not to say that fighting for independence should necessarily bar such an organization from contributing to nation-building). Functionally, the party should have been doing what President Kenyatta told the conference of party workers.[33]

There are many reasons for the post-independence decline of the party. Perhaps when the original major opposition party dissolved itself at the end of 1964 it removed any threat to the ruling party. It may be that the ruling political elite never liked strongly organized and disciplined political parties, as the *Daily Nation* seemed to suggest.[34] But perhaps more fundamental is the fact that at the time of the struggle for independence, all ruling elites were in the party because that was the only place they could have conducted their struggle against colonialism. With the advent of independence and the subsequent process of Africanization of both political and civil service positions, party personnel decreased. In other words, most former party officials and workers seized upon jobs in the government service, leaving their former political functions without anyone (or without anyone comparable) to oversee party affairs. Many present Cabinet members and Members of Parliament were formerly political leaders in their districts and provinces. When they joined the government, they took with them their loyal local supporters, who had hitherto been engaged in party affairs. This change of personnel deprived the party of valuable and devoted workers. Without further recruitment and training to replace those who left, it is difficult to see how Kenya's political development could have kept pace with bureaucratic development. It is also difficult to regard the President's initial call for training of the party workers for national development as anything more than a rhetorical flourish.

Illustrative of this last observation is the brief history of the Lumumba Institute, which was supposed to be the training ground for party officials and workers. After the unfortunate incident on July 6, 1965, when 27 party trainees and officials attempted to take over the headquarters of the party and ended up in jail, the Institute was closed down by the Government. While such action may have been justified by existing circumstances, it also clearly shows that the Government did not fully appreciate the usefulness of well-trained party personnel. The fact that the first graduates of the Lumumba Institute did not support the government's policies and programs is itself evidence that the government did not realize fully what it was getting into when it established the Institute. Perhaps the most sensible thing would

have been to revise the syllabus of the Institute
to reflect national aspirations as seen and understood by the ruling elites. Other improvements that
could have been instituted include the careful selection of teaching staff and quality students so that
the existence of the Institute, its operation, and
output would be consonant with national plans and
objectives.

Before further examination of the rise of the
bureaucracy, it should perhaps be pointed out that
without effective political organization and education, political participation is difficult to
accomplish.[35] With the President's appeals for
mass mobilization to facilitate both political participation and integration, the lack of any definitive organizational pattern, the muzzling of
the party by bureaucrats, and the general weakening of the party, it is difficult to talk of political participation, let alone equality. For in
the final analysis the only meaningful way the
masses can participate in politics is to take part
in local political activity. Of course one can
speak of elections as the most meaningful way of
influencing public officials, but this is only one
way.[36] People can and do organize at the local
level to influence local authorities in various
ways. But with the apparent downgrading of the
party, people naturally get the impression that it
would not be worth their time and effort to be involved in politics. An indirect consequence of
all this is that Kenya today cannot be said to be
politically integrated, despite the existence of a
one-party government. Maybe it is asking or expect-
ing too much, but the plain truth is that Kikuyus
elect Kikuyus to the national Parliament, Luos elect
Luos, Kamba elect Kamba, etc. In other words, Kenya
has not yet reached the point where an individual's
merit and qualifications can cross tribal lines.
Ironically, in the early 1960's it appeared that an
individual of one ethnic group could represent a
constituency inhabited by another ethnic group; a

good example of this was the late Tom Mboya, who always depended upon Kikuyu votes, though he himself was a Luo.

Also, to speak of Kenya's masses being mobilized is to overstate the situation. This is not to say that various individuals and groups have not responded to government appeals for self-help, etc. Being mobilized conveys, here, a notion of people who are actively involved in making decisions which affect many phases of their lives. To be involved in only one or two activities is not to be mobilized.[37] The point is that full and conscious mobilization requires more than bureaucratic maneuvers and elitism; it requires individuals like those the President mentioned, who are "locally known and trusted" and who are the links between the ruling elite and the masses. Looked at from this perspective, the decline of the party can be said to have negatively affected the level of the people's political participation. Kenneth Good has observed:

> At the end of 1967 the Kenyatta elite confidentially viewed KANU (Party) as neither a national front which loyally and unquestioningly supported the government, nor a policy-influencing body. Somewhat surprisingly, they may have come to see KANU as a source of desired prestige for their incumbency. In December (1968) the Government announced its intention of spending 1,800,000 pounds (Kenya pound = $2.80) on the construction of a 27-storey building in Nairobi — it would be the city's biggest and costliest — for KANU. In endeavouring to meet some of the public criticism at such an outlay, Arap Moi (the Vice- President) reportedly said that the party building might also house some government organizations. Kenyatta has previously insisted upon the maintenance of a strict separation between party and administration but, of

course, with the thought of the possible subordination of the administration chiefly in mind. Such a building would indeed be a fine acquisition for any group. Yet the money and the building might also be seen as something of a measure of Kenyatta's private assessment of the extent of KANU's decline.[38]

Good has gone further to examine the various implications of this party decline. At one point, he says that there is no evidence to suggest that the Kenyan masses show particular apathy toward politics:

And given the record of the fifties, and such slighter prosaic evidence as large attendances at political meetings and in the public gallery of the Kenyan Parliament, there is something to suggest that the Kenyan people would seek to display an interest in their political life if, that is, such participation should appear meaningful. However, in their determination to form an all African and a KANU government, under Kenyatta, most elites' energies and concern seem to have been given to the promotion of their own nebulous unity and little to the detail of the relationship between the higher levels of the party and the mass of the people.[39]

From the foregoing remarks, it would seem that the decline of the party may have serious implications for the political growth of Kenya. It is helpful here to stress Good's point that the elite may have come to regard the party as a prestige symbol serving their political interests. The question is certainly not one of whether Kenya can develop without a strong party but, rather, of whether it is proper to compare the role of a

party in such a developing society with that of a
party in a developed society. Given the level of
education of the masses, their general poverty,
and the social disruptions that have necessarily
come with both colonial and nation-building programs,
it is difficult to see how this great mass of people
could be effectively involved in both the decision-
making process and nurturing of a common national
awareness. This paper takes the view that political
involvement and the growth of a national consciousness can be created only through organization along
particular political lines similar to those President Kenyatta mentioned in connection with mass
mobilization.

Rise of the Bureaucracy

     The decline of the party and the rise of bureau-
cracy have implied, as has already been said, that
bureaucracy has assumed at least some political
functions that one might expect the party to undertake. It would appear logical, therefore, to examine the extent to which bureaucracy may have influenced both political integration and participation.
     Reciprocal relationships between the bureau-
cracy and the political elites can be traced to
the time of independence.[40] Kenya's independence
came at a critical period, when the newly independent state was experiencing serious internal tribal and factional dissent and secession threats.
Obviously, the African leadership desired and
was determined to keep Kenya united.[41] The party
that they had successfully employed against the
colonialists was evidently considered inadequate
to handle the situation.[42] So the decision to
build upon the British-made bureaucracy was apparently the most sensible under those circumstances. The new government put emphasis on maintaining as efficient a civil service as existed

during the colonial period. In order to assure themselves that they were in power, they used the bureaucracy to consolidate their newly acquired power; it was the bureaucracy that was instrumental in resisting the new government's political enemies — whether traditional or radical ones.[43] That at is to say, some traditional elements may have felt that independence was a license to revert to the traditional patterns of life; the radical ones may have felt that independence meant doing away with the existing order.[44] There is no question that were it not for this bureaucracy, the elites would have had serious difficulties in establishing control.

That the bureaucracy assisted the leadership in establishing control does not mean that the bureaucracy gained nothing from this relationship. Indeed, the very fact of being so tremendously useful to the incoming rulers enhanced or promoted such bureaucratic interests as prestige, tenure, higher salaries, promotions, and other fringe benefits such as were enjoyed by the colonial civil servants.[45] Precisely because this bureaucracy has changed little, nation-building efforts have tended to stagnate Kenya's political growth toward fuller participation and national awareness. As implied above, the President is on record as opposing any hasty move on these matters; he has said, "I must warn you not to start by demolishing the whole structure created by the colonial government because of some untried experiment."[46] This indicates the influence (or perhaps the support) underlying the bureaucracy.

During the early years of independence, many non-Kenyan bureaucrats were to be relieved of their duties because of the pressures exerted by a combination of indigenous political forces and pre-independence political promises. This replacement of expatriates by Africans is generally referred to as "Africanization." Those being replaced were an extremely vocal group, supported by the British

Government, who demanded fair compensation for the loss of their careers. They spoke very pessimistically, predicting administrative disasters if they were forced to leave their positions before they had trained their successors. They also demanded compensation in advance of their early retirement. The point to be emphasized here is that this kind of talk, with its threatening overtones in an atmosphere already infused with racial and political tensions, tended further to soften the attitudes of incoming rulers toward the established bureaucracy. It also tended to give some leeway to the departing expatriates to recommend for promotion those Africans they knew and thought most capable of retaining and operating the form of institutional structures which they had established.[48] In the eyes of local people, such promotions to high positions hitherto occupied by Europeans tended to enhance the relative importance of the civil servants as well as their prestige and prerogatives. This civil-service-oriented mentality is especially obvious particularly among the school leavers, most of whom aspire to high positions in the Government.[49] By inference, it may be observed here that Kenyan youth, particularly the educated youth who are likely to be tomorrow's leaders, have become civil-service-oriented as opposed to party- or politics-oriented (which was the case during the pre-independence struggle).

From the foregoing, it may be said that the Africanized bureaucracy has been able to bridge the gap that existed between it and the nationalist who, after independence, assumed leadership. The pre-independence conflict was probably unavoidable if one allows for the inevitability of this bureaucracy's having been more conservative than the nationalists.

Clearly, the bureaucracy has succeeded in completely dominating both the party and the national scene; it has also moved from its former narrowly conceived role of simply keeping order to a more involved and challenging role of active nation-

building. Social and economic programs for national
development are designed and implemented almost exclusively by a coalition of Kenya bureaucrats and
foreign experts. Perhaps this is as it should be,
but the main question that such a pattern of development (which, incidentally, relates very much to
the basic argument of this paper) poses and leaves
unanswered is when and how the masses of people are
involved in a participatory capacity. How do we
create a feeling of oneness among villagers? It
is a difficult task but, however looked at, it does
not appear that bureaucracy alone or in coalition
with foreign expertise will actively involve the
masses in nation-building.

Here we may note Fred Riggs's observations on
situations that appear to be similar to that of
Kenya. At one point he seems to say that bureaucratic penetration and control of local affairs
undermines the base of the parliamentary system and
that bureaucratic expansion needlessly controls the
local electorate.[50] Kenya's case is one of an
elected chief executive (including his Cabinet and
some Ministers) using the bureaucratic chain of
command to control and manipulate the electorate
at all levels.[51] Politically speaking, what has
happened in Kenya is that bureaucracy has become
the sole (or nearly the sole) mediator between the
elites and the people, with the consequence that the
line and medium of communication between the people
and politicians (their representatives) have been
distorted. Popular "messages" pass through the
bureaucrats who have a vital stake in what is decided. When the political party is weak and cannot control the bureaucracy, political assemblies
tend to be tolerated and accepted by bureaucracy
only as they give the bureaucratic administration
some semblance of democratic legitimacy.

In the passage cited above, Riggs expresses
concern over the possibility that a one-party system may turn the parliamentary system into its
puppet; but while this may be the case elsewhere,

it is not the case in Kenya.[52]   Indeed, if the trend
discussed above does not change, perhaps the real
concern in Kenya's case is that the parliamentary
system will become a puppet of the bureaucracy.
Structurally, the provincial administration in Kenya
is linked directly to the President's office (notwithstanding a Ministry of Local Government that
could easily assume such a role), which would seem
to imply that the provincial bureaucrats enjoy the
advantages of direct access to the Chief Executive
and by use of it they can put their case directly
to the President instead of to a Minister.   Finally,
one might close this discussion of the relationship
between a powerful bureaucracy and a weak party by
saying that a bureaucracy without effective political
checks at all levels (excep the top leadership, which
it serves), a bureaucracy insufficiently supplied
with political ideology, and a bureaucracy functioning as the only medium of communication between the
masses and the top political elite is, in fact, most
unlikely to bring about national consciousness and/or
political participation.[53]   In other words, the
function of such a bureaucracy may ultimately make
both integration and participation more difficult.
Bureaucratic functions are necessarily closed to the
majority of Kenyans, who lack sufficient skills;
participation is thus out of the question for them.
In regard to integration the situation is very similar.   Integration implies participation; one feels
an integral part of a group because he shares and
takes part in the group's activities.   It is therefore difficult to envisage integration without at
the same time instituting participation.[54]

Interest Groups

     Like many underdeveloped countries, Kenya is
not blessed with many effective interest groups
which, in the developed countries, cast weighted
"votes" in the political process by representing

their special interests to the decision-makers. There are, however, a few interest groups whose activities and influences may be of some help to the general arguments of this paper. We are concerned here with the elitist phenomenon as manifested by various interest groups. The basic units of such interest groups do exist in Kenya, but they are too weak or too small to make their voices heard. The weaknesses of such interest groups may be due to a number of factors, including low literacy, lack of ability to finance private endeavors and to generate domestic capital, lack of organization, and bureaucratic hostility to such organizations operating outside their area of jurisdiction.

The most active vocal interest group in Kenya is probably the labor movement. The influence of labor on Kenya's politics is a consequence of its role during the pre-independence struggle.[55] The Kenya Civil Service was so racially and discriminatorily structured during the colonial era that almost all Africans who entered it were in the lower, manipulable segments, commonly called the "Junior Service."[56] Those in this section found it necessary to organize "themselves as trade unions and as an instrument for fighting for raising their status in the service."[57] In government as well as in private industries and on the farms, workers organized themselves into unions in order to advance their interests more effectively. All these unions joined together in the early 1950's to form the now-defunct Kenya Federation of Labour led by Tom Mboya.[58]

Since the advent of independence, the labor movement has never lacked representation where its interests were involved. First, when Mboya became the Minister of Labour, he still maintained his General Secretaryship of the labor movement. Later some indications appeared that the Kenya Federation of Labour leadership always consulted with the Minister of Labor before going on strike.[59] When Mboya ceased to be the General Secretary, his successor was also elected to Parliament. There have also

212

been a number of Assistant Ministers and Members of
Parliament whose connections with the labor movement
have remained strong. From all this, one would get
the impression that labor interests were well attended. But here, as in the political arena, two
groups existed and still exist — the elites and the
rank and file of workers. In the final analysis,
what is in the interest of the elites (in this
case the labor elites) is not necessarily what the
rank and file of workers want. So, like any other
elite, labor leadership continues to speak in the
name of the workers who, in most cases, may not
even know what is going on.

Internal disputes among the various office holders and aspirants caused schisms which led to the
formation of rival labor groups. These internal
dissensions ran so high in 1966 that a member of
one rival faction was killed in a riot, which prompted
President Kenyatta to abolish the rival labor groups
by Presidential decree. He ordered the formation
of the Central Organizations of Trade Unions (C.O.T.U.)
as the single official nationwide labor organization.
The head of this new organization is nominated or
selected by the President from a list of three leading candidates elected by the entire labor movement
through their representatives.[60] Such a reorganization could not have improved the labor movement,
because the person nominated by the President to
head the organization was the man who had been head
of the dissolved K.F.L.[61] Thus this story ends just
about where it began: with an elite group in the
labor movement that seems to toe the government line
without acknowledging this to the general membership. In fact, it appears that, since this same
group obtains their jobs from the President, they
are rather unlikely to bite the hand that feeds them.
Labor's integration role was a significant one before independence; but, as with the political party,
this role has diminished recently because of internal struggles, bureaucratic pressures, or, as the
late Tom Mboya said, in the official view, because
they should not oppose the African government.[62]

Bureaucracy has some characteristics which tend to make it function as a pressure group in some situations. For instance, the British civil service is in theory and general practice organized outside British politics. It represents its interests through unions which bargain with the employer's (government) representatives. Kenya's bureaucracy as a pressure group must be viewed from a rather different perspective. In the first place, the higher bureaucrats hold all the important positions which relate to the formulation and implementation of policy; they have prestige, power, and good financial renumeration. At this high level these bureaucrats not only identify with the political elite (on the grounds that their basic interests tend to be similar); they also tend to be the bulward of conservatism, inclined to maintain the status quo or at least to check any reform that may be unfavorable to their positions and interests. It can therefore be seen that to such bureaucrats, trade unionism is not of much consequence.

But for the lower echelons of the service — say, below the technical and executive grades — unionization is the only means of obtaining better opportunities for promotion and salary increases. Through trade unions they get shorter working hours, tenure, promotion, fringe benefits, leave allowances, reasonable disciplinary procedures, etc. As such, bureaucracy can be taken as an interest group, although not all segments of it belong to the same interest group. As in the labor movement, there is an elitist group among the bureaucrats that may be used by the rulers to manipulate the rest of Kenyan bureaucracy. Also implied in this elitism is the fact that the level of involvement of the rank and file is necessarily affected.

Another potentially influential group is the chamber(s) of commerce. There are two main associations of chambers of commerce in Kenya organized on an East African basis — the Association of Chambers of Commerce and Industry of Eastern Africa

214

and the Federation of Commerce and Industry of
Eastern Africa.[63] These chambers of commerce are
located in the urban areas, although their membership may be somewhat scattered around the small
towns. They are heavily dominated by immigrant
communities like the Indians and the Europeans, who
still own and operate much of Kenya's commerce and
industry.[64] There are several African chambers
of commerce which, until recently, were not affiliated with the two major ones. These two main
commercial groups are economically powerful, which
means that they can influence government policies.
One indication of such influence may be seen in the
fact that the government has taken great pains to
guarantee the safety of private capitalists operating in Kenya to expatriate their profits.[65]

Before independence, demonstrable conflict had
existed between the African nationalists and the
foreign business community operating in Kenya.
This conflict was a natural consequence of the
latter's domination of Kenya's economic life —
which, incidentally, foreigners still very much
dominate.

The politico-commercial disagreement may be
validly projected to the bureaucratic circles for
two reasons: (1) the bureaucrats tend to support
their superiors in the event of a contest between
the two and (2) the financial support of the bureaucracy is directly related to tax collection and
laws that govern it. However, this conflict need
not be overemphasized, since these three groups —
political leaders, top civil servants, and the
business community — are now cooperating in nearly
every aspect.[66] The point is that these groups
have recognized their interdependence. Such cooperation was alluded to by the Minister for Commerce
and Industry when, addressing a meeting of the
Chamber of Commerce, he said:

> In several cases a few leading Africans with
> big names or big positions have . . . ac-
> cepted appointments as directors in com-

215

panies where no functions are given them,
and the African name is used as no more
than a decoration . . . they have an
African member on the Board of Directors
in the hope that they will receive special
considerations or special favours by the
government agencies or foreign corporations from friendly countries. . . .[67]

In other words, the restrained relationships that
existed between the business community and the nationalists during the struggle for independence does
not seem to be so evident these days, primarily because the African top echelons are to a degree co-
opted by the business community, so that they now
talk the same language, with apparently identical
interests. Again, given the structure and operation of the business community, it is impossible
to tell exactly what they could have done to facilitate African participation in the undertaking
except using rhetoric not unlike the political
flourishes referred to earlier.
    Kenya's press may possess the greatest poten-
tial influence; but so far, with a few exceptions,
the press has not been at variance with the elites.[68]
Since independence the foreign owners and managers
of the press, with their newly appointed African
editorial staff and/or board members, have recognized and deferred to those who wield power. What the
President, his Ministers, and the higher bureaucracy
say receives maximum coverage, as would be the case
anywhere else. But criticism of political leadership or the government is tangential. It may be
said that criticism of government is constitutionally
allowed but in practice does not occur. The probable explanation for this is that the press may
consider subservience a means of protecting its
interests. However one may explain this behavior,
it is certainly self-protecting. Considering the
government's monopoly on radio, television, the
Kenya News Agency, and other media, the press has

little leeway. Censorship does not exist as such;
there is no need for it. But the fact that the
government chooses what to reveal and what not to
reveal about its activities appears to make legal
restrictions unnecessary. As has already been
mentioned, the mass media, in particular the press,
seem to possess the greatest potential for influencing the course of events; but because the press
is still foreign-owned, and like labor or other interest groups has co-opted and been co-opted by some
of the elites, its interests tend to coincide with
those of the elites. Thus the impact of the press
on processes of political participation, integration,
and propagation of a national consciousness is relatively insignificant if one is not thinking of the
press's role of transmitting the elite's message to
the masses — a one-sided form of communication.

Conclusions

    In conclusion, it should be emphasized that
the recent trend in Kenya has been, and still is,
toward an increasing role in rule-making and implementation for both the bureaucracy and the Chief
Executive. As the power of the party wanes, it
is becoming increasingly clear that in the absence
of strongly articulate non-bureaucratic groups and
institutions to check or share the excesses of
power wielded by the elites, there is a danger of
losing the masses. Indeed, political impotence
such as may be experienced by the party is directly
related to economic impotence. Conversely, political power has often led to economic power. A
marriage of convenience has been contracted between
the elitist groups in the various sectors of Kenya's
life. In this connection, it has been observed:

        Kenya's economy is growing very rapidly, but
        the gap between classes or between the haves
        and the have-nots seems to be widening. There

217

is clear evidence of a few African political and bureaucratic elite who are
slowly merging with the commercial elite,
while the majority of African's linger
helplessly below the totem pole. This
trend may defeat the very tenet of African
Socialism which in effect may lead to another revolution of an unanticipated nature and which may end up in the disin-
tegration of the whole Kenyan society.[69]

Here we emphasize the phenomenon of elitism,
which has been depicted as present in all major
sectors on Kenyan life and which coalesces to
protect its status. This coalition of various
sector elites is argued to be the inevitable consequence of an unchecked, unhampered bureaucracy
which has, throughout the post-independence period,
dominated and outmaneuvered both the political and
the nonpolitical elements in Kenyan society.
Another significant trend discernible from the
foregoing is a political and economic convergence.
Clearly the politics of nation-building and the
economics of nation-building are so intertwined
that one cannot be discussed without involving the
other. Specifically, the problem of elitism in
both politics and economics is unavoidable. The
intimation here is that the lack of political accountability to which we have attributed the dominance of bureaucracy has led to a lack of economic
accountability which, for reasons of space and
brevity, we shall not discuss here.[70] This lack of
accountability has, in its turn, produced a socioeconomic polarization of Kenyan society into groups
that are not very alike, either in interests or in
general outlook. Inevitably, the processes of
political participation and the growth of a national
awareness have been negatively affected. In order
to reverse the trend, one is compelled to agree
with the Christian Council of Kenya that class and
social polarization are not inevitable dictates of
nature and that serious

. . . vigilance and resolution are needed
if the tenets of Democratic African Socialism are to be implemented in such a
way as to draw every citizen into a real
participation in both the sacrifices for,
and the rewards of, rapid modernization.[71]

We have already suggested that questions of
political integration and participation are closely
linked. We now suggest that political integration
and participation can best be achieved through political organization and leadership. This is not,
of course, to say that there is only one way of
inculcating particular attitudes among a people;
but given the experience of the developing world
to date, the most momentous social changes have
occurred in those countries where sociopolitical
organization has been undertaken seriously. Again,
this is not saying that sociopolitical organization
or even social change necessarily indicates superior
development. The difficulty here is that, in the
face of a problem of bureaucratic elitism and its
twin sister, apathy, the social, political, and
economic gaps existing between the mass of the people and the ruling class inhibit the possibility
that a national social and political consciousness
will be achieved.

Kenya's difficulties in integration and participation are somewhat explained by the fact that:

The major decisions are likely to be made
on the basis of what works, rather than on
the basis of rigid adherence to any dog-
matic theory. It has been said that the
intellectuals should be aware of arguing
African Socialism to its death. (What is
left unsaid here is that) the refusal to
theorize may easily slip into the refusal
to think straight, and this can amount to
a surrender of the initiative and a failure
to make responsible decisions.[72]

There may thus be some correlation between bureaucratic pragmatism and the party's intellectual ideologization of its intents and policies. To the extent that bureaucracy feels hampered by the party's intellectual ideologization of national programs (as was evidenced by the announcement and formulation of the Government Sessional Paper No. 10 on African Socialism), it may be said that bureaucracy ignores or emasculates these ideologizations in favor of something more practical that does not require too much adjustment to fit bureaucratic routines. To the extent that this may have been true in Kenya, the above conclusion would not appear to be far-fetched.

Research and methodological studies have indicated clearly that theorization of the situation under study is a necessary condition of rationality and coherence. Conceptualization and formulation of nation-building programs thus needs both aspects: theory and pragmatism — the latter always striving to achieve the level of the former. In this way, perhaps, the party's intellectual ideologization of national goals could guide an otherwise directionless bureaucratic pragmatism; but once party goals are overshadowed by bureaucratic pragmatism, the possibility of a national consciousness built on an integrated, participating society is somewhat diminished.

NOTES

1. Guy Hunter, *Modernizing Peasant Societies: A Comparative Study in Asia and Africa* (London: Oxford University Press, 1969), p. 218.

2.   David E. Apter, *Some Conceptual Approaches to the Study of Modernization* (Englewood Cliffs, N.J.:   Prentice-Hall, 1969), p. 357. Apter seems to differentiate authority from power by associating the former with a sense of duty or having a right over something; power is ability to compel or to use coercive sanctions to achieve an objective.

3.   Susan Wood, *Kenya: The Tensions of Progress* (2nd ed.; London: Oxford Univeristy Press, 1962), p. 100.

4.   Fred W. Riggs, "Bureaucrats and Political Development: A Paradoxical View," in Joseph La Palombara, ed., *Bureaucracy and Political Development* (Princeton: Princeton University Press, 1963), p. 125.

5.   Wood, *loc. cit.*

6.   *Ibid.*

7.   Irma Adelman, George Dalton, and Cynthia T. Morris, "Society, Politics and Economic Development," in G. Carter and A. Paden, eds., *Expanding Horizons in African Studies* (Evanston, Ill.:   Northwestern University Press, 1969), pp. 209-42; see especially p. 220, where they note: "The great need for political integration is emphasized by the fact that in some of these countries the adoption of Western-type parliamentary institutions at the time of independence led to struggles for national power among different (groups). In several instances these power contests were so sharp that they posed serious threats to the stability of the new national polities" (e.g., Nigerian civil war, numerous coups d'état, boundary wars between Somalia and Kenya, Ethiopia and Somalia, etc.).

8.   During the early years of independence,
President Kenyatta, then the Prime Minister, seemed
to argue on the same lines when he said that one
party "was the most prudent method of attaining
those aims and objects which our people hold so
dear." See *Daily Nation*, August 14, 1964. But a
different impression is given by later development.
See, for instance, *Kenya Weekly News*, September 1,
1967, p. 18. In this article an impression is given
that Kenya did not really need a strongly organized
and disciplined political party and that the need
was for a mass movement as existed or similar to the
one existing during the struggle for independence.
This view has been attributed to the late Tom Mboya,
who was the General Secretary of the ruling party
(K.A.N.U.). Mboya himself confirms this view. See
Mboya's *The Challenge of Nationhood* (New York: Praeger, 1970, p. 48. Kenneth Good, in *Canadian Journal
of African Studies* (Autumn, 1968), pp. 130-35, suggests that not even the President himself is anxious
to have a well-organized and disciplined party.

While on this, perhaps it is helpful to point
out that the theory and practice of mass politics
seem to have worked reasonably well in such African
countries as Tanzania, Guinea, and pre-coup Mali
and Ghana. But, as just hinted, it has not worked
in Kenya.

9.   "Mzee Kenyatta's Statement on the One-Party
State," *Daily Nation*, August 14, 1964.

10.   This refers to the coastal strip (locally
known as the Mwambao) and the Somali in the north,
all of whom demanded secession from independent
Kenya. Indeed, blood had to be shed to keep Somalis
within the boundaries of independent Kenya. See
Colin Legum, "Somali Liberation Songs," *Journal of
Modern African Studies*, I, 4 (December, 1963), 511.

222

11.   Government of Kenya, *Kenya News Agency Handout*, No. 1842 (December 12, 1964), pp. 1-2. Quoted from a speech delivered by the President at the opening of the Lumumba Institute, Nairobi. Also see *Daily Nation*, August 14, 1964.

12.   Government of Kenya, *Kenya News Agency Handout*, No. 768 (December 12, 1965); quoted from a speech delivered at a conference of public servants and party officials.

13.   Examples of this are the 1965 arrest of 27 party workers on grounds of breach of peach because they objected to the manner in which the party headquarters was run; but when the government-favored factions conducted irregular party elections, the bureaucracy did not consider such actions as breaches of the peace. Even when 22 branches of the Party complained of irregularities, the governing bureaucracy did not think peace had been breached. (See Oginga's statement of resignation, *East Africa Standard*, April 15, 1966). At the other times, provincial administrators intimidated citizens who did not support the governing party (as decreed by them). (See *Official Report*, House of Representatives, 1st Parliament, 4th Session, Vol. X, Pt. I (September 28, 1966), cols. 159-66. Perhaps one should note, too, that similar difficulties have arisen in Tanzania, pre-coup Ghana, Mali and in Guinea where they were resolved, or at least so said, by politicizing the civil service which President Kenyatta clearly refused to do.

14.   *Kenya News Agency Handout*, No. 768.   See also Republic of Kenya, *Code of Regulations*, Sec. 1 (b).

15.   President Kenyatta seemed to imply that civil servants' political involvement should be kept secret in the interest of professional effi-

ciency. See the Presidential Address at the K.A.N.U. Delegates Conference, March, 1966, published by the Ministry of Information, Nairobi. Also see G. E. Caiden, "The Political Role of the Commonwealth Bureaucracy," *Journal of the Australian Regional Groups of the Royal Institute of Public Administration*, XXIV, 4 (December, 1965), 312.

16. John Spencer, "Kenyatta's Kenya," *Africa Report*, Vol. II, No. 5, May, 1966, p. 6. Also see Mzee Kenyatta's Speech to the KANU Delegates Conference 1966, cited above: he conceded this point.

17. Caiden, *loc. cit.*

18. *Ibid.*

19. Since the merger of the two major parties in 1964, there have been at least two opposition parties: the African People's Party dissolved itself and rejoined the ruling Kenya African National Party, and the Kenya People's Party was banned by the Government. Besides, the Government controls all public meetings, which means that bureaucracy does sit on the seat of political judge and arbiter.

20. *Africa Digest*, October, 1965, pp. 32-33.

21. Mboya, *op. cit.*, pp. 59-62; Republic of Kenya, *Official Report*, National Assembly, 1st Parliament, 3rd Session, Vol. VIII (March 2, 1966), cols. 1669-73; (March 3), cols. 1720-25.

22. Spencer, *op. cit.*, p. 9.

23. Oginga's resignation statement, *East African Standard*, April 15, 1966.

24. *Kenya News Agency*, Press Release No. 7 (December 8, 1964).

25. *Kenya News Agency Handout*, No. 1867 (December 16, 1964).

26. *Kenya Calling: Weekly Digest*, January 8, 1966.

27. Spencer, *op. cit.*, p. 6.

28. *Ibid.*

29. Jomo Kenyatta, *Suffering Without Bitterness: The Founding of the Kenya Nation* (Nairobi: East African Publishing House, Ltd., 1968), p. 62, mentions that he "steeped himself in the solid work of Party Organization," but this writer could not find any trace of such solid work or even reference to it except by himself.

30. *Afica Diary*, February 3-9, 1962, p. 381.

31. Cited in Kenyatta, *op. cit.*, p. 158.

32. Tom Mboya, "The Role of the Party in Independent Kenya," *Pan Africa*, February 21, 1964, p. 5.

33. *Daily Nation*, April 16, 1965, p. 19. Similar sentiments were expressed by the late Tom Mboya. See *The Challenge of Nationhood*, p. 48.

34. Government of Kenya, *Kenya News Agency Handout* No. 1842, December 12, 1964, pp. 1-2. Quoted from a speech delivered by the President at the opening of the Lumumba Institute, Nairobi.

35. The late Tom Mboya, in a speech made on February 20, 1967, at the opening of National Book Week in Nairobi, argued, at one point, that "We believe that the ordinary people in villages and towns must participate in the policy formulation process." He just believed; he did not say or imply that they did take such part.

36. The last general election in Kenya (December, 1969) produced startling results, especially in turnover of the incumbent Members of Parliament; 65 percent, including five Cabinet Ministers, were defeated at the polls.

37. Most self-help projects are schools — Harambee schools and health centers — many of which cannot be sustained by local resources and have either to be closed down or taken over by the government.

38. Good, *op. cit.*, p. 131.

39. *Ibid.*

40. It is important to note that during the struggle for independence, the current ruling elites were in opposition to the colonial administration while the incumbent bureaucracy, though on a much lower level (usually clerical and auxiliary), was working for, and therefore with, the colonial administration. Their relations at this time were anything but reciprocal. Indeed, the African auxiliaries to the colonial administration were usually the ones who were used to counter the effects of the latter's political agitation.

41. Donald Rothchild, ed., *Politics of Integration: An East African Documentary* (Nairobi: East African Publishing House, 1969), pp. 134-54; Rothchild quotes the President in connection with the political integration of the three East African states. The President was, in effect, tongue-lashing Kenya's opposition party for the difficulties (regional) it had created even within Kenya. The President argued that he wanted a united Kenya in the federation.

42. Mboya, *The Challenge of Nationhood, loc. cit.*

226

43. Witness the firing of the chiefs and the detention and imprisonment of the recalcitrant political elements.

44. Rothchild, *op. cit.*, pp. 134-154 In these same speeches, the President's remarks do imply the avoidance of any hasty or radical move such as would jeopardize his gradual approach to these matters.

45. A. L. Adu, *The Civil Service in the New States of Africa*, New York: Praeger, 1965, pp. 96-115.

46. Government of Kenya, *Kenya News Agency Handout*, No. 189, 1965.

47. *Localisation and Training of Kenya Civil Service: Interim Report* No. 2. "Revised Conditions of Service for the Kenya Civil Service," Issued by the Director of Personnel, Office of the Prime Minister, Nairobi, 1964.

48. Oginga Odinga, *Not Yet Uhuru* (New York: Hill and Wang, 1966), pp. 256-57.

49. David Koff and George von der Muhll, "Political Socialisation in Kenya and Tanzania — A Comparative Analysis," *Journal of African Studies*, V, 1 (1967), 35-48; Tom Mboya, "The Future of Africa — A Challenge to African Youth," *Kenya News Agency Handout*, No. 452, December 28, 1966, pp. 5-7.

50. Riggs, *op. cit.*, p. 146.

51. "Chain of command" here means the Provincial and District Commissioners, District Officer, Assistant District Officer, Chief, Headman.

52. Countries like Guinea, Tanzania, pre-coup Ghana, and Mali are good examples of this situation where party dominated bureaucracy.

53. Riggs, *op. cit.*, p. 129. Here, Riggs seems to be alluding to a situation very much like this description.

54. Richard R. Fagen, *The Transformation of Political Culture in Cube* (Stanford: Stanford University Press, 1969), pp. 4-10. For further details on the various aspects of both integration and participation, see S. Verba, "Comparative Political Culture," in Lucian Pye and Sidney Verba, eds., *Political Culture and Political Development* (Princeton: Princeton University Press, 1965); Gabriel Almond and Sidney Verba, *The Civic Culture: Political Attitude and Democracy in Five Nations* (Princeton: Princeton University Press, 1963); Gabriel Almond and Bingham B. Powell, *Comparative Politics: A Developmental Approach* (Boston: Little Brown, 1966).

55. It should be noted that when all political organizations were banned in Kenya in 1953, the nationalists used the labor movement to air their grievances, which provided raw material for the nationalists. Also, some of the African grievances were related to the union movement, such as discriminatory hiring or promotion practices or laws. In addition, the labor leaders at this time also happened to be the political leaders — such as the late Tom Mboya.

56. Adu, *op. cit.*, p. 153.

57. *Ibid.*

58. Oginga Odinga, *op. cit.*, p. 108.

59. *Ibid.*, pp. 305-08.

60. *Reporter* (Nairobi), September 10, 1965, p. 23.

61. He has since been succeeded by his rival.

62. *Kenya News Agency Handout*, No. 452, p. 6.

63. Government of Kenya, *Commerce and Industry in Kenya 1961* (Nairobi: Ministry of Commerce and Industry, 1962), p. 45. The names of Chambers of Commerce have changed with time, so that instead of being East African, they are Kenyan. See *East African Standard*, February 23, 1968.

64. *Who Controls Industry in Kenya*, a report of a Working Committee of the Christian Council of Kenya (Nairobi: East African Publishing House, 1968), p. 250. This document clearly indicates in its listing of all major business establishments in Kenya that Kenyans do not own or operate these business enterprises and that, by and large, all of them are subsidiaries of overseas corporations registered locally (in Kenya) as private companies.

65. Jacob Oser, *Promoting Economic Development* (Evanston, Ill.: Northwestern University Press, 1967), pp. 196-208.

66. *Kenya News Agency Handout*, No. 745 (December 15, 1965).

67. *Ibid.*

68. When the press reported various oath ceremonies taking place in Central Province, just before the last general election on December 6, 1969, in a manner disapproved by the government, a few of the foreign correspondents were deported. See *Daily Nation*, October 3, 1969.

69. *Who Controls Industry in Kenya*, p. 259.

70. By "lack of accountability" is meant the lack of African control over the means of production and distribution (in the case of economics) and a lack of African political control over the bureaucracy (in the case of politics).

71. *Who Controls Industry in Africa*, pp. 270-72.

72. *Ibid.*, p. 272.

PART III

Case Papers on Development Administration in Africa

Administrative Structure:
Situation and Culture
in the Case of Urambo

by Kenneth L. Baer

Urambo is a Tanzanian tobacco-growing settlement scheme in the Tabora Region. In the Tanzanian context, a settlement scheme was an agricultural development project which attempted to transform the production techniques and life styles of the participants.[1]

Bureaucratically, Tanzanian settlement schemes fell under the jurisdiction of the Ministry of Lands, Settlement and Water Development rather than the Ministry of Agriculture. Although settlement schemes still survive in Tanzania, they have been significantly deemphasized in terms of both ideological praise and financial support since April, 1966. An understanding of settlements and their subsequent decline gives a processual insight into the changing nature of developmental administration.

Developmental administration can best be understood by combining macro-theory with micro-level analysis, an attempt to fill the gap to which Brokensha refers when he says:

Scarcely any realistic detailed studies have
been made on administration. The general
and hortatory abound, but the specific is
rare.[2]

An analysis of the Urambo scheme is helpful in
filling this gap on the micro-level, and developments in Urambo relate to and inform our understanding of the macro-setting of developmental administration in Tanzania.

This subject may be approached by tracing the
historical development of Urambo as a settlement
scheme and by relating this settlement scheme to
its own particular administrative ecology. Finally,
through a situational analysis as well as questionnaire data, information which tends to confirm that
developmental administration requires a cultural
base to operate successfully within the awareness
of its clients will be offered.

The Development
of Urambo

Initially it is useful to summarize significant events in Urambo development and administrative history.* In sketching the history of Urambo,

---

*April, 1948: Overseas Food Corporation (O.F.C.)
initiated work at Urambo.
October, 1952: Co-operative African Tenant
Scheme started.
April 1, 1955: Tanganyika Agricultural Corp-
oration (T.A.C.) replaced O.F.C.
October 1, 1955: 12 large farms leased to
former European O.F.C./T.A.C. employees.
October 1, 1956: First medium farms established
for Africans.

234

I have emphasized the evolution of the settlement
scheme from a European-inspired and -dominated venture in plantation agriculture to an African-con-
trolled scheme administered both by the Urambo
cooperative and the Division of Village Settlement.
While this paper concerns a particular settlement
scheme and uses it as an example, the conclusions
have an application which transcends Urambo and
Tanzania and informs our understanding of development administration in a general context.

Urambo was from the first a transformational,
production-oriented undertaking. It was one of
three large areas in Tanzania which constituted
the British-initiated Groundnut Scheme.[3] This
scheme was originally mandated for the large-scale
production of groundnut (peanut) oil, a project

October 1, 1958:   First small farms with separate curing barns established for Africans.

December, 1958:   Tanganyika Plantation Workers
Union established a regional office at Urambo.

December, 1958:   Urambo Employers' Association
formed.

1960 season: Tanganyika African Tobacco Growers Association formed.

November 15, 1962:   Urambo Farmers' Co-operative Society, Ltd., registered.

March, 1963:   Rural Settlement Commission
created.   The Village Settlement Agency (V.S.A.)
formed as its executive branch.

May, 1964:   Ministry of Lands, Settlement and
Water Development created.

January, 1965:   V.S.A. assumed control of the
seven schemes formerly under T.A.C. jurisdiction.

December, 1965:   Rural Settlement Commission
and the Village Settlement Agency dissolved.   The
Division of Village Settlement (D.V.S.), within
the Ministry of Lands, Settlement and Water Development, assumed the functions of the V.S.A.

designed to alleviate the vegetable oil shortage
in Europe after World War II. Efforts to grow
groundnuts commercially eventually failed in all
three areas — Kongwa, Nachingwea, and Urambo. The
failure of all three areas did not terminate the
project; in each case the administrative structure,
techniques, and skills were redeployed. In Urambo
an early attempt was made to find an alternative
cash crop. One hundred acres of Virginia-type
tobacco were grown experimentally in the 1950-51
season. The crop was successful; from this modest
beginning, tobacco has grown into the dominant cash
crop in Urambo, and indeed in all of the Tabora
region.

The Overseas Food Corporation's interest was
in production — initially in groundnuts and ultimately in tobacco. At the very beginning, the O.F.C.
established two production units of 20,000 acres
each, a plantation approach to tropical agriculture.
Because these units proved unmanageable, 25 large
farms of various sizes were created in the 1950-51
season, including the experimental farm which produced Virginia-type tobacco. Each farm was to have

----

April 4, 1966: Speech by the Second Vice-
President, Mr. R. M. Kawawa, announced the end of
the settlement approach.

May 29, 1968: Urambo small farmers met in
front of the T.A.N.U. office, demanding a change
in the cooperative leadership.

May 30, 1968: An elected group of the small
farmers met with the Area Commissioner and T.A.N.U.
officials.

July 24, 1968: General open meeting at which
the Cooperative Committee and the top administrative
staff were expelled from office.

August 8, 1968: New Cooperative Committee
elected.

a European manager, a European assistant manager, and, in the case of especially large farms, a European mechanic.[4] While this restructuring of the land proved a useful device for administration, it also laid the foundations for the development of a land-based rather than a managerial-based class system. Thus, the attempted agricultural transformation of Urambo involved importing a European technical and managerial class as well as developing an African semiskilled labor force.

The supplanting of groundnuts by tobacco had far-reaching effects. The nature of groundnut cultivation lends itself to large-scale mechanized farming. The conception of the Groundnut Scheme was capital-intensive plantation production. Tobacco is quite different. It is a difficult, labor-intensive crop, requiring much care and constant attention. Because of the nature of this crop, as well as the fact that the O.F.C. favored the development of a class of African farmers, Africans were brought into the scheme as actual producers rather than as O.F.C. plantation employees. In the 1952 season African farmers were able to grow tobacco on contiguous farming units under the supervision of agricultural personnel of the O.F.C. The O.F.C. supplied necessary credit and used the crop as collateral for this credit in a standard sharecropping arrangement. Any final profit was to be divided equally between the O.F.C. and the tenant, though in the following season this arrangement was changed to a 60/40 percent division in the farmer's favor. During this period and until 1958, this farming arrangement was known as the Green Leaf Scheme because no individual farmer cured his own tobacco; he cultivated and harvested the tobacco, and the curing was done in large, centrally located O.F.C. curing barns.

When the Tanganyika Agricultural Corporation replaced the O.F.C. in 1955, the relationship of this new paragovernmental agency to the land changed. The T.A.C. did not aim to continue directly in farm-

ing, but instead offered leases on the large farms
to Europeans. These Europeans, who were drawn from
the technical and managerial class of the O.F.C.,
then had the option of farming themselves or, in
the case of a few, of remaining attached to the
bureaucratic structure.

The T.A.C., like the O.F.C., was firmly committed to the notion of maximum production, but
with a different relationship to the land. Though
not bureaucratically oriented for production, the
T.A.C. occasionally found itself with farming units
for which qualified farmers could not be located.
However, the T.A.C. at Urambo was essentially an
administrative structure for a series of privately
managed units which, at this stage, consisted of
small farms managed by Africans and large farms
managed by Europeans. T.A.C. provided the farmers
with services similar to those provided by the
O.F.C. — purchasing, marketing, and various forms
of credit. As tobacco farming evolved at Urambo,
there developed, in addition to small and large
farms, two other categories of farms based on
size: the 10-acre farm and the medium farm.

While there were very close informal, personal
ties between the landed European farmers and the
T.A.C. administrators at Urambo, no identity of
interested existed. While the long-term European
farmer's aspiration was the creation of a viable
economy, T.A.C. also listed social objectives of a
related nature.

> Amongst the experiments which are proceed-
> ing is one to which the Corporation attaches
> much importance, namely the African Tenant
> Scheme (commenced 1952) with a view to en-
> suring the evolution of the African yeoman
> farmer from the peasant to the final stages
> of owning his own land of sufficient area
> to ensure independence and a reasonable
> standard of living.

The Corporation believes that, if successfully developed, established and expanded, the Scheme should contribute substantially to the evolution of a sound economy in this Territory; an economy which is, at present, based preponderantly on agriculture and, subject to any significant mineral discoveries that may be made, is likely to remain so in the foreseeable future.[5]

It is not clear whether the European administrators and farmers ever anticipated the African's rising to the status of an equal in the large farmer category, or whether the Europeans ever visualized themselves as tenants of anything other than large farms. In any case, two developments strengthened the position of African farmers at Urambo. In the first development, starting with the 1956 tobacco season, three Africans farmed medium holdings. These three farmers, in the estimation of the T.A.C., were the best African farmers participating in the Green Leaf Scheme. In the second development, a significant addition to the African Tenant Scheme began in 1958. The African farmer became totally responsible for every aspect of his crop, including curing. The delay in initiating this program was caused partly by the technical problem of tobacco curing.

The Corporation and its African tenants on the Scheme have given much thought to and have held many discussions on the problems of how the African farmer can most profitably undertake the growing of Virginia Flue Cured Tobacco. These consultations have resulted in a new system being evolved. The plan is based on the use of small tobacco barns built of mud and wattle walls, with a thatched roof, and a furnace made from disused drums. Each barn is large enough to cure the

crop for 1 1/2 acres. . . .They can be
built by the growers themselves and there
will be either 2 or 3 on each holding.[6]

Once the T.A.C. set this direction and it became
known that tobacco growing was profitable, the number of African farmers of small farms grew steadily;
by the end of the 1968 season, there were over 2,000.
Concurrent with the development of this class
of small-holder African farmers was the decline in
importance of the European farmers. At the end of
the 1959-60 season, after suffering from a strike
organized by the Tanganyika Plantation Workers
Union, eight of the 18 European farmers left. The
last three European farmers left at the end of the
1964-65 season, and then the tobacco scheme in
Urambo had only a few European personnel in administrative positions. The end of the era of the
European presence in Urambo occurred in 1968, when
the European Regional Settlement Officer, employed
by the T.A.C.'s successor, the Village Settlement
Agency, to work in Urambo and the surrounding area,
did not take up his renewed appointment.
Given an historical perspective on Tanzanian
nationalism, it is possible to understand that
the European farmer could not survive in Tanzania,
though the T.A.C. had granted the farmers leases
of 33 years. Though the Europeans did not remain
to prosper in Urambo, the Africans did, giving
proof to the statement recorded by a T.A.C. official: ". . .that whenever the African becomes
established as a grower of a European crop, he
ultimately sees the European out."[7]
The Africans, however, were greatly influenced
by the bureaucratic and farming patterns established
by the Europeans. Most influential was the tobacco
technology itself, which evolved over the years from
1950. This technology made tobacco a viable crop
in Urambo but in itself did not predicate any particular form of social organization, landholdings,
or administrative institutions. The land-holding

system (a gradation from large farms to small farms) was retained, though political and economic pressures exerted against the large farm holders eventually reduced their number from 22 to four. There was, however, starting in the 1964 season, a great expansion in the number of medium and 10-acre farms, the latter being intermediate between the medium and the small farm.

For all the Europeans and for many of the Africans, tobacco cultivation was based on utilizing wage labor, often only for a small part of the year. While the small farms originally were designed as family-operations growing from three to five acres of tobacco, acreage restrictions were difficult to enforce. Therefore more acreage than could be handled by the family unit was planted. This resulted in the maintenance of another social layer in Urambo, that of the part-time agricultural worker.

Urambo within the
Administrative Ecology

Urambo has had a developmental emphasis for more than 20 years; since it has survived in spite of shifting government policies, a detailed analysis of its most recent administration and the administrative culture of its peasant farmers will highlight the problem of developmental administration on the micro-level.

Urambo as a settlement was unique in that administrative responsibility resided in both the Division of Village Settlement and the Urambo Cooperative. The Village Settlement Agency, followed by the Division of Village Settlement, assumed administrative jurisdiction over Urambo in January, 1965. This was part of a larger attempt by the Tanzanian government to consolidate the administration of several different types of settlement schemes within one bureaucracy. The Division of

Village Settlement assumed many functions which previously had been performed by the resident staff of the Tanganyika Agricultural Corporation. In fact, the agent of the T.A.C. became the manager of the settlement scheme at Urambo, and the agricultural assistants and clerks then became government employees. The consolidation of settlement schemes within a single bureaucracy — the Division of Village Settlement — allowed, at least in theory, greater coordination of policy and personnel.

Official Division of Village Settlement policy favored the developement of cooperatives on their settlements.[8] This policy was implemented by creating a training phase designed to instruct the farmers in cooperative management. The duration of this pre-cooperative phase was not specified. At the time of this study, Urambo was the only settlement scheme where the cooperative had fulfilled its original intention and actually assumed a large degree of administrative control. In terms of the previous Urambo history of African pressures for greater participation and benefits, this was a logical development. This autonomy was achieved during the administrative hiatus between the policies of the T.A.C. and those of the Division of Village Settlement. Though the Urambo cooperative had almost total authority, the same governmental structure existed at Urambo as at any other settlement scheme where the cooperative was less powerful or nonexistent.

Therefore, among government-sponsored settlement schemes, Urambo was unique in that its cooperative was not under the control of the Division of Village Settlement. The Urambo cooperative had total administrative responsibility for the small farmers. Farmers in any category other than the small farm could not be members of the cooperative and were not allowed, at least in theory, to receive supplies from it. The small farmers, at least numerically, totally dominated the Urambo settle-

ment. Of all farmers in Urambo, 96 percent were
small farmers: and this percentage was increasing
as Urambo continues to expand.

Type of Farm	Average Tobacco Acreage	Number	Percent
Large	60	4	0.2
Medium	15-20	20	0.9
10-Acre	10	52	2.5
Small	3-5	2,019	96.4
		2,095	100.0

The Urambo cooperative performed many services related to tobacco production for the small farmers.
Each year it ordered tobacco supplies for the
coming year's production. In order to finance the
purchase of these supplies, the cooperative borrowed
money from the National Development Credit Agency.
The very size of these loans indicates the relative
size of this organization.

Season	Amount of Loan	Equivalent in dollars (approximate)
1964-65	344,400 shs.	$ 49,000
1965-66	4,382,300 shs.	$626,000
1966-67	2,086,500 shs.	$298,000
1967-68	2,378,900 shs.	$340,000

In the last season for which I have the figures,
the Urambo cooperative borrowed approximately
$340,000. This operation was impressively large
and involved the administration of a complex organization attempting to perform numerous agricultural functions.

Figures 1 and 2 illustrate the administrative structure of the Urambo cooperative and that of the Division of Village Settlement.

It can be seen from these two figures that the potential for conflict existed. There was an obvious duplication and overlapping of personnel in the areas of agricultural assistance, tractor use, and ultimate authority.

1. Lobby for policy most advantageous for tobacco growers.

2. Provide essential services for the farmers.
   Tractor service
   Agricultural advice
   Credit and supplies
   Accounting system
   Selling mechanism
    for crops other
    than tobacco

1. Coordinate and convey government policy to the farmers.

2. Provide essential services for the farmers.
   Tractor service
   Agricultural advice
   Provide a selling
    mechanism for tobacco

While in a strictly administrative sense, official government representation was unnecessary at Urambo, this presence did serve an important latent function. Government representatives were a sounding board for dissatisfied peasants who felt that the cooperative did not serve their best interests. The manner in which this dissatisfaction could manifest itself can be seen in terms of alternative communication patterns, Figure 3.

The local farming unit was composed of all those farmers whose farms lay within the boundary of a previously demarcated large farm. This group of farmers elected a farm committeeman who could situationally represent them. The committeeman's primary responsibility, however, lay in coordinating the distribution of services and supplies and working at the distribution center when the tobacco was being pressed into bales. The cooperative compensated him for this latter work. Often, when a T.A.N.U. representative lived on a

Figure 1

Administrative Structure of Urambo Farmers' Cooperative
Society, Ltd.

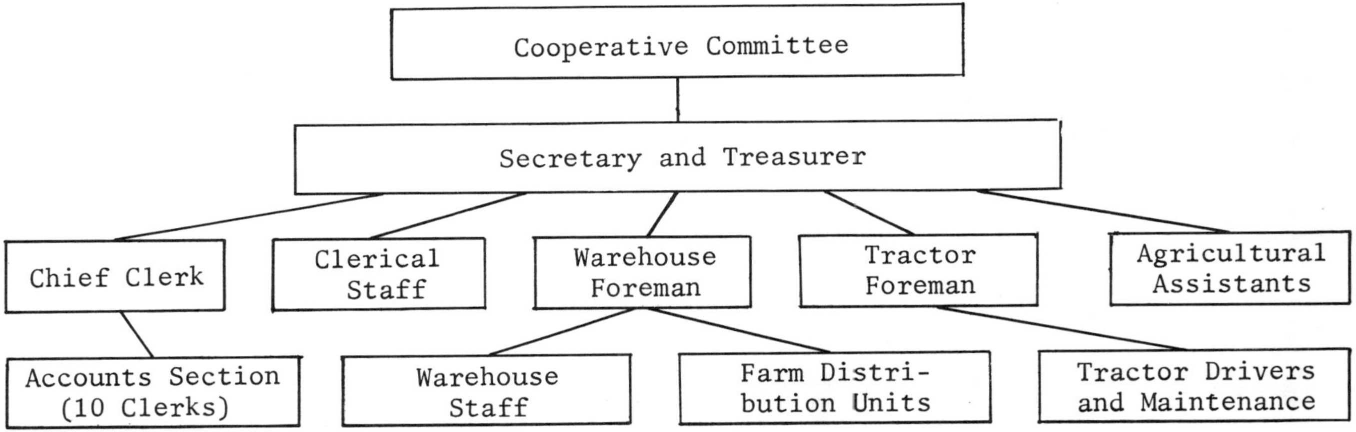

Figure 2

Administrative Structure of Division of Village
Settlement at Urambo

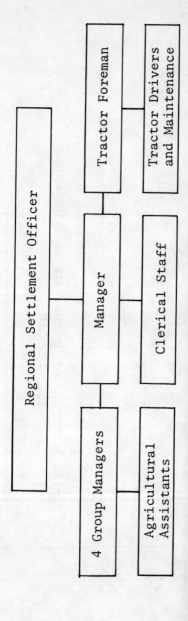

Figure 3

COMMUNICATION FLOW: URAMBO FARMERS

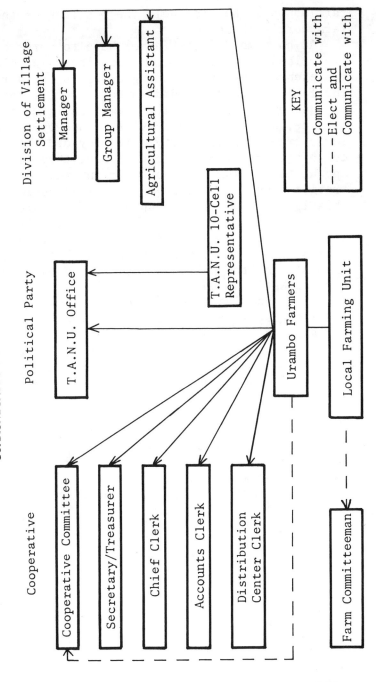

247

farming unit, he also held the position of the farm committeeman.

At no time did the farmer have to work through prescribed channels of communication using elected representatives or ascending orders of authority. The farmers could and did appeal directly to the manager or the Cooperative Committee in matters of finance, supplies, and services, thus bypassing lower orders of authority. If they did not receive satisfaction from one source, they would appeal to another, thereby blurring the administrative boundaries between these institutions. This ignoring of clear channels of communication and of orders of authority created a conflict situation involving the jurisdictions of the Urambo cooperative, the Division of Village Settlement, and the political party, the Tanganyika African National Union (T.A.N.U.).

This conflict situation bears scrutiny as a model of developmental administration. It is a variation of the inter-institutional competition which the French agronomist René Dumont felt was necessary. In his 1967 survey of Tanzanian settlement schemes, Dumont noted:

> To quicken progress, a socialist economy must recognize and correct quicker her mistake than has been done until now. In my opinion, *a limited amount of competition,* between public, semi-public and private enterprises appear necessary, to improve the efficiency of socialist organization. . . Co-operatives also need some kind of *limited* competition to improve quicker their efficiency.9

It would be difficult to argue that tension and conflict within an administrative context are necessarily beneficial or creative; possibly, developing countries cannot afford the duplication of supervisory personnel and services. Conflict developed at Urambo certainly not because of deliberate policy but because two different ministries — the Ministry of Agriculture and Cooperatives, under whose jurisdiction the Urambo cooperative operated, and the Ministry of Lands, Settlement and Water Development — were not able to reorganize overlapping authority. Despite the potential waste of government personnel in this arrangement, the peasants benefited from the leverage given them by this inter-institutional competition.

Situational Analysis

The overthrow of the Cooperative Committee in July, 1968, illustrates the process of administrative change through inter-institutional competition and the resulting reorganization of institutional control. It also clarified the position of the Division of Village Settlement toward control of the Urambo settlement scheme. At Urambo, the Division of Village Settlement had maintained an elaborate administrative structure, as is show in Figure 2. This administrative group had often clashed with cooperative officials. Judging from this history of conflict as well as the administrative control on other settlement schemes, the farmers and the cooperative officials thought that the Division of Village Settlement intended to wrest total control over the Urambo scheme. After all, the simplest resolution of this conflict would have been for either the cooperative or the Division of Village Settlement to assert total control. The account of this incident which follows, however, indicates that the Division of Village Settlement was in fact not at all anxious to accept total responsibility for the scheme, even though the dissident farmers themselves appealed for government control.

The actual situation occurred at an open meeting for all small farmers on July 24, 1968. Formal

249

announcement of the meeting was posted July 2 and
sent to the government officers listed below. The
number of high-ranking officials invited indicated
the seriousness of this meeting.

1. Acting Commissioner of Village Settlement, Dar es Salaam
2. Regional Commissioner, Tabora
3. Regional Cooperative Officer, Tabora
4. Regional Settlement Officer, Tabora
5. Regional T.A.N.U. Chairman, Tabora
6. Regional Information Officer, Tabora
7. Area Commissioner, Tabora
8. District T.A.N.U. Chairman, Tabora
9. District Agriculture Officer, Tabora
10. Manager, Urambo Settlement Scheme, Urambo
11. Officer in Charge, Police Station, Urambo
12. Divisional Executive Officer, Urambo
13. Branch T.A.N.U. Chairman, Urambo

Not all of these officials responded, but the
Acting Commissioner of Village Settlement attended
as did representatives from the regional, district,
and divisional (Urambo) level.

While this meeting began like so many previous
meetings in Urambo — two hours late — it was obviously quite different from the previous general
meetings of the Urambo cooperative. By noon more
than 500 farmers had arrived, many having walked
since morning from outlying farms as far away as
20 miles. They assembled at the Jamhuri (Independence) Community Center, a large aluminum-roofed
building built during O.F.C. days and called, then,
Coronation Hall. On the stage, in two rows facing
the farmers, sat an impressive group of national
and local functionaries. The chairman of the
meeting was the chairman of the Urambo Cooperative
Committee; at the same table with him were the
Acting Commissioner for Village Settlement and
his Assistant Commissioner, the Regional and the
District Cooperative Officers, a Regional and an

Area Commissioner, and the Regional Settlement Officer. Parallel with this row but separate from it sat the secretary of the cooperative, managers of the near-by tobacco schemes, and the members of the Urambo Cooperative Committee.

The actual sequence of the meeting's events was relatively simple. The Chairman of the Cooperative Committee read a history of Urambo from the beginning of the O.F.C. until the present, the secretary of the elected representatives of the farmers read a list of complaints, and then the meeting was temporarily adjourned. After a two-hour break, the Cooperative Chairman delivered what was, in effect, an abdication speech on behalf of himself and the entire Cooperative Committee. He emphasized, however, that his administration had not stolen the farmers' money — the farmers' chief grievance.

Various complaints against the cooperative, founded in 1962, had a history nearly as long as the cooperative itself. The complaints concerned poor management and accusations of corruption. While the farmers had contemplated action previously, this was the first time they had successfully forced change. Their success in this venture can be attributed to a pre-meeting mobilization and to their willingness and ability to use other institutions to effect change.

The farmers had had a meeting on May 29 in preparation for the general and official meeting on July 24. The May 29 meeting had been mediated by the local officers of the political party, T.A.N.U. At this meeting, the farmers elected a committee to represent them; the secretary of this committee read the list of complaints at the July 24 meeting. In the context of the farmers' complaints against the cooperative, he described the meeting at the T.A.N.U. office.

> When the meeting opened at the TANU office, at 9:30 a.m., there were 769 farmers in attendance, and when it ended at 2:30

p.m. the number had swelled to double that
figure. A Secretary and Chairman were
chosen before the proceedings, and representatives were selected after the meeting,
for the purpose of presenting their grievances and intentions both to TANU and the
government. Accordingly, on the following
day, May 30th, those representatives met
with the District Commissioner in the TANU
office. . . .

　　After hours of discussion — from 9:30
a.m. to 2:30 p.m. — the farmers agreed upon
a resolution which was stated thus: "Remove the Managers and Leaders: Let the
Government lead us; Let us form our own
society later on."[10]

Most of the small farmers, united as a group
against the clique of cooperative officials in
power, thus managed to win control of the cooperative. Their desire, however, was not to keep
control of the institution but to turn that control back to the government, represented by the
Division of Village Settlement. There was indeed
some logic in this desire. The farmers wanted to
abandon the very type of institution (the cooperative) that the Tanzanian government was trying
to encourage. The farmers were entrepreneurs who
wanted to maximize their profits and minimize their
losses. This situation was possible, they argued,
only if some government agency was willing to provide credit for the crop, extend this credit over
several years in case of crop failure, and supply
supervision of those concerned with the daily administrative details of running this large organization.

　　The farmers desired a situation which in theory
already existed. They did receive credit, and no
attempt was made to recover this credit if the
crop proceeds were not adequate — though of course,
the debt was carried over to the following year.

Regional and District Cooperative Officers had
the responsibility of supplying supervision,
though none of them was actually stationed in
Urambo. The difficulty in Urambo did not lie
in the conception of the administrative structure; it lay in the inability of the farmers
themselves to exert a constant influence in the
running of the cooperative in ways other than
periodic outbursts of discontent.

There were two bureaucratic responses to the
attempt by the farmers to seek government control
of their cooperative. The Regional Cooperative
Officer noted that the cooperative had to continue
in order to be responsible for its large debt,
which he estimated at 1,000,000 shillings, approximately $144,000. Primarily because of this debt
position and its effect on their receiving any
profit, the farmers were prompted to appeal for
government control. The National Development
Credit Agency had the prior right to 75 percent of
tobacco monies generated through the sale of the
tobacco to the Tanganyika Tobacco Board. Because
of this arrangement, a condition of the loan, it
was possible (and in fact often happened) that
farmers who had earned a profit did not receive
their full profit or even a significant percentage
thereof.

The response of the Acting Commissioner for
Village Settlement was relevant in a wider sense
to problems within development administration.
He initially noted that the farmers should not
make a distinction between their cooperative
and the Division of Village Settlement; both are
governmental units working for the people, he
asserted. He continued by noting that, though
the Urambo cooperative had problems, it nevertheless served as an example to other farmers. The

Urambo cooperative had achieved its self-government,
and hence should not ask the government to resume
control. The farmers in a self-governing cooperative had to live up to certain responsibilities,
he maintained.

The meeting ended on that note. The farmer
who had been elected chairman of the May 29 meeting was to serve as acting chairman of the cooperative until formal elections. In those elections
at a general meeting the following month, the same
man was elected chairman together with a new Cooperative Committee. The same structure of the cooperative and its relationship to the Division of
Village Settlement was maintained.

At the micro-level of Urambo, administrative
change simply involving a shifting of personalities
rather than any fundamental reorganization. Essentially the farmers were looking for mechanisms
which would alleviate their administrative exploitation. They appealed to the Government but were
rejected.

The new Cooperative Committee renegotiated the
loan with the National Development Credit Agency
and thus stayed the financial crisis. One of its
first acts was to participate in choosing those
farmers who would be given larger acreages for
the coming season. The Cooperative Committee
Chairman and four committee members thus acquired
10-acre farms.

Administrative Culture

Ultimately our concern with Urambo is with the
larger problem of an administrative culture and
its implications for rural development. In this
area of administrative culture, the emphasis is
on the farmers' perception of bureaucratic structures and functions, and of their ability to gain
and to attempt to gain satisfaction from that
structure. The farmers' ability to deal with the

external agencies which impinge upon them is crucial to the success of any government-administered peasant economy. President Nyerere has made this point quite clear in his discussion of rural development in *Freedom and Development:*

> When we tried to promote rural development in the past, we sometimes spent huge sums of money on establishing a Settlement, and supplying it with modern equipment, and social services, as well as often prividing it with a management hierarchy.
> What we were doing, in fact, was thinking of development in terms of things, and not of people. Further, we thought in terms of monetary investment in order to achieve the increases in output we were aiming at. In effect, we said that capital equipment, or other forms of investment, would lead to increased output, and this would lead to a transformation in the lives of the people involved. The people were secondary; the first priority was output.[11]

Some data reflecting the perceptions and orientations of the Urambo farmers toward the administrative structure is illustrative. The following information on Urambo is based on a survey of 85 farmers.[12] The answers which the farmers gave tended to confirm that the complexity of the administrative culture reduced the ability of the farmer to master his administrative environment. The previous situation indicated that the farmer could make short-term changes, but not necessarily long-term or fundamental changes.

Government Structure

1. What is the work of the agricultural extension agent?

Answers:	Number	Percent
To help the farmers	48	56.4
To talk and teach tobacco	26	30.6
To look after the fields	11	13.0
	85	100.0

2. What is the work of the group manager?

Answers:	Number	Percent
To aid and supervise the agricultural agents	66	77.6
Not sure	19	22.4
	85	100.0

3. What is the work of the manager?

Answers:	Number	Percent
To look after the civil servants (group managers and agricultural extension agents)	25	29.4
To look after the settlement scheme and its property	37	43.5
To work for all the farmers	12	14.1
Not sure	11	13.0
	85	100.0

The questions concerning structure started at the level of most immediate contact and then proceeded to higher forms of authority. The Urambo peasant farmer had an absolutely clear idea of the function of the one governmental civil servant with whom he had the most immediate contact, the extension agent. The fact that many of the farmers were not sure of the function of the group manager reflected the failure to decentralize the settlement scheme and to give meaningful authority to this intermediate position between manager and extension agent. The farmers had divergent ideas as to the manager's work. They did not have extensive contact with the manager, and their divergent views correspond to the reality of the administrative ambiguity in which the manager found himself at Urambo.

Cooperative Structure

4. What is the function of the cooperative?

Answers:	Number	Percent
To aid the farmer	47	55.3
To unite the people	26	30.6
Not sure	12	14.1
	85	100.0

5. Who runs the cooperative?

Answers:	Number	Percent
Co-operative Committee Chairman, Secretary, and Treasurer	29	34.1
Secretary and/or Treasurer	28	32.9
Co-operative Committee	17	20.0
Not sure	11	13.0
	85	100.0

6. What is the work of the Cooperative Committee?

Answers:	Number	Percent
To solve the problems of the farmers	59	69.4
To run the cooperative correctly	11	13.0
To force the people forward	7	8.2
Not sure	8	9.4
	85	100.0

While the farmers were not sophisticated in the
rhetoric of the cooperative movement, they did
conceptualize the cooperative as either aiding
or uniting the people. Particularly striking
about the responses to question 5 was the fact
that the farmers saw administrative control not
so much in their own committee but predominantly
in the two highest appointed positions: the
cooperative's Secretary and Treasurer. Another
aspect of this same perception was seen in the
responses to question 6. A large majority of
the farmers looked upon the Cooperative Committee
as an administrative mediating agency, and not as
that core unit of the institution with the highest
amount of control. There was a tendency to view
the cooperative as an institution comparable with
other institutions but not essentially different
because of farmer control.

Administrative Participation: The Cooperative

7a. What do you think of the leadership of the
     Cooperative?

Answers:	Number	Percent
Good	8	9.4
Bad	66	77.6
Not sure	11	13.0
	85	100.0

7b. If the leadership is bad, what is the prin-
     ciple problem?

Answers:	Number	Percent
Problems with money	45	68.1
Problems with coopera- tive servants	16	24.2
Problems with tractors	5	7.7
	66	100.0

8. What are the qualifications of a man to become a Cooperative Committeeman?

Answers:	Number	Percent
Problem-solving ability, especially with money	27	31.7
Respectful of other farmers, so that people like you	11	13.0
No qualifications necessary	9	10.6
Literacy	4	4.7
Not sure	34	40.0
	85	100.0

9. What changes are necessary in the society so that there will be more benefit?

Answers:	Number	Percent
More loans necessary for the small farmers	36	42.3
Cooperative needs to be completely changed	22	26.0
The cooperative servants should be terminated	12	14.1
There should be more tractors	7	8.2
Not sure	8	9.4
	85	100.0

If the farmers did not feel that they exercised control, or were able to exercise control, they tended to feel that the existing leadership was bad. This leadership was conceptualized as bad because of financial affairs. This response was understandable in the context that often those small farmers who had profitable seasons did not receive their full compensation. While a plurality of the farmers felt that additional loans would be most helpful, a full quarter of the farmers noted the need to change the cooperative completely.

Administrative Participation: Farming Activities

10. What will you do if you want to use a tractor?

Answers:	Number	Percent
Go to the agricultural extention agent	36	42.3
Go to the local store clerk	22	26.0
Go to the office	16	18.8
Go to the farm committeeman	8	9.4
Use the private tractor of another farmer	3	3.5
	85	100.0

11. What would you do if you want to get a 10-acre farm?

Answers:	Number	Percent
Apply to the manager	25	29.4
Apply to Cooperative Committee	31	36.5
Not sure	29	34.1
	85	100.0

The purpose of these last two questions was to determine how the farmers worked their way through
the administrative maze in order to accomplish
practical but somewhat difficult tasks. The settlement scheme had access to a limited number of
tractors, some belonging to the Division of Village
Settlement and some to the cooperative. The farmer could hire these tractors to plow his fields,
carry his wood for tobacco curing, and transport
his tobacco to the sales floor. The last question
raised the whole issue once again of an administrative conflict between the cooperative and the
manager. The farmers themselves were not sure
how best to proceed in this matter. They did in
general desire larger land holdings, and working
through either the cooperative or the government
was a recognized channel toward this goal.

Conclusion

The previous section on administrative culture has discussed the farmers' awareness and perception of the administrative structure in which they worked. The administrative culture of Urambo was a complex one which involved many alternatives. To understand what constituted this administrative culture, one must know the farmers' conception of administrative structure and function, and the results of a situational analysis. There are some general conclusions to be derived from all of this information.

1. The total institutional ecology included the cooperative, the political party, and the government, in the form of the Division of Village Settlement.

2. Administrative change involved an ability to manipulate the countervailing powers within the institutional framework.

3. The farmers were able to recognize and identify their individual self-interest, and were able to mobilize in attempting to satisfy that self-interest.

4. The farmers did not aspire to control their administrative institutions.

5. The farmers were unsure of the administrative culture.

The case of Urambo thus could justify the Tanzanian retrenchment from large-scale settlement schemes. Though there are numerous problems in such government-operated settlement schemes, one must also consider that the inability to develop mechanisms to transmit an administrative culture or to develop a culturally integrated administrative culture may cause any peasant-controlled rural development to fail.

> Development brings freedom, provided it is development *of people*. But people cannot be developed; they can only develop themselves.[13]

NOTES

1. For an overview discussion of settlement schemes, see Robert Chambers, *Settlement Schemes in Tropical Africa, A Study of Organizations and Development* (London: Routledge and Kegan Paul, 1969).

2. David Brokensha, "Trends in Development Administration," *Canadian Journal of African Studies*, III, 1 (Winter, 1969), 111.

3. A general history of this episode is Alan Wood, *The Groundnut Affair* (London: The Bodley Head, 1950). There is, however, very little attention given to the Urambo scheme in Wood's study.

4. Overseas Food Corporation, *Annual Report and Statement of Accounts for the Year ended 31st March 1955* (London: Her Majesty's Stationery Office, 1956), p. 34.

5. Tanganyika Agricultural Corporation, *Report and Accounts for the Period 1st April to 30th September 1955* (Dar es Salaam: Government Printer, 1956). Foreword by Stuart Gillett, Chairman of T.A.C.

6. Tanganyika Agricultural Corporation, *Annual Report and Statement of Accounts for 1957-1958* (Dar es Salaam: Government Printer, 1959), p. 36.

7. General Manager's File, A.1, "Agricultural General," Vol. I, letter from Agent to Chief Administrative Officer, November 21, 1958.

8. Ministry of Lands, Settlement and Water Development, *The Rural Settlement Commission* (Dar es Salaam: Survey Division, 1966), p. 43.

9.   René Dumont, "Short Notes on Tabora Region, 3rd to 5th September 1967" (Dar es Salaam, 1967), p. 5.   (Mimeographed.)

10.   Bruno John, "Complaints of the Farmers Regarding the Leadership of the Society" (Urambo, 1968), pp. 4-5.   (Mimeographed.)

11.   J. K. Nyerere, *Freedom and Development* (Dar es Salaam: Government Printer, 1968), pp. 6-7.

12.   This material was gathered by the author during the period from October, 1967, through October, 1968. The author was attached in a research capacity to the Division of Village Settlement and supported on a grant from the Program of Eastern African Studies, Syracuse University, and the Shell Foundation.

13.   Nyerere, *op. cit.*, p. 2.   Italics in the text.

BIBLIOGRAPHY

Books and articles

Brokensha, David. "Trends in Development Administration," *Canadian Journal of African Studies*,
III, 1 (Winter, 1969, 104-12.

Chambers, Robert. *Settlement Schemes in Tropical
Africa, A Study of Organization and Development*.
London: Routledge and Kegan Paul, 1969.

Nyerere, Julius K. *Freedom and Development*. Dar
es Salaam: Government Printer, 1968.

Wood, Alan. *The Groundnut Affair*. London: The
Bodley Head, 1950.

Official publications

Ministry of Lands, Settlement and Water Develop-
ment. *The Rural Settlement Commission: A
Report on the Village Settlement Programme
from the Inception of the Rural Settlement
Commission to 31st December*. Dar es Salaam:
Survey Division, 1966.

Overseas Food Corporation. *First Annual Report
and Statement of Accounts for the Period ended
March 31, 1949*. London: H.M.S.O., 1949.

_____. *Annual Report and Statement of Accounts
for the year ended 31st March, 1950*. London:
H.M.S.O., 1950.

_____. *Annual Report and Statement of Accounts
for the year ended 31st March, 1952*. London:
H.M.S.O., 1952.

264

_____. *Annual Report and Statement of Accounts for the year ended 31st March, 1953*. London: H.M.S.O., 1953.

_____. *Annual Report and Statement of Accounts for the year ended 31st March, 1954*. London: H.M.S.O., 1954.

_____. *Annual Report and Statement of Accounts for the year ended 31st March, 1955*. London: H.M.S.O., 1956.

Tanganyika Agricultural Corporation. *Report and Accounts for the Period 1st April to 30th September 1955*. Dar es Salaam: Government Printer, 1956.

_____. *Reports and Accounts for 1955-56*. Dar es Salaam: Government Printer, 1957.

_____. *Annual Report and Statement of Accounts for 1956-1957*. Dar es Salaam: Government Printer, 1958.

_____. *Annual Report and Statement of Accounts for 1957-1958*. Dar es Salaam: Government Printer, 1959.

_____. *Annual Report and Statement of Accounts for 1958-1959*. Dar es Salaam: Government Printer, 1960.

_____. *Annual Report and Statement of Accounts for 1959-1960*. Dar es Salaam: Government Printer, 1961.

_____. *Annual Report and Statement of Accounts for 1960-1961*. Dar es Salaam: Government Printer, 1962.

Unpublished sources

Dumont, René. "Short Notes on Tabora Region, 3rd
    to 5th September 1967." Dar es Salaam, 1967.
    (Mimeographed.)

John, Bruno. "Complaints of the Farmers Regarding
    the Leadership of the Society." Ref. No.
    WTU/6. Urambo, 1968. (Mimeographed.)

266

Institution-Building and Rural
Development in Malawi

by Robert A. Miller

As an administrative officer in the Ministry of
Development and Planning of the Malawi Government,
the writer was responsible for the District Development Committees established by the Minister
of Development and Planning, Aleke Banda, in
January, 1965. When the writer joined the Malawi
Government in August, 1966, the District Development Committees were a nascent organization which
had not yet begun regular meetings. Thus he was
able to view their development almost from inception.

The Minister established the committees in
the hope that they would become a major catalyst
in rural development. The involvement of district,
area, and village leaders in the process of planning and implementing rural programs was expected
to act as an inducement for their active support.
Aleke Banda was greatly impressed by the success
of a similar venture in Malaysia and hoped to
emulate its example, though he recognized that
such an organization would have to be tailored
to Malawi.

Part I of this essay discusses the differences between decentralization and devolution, stressing that rural participation in national development may take more than one form. District Development Committees were established along decentralized lines and thus differed considerably from district councils. Part I is devoted largely to a discussion of District Development Committees in Malawi and should be of general interest to those concerned with rural development in Africa.

Part II, more theoretical, attempts to place the committees within the perspective of institution-building theory. The value of this exercise lies in permitting this case study to be related to similar studies of institution-building. Despite some weaknesses in the concept, "institution-building" as a comparative tool is useful. While its shortcomings are pointed out, and while suggestions toward overcoming them are made, it is beyond the scope of this paper to redevelop or operationalize the concept of institution-building; such an exercise would certainly be worthwhile.

There are two main reasons why the institution-building model is not presented at the beginning of the paper. For one, many readers who are concerned with rural development may find the conceptual discussion outside their interest; they are spared working through such discussion in order to reach the case study. Secondly, as explained in the body of the paper, institution-building seems most valuable as an evaluative tool; its overlapping categories are likely to cloud description of the District Development Committees. Thus, Part I is mainly descriptive and Part II, analytic.

PART I: DISTRICT DEVELOPMENT COMMITTEES IN MALAWI

It is a mistake — where rapid development
is the primary objective — to maintain

268

"local autonomy" or "freedom from central government interference" as the governing principle in central-local relations. Poor local governments, like poor people, are likely to get poorer if left to their own resources. They need help if they are to overcome their disabilities and realize their potentialities for useful service.[1]

It is my intention to make District Development Committees the main instrument for securing rapid progress throughout the country and to expand the responsibilities of the Committees in this field in accordance with their capacity.[2]

Decentralization and
Development

Governments cope with centrifugal forces in different ways. They may enlarge the scope of their administrative systems to penetrate localities more thoroughly, or they may recognize, even establish, more autonomous units which are able to exercise authority primarily upon their local constituencies. Frank Sherwood has stressed this point.

Centralization is best defined as involving the concentration of power at the top of the pyramid and decentralization as indicating the dispersal of power throughout the structure. . . (devolution) means the transfer of power to geographical units of local government that lie outside the formal command structure of the central government.[3]

In some countries more centralized organization might produce societies more conducive to change.[4] Yet in many developing countries, the danger lies in excessive centralization. It may cause interminable delays, is often based on a lack of reliable information about outlying areas, and suffers from poor communication with rural areas. The problem becomes one of reconciling the need for a strong central government with the dangers of a remote, sluggish central administration which stifles what Jawaharlal Nehru called the "conditions in which a spontaneous growth from below is possible."[5] David Lilienthal, the distinguished former administrator of the Tennessee Valley Authority, concluded that decentralization rather than devolution is the answer, and proposed "the decentralized administration of (central) functions which lend themselves to such a technique . . . (and) the active participation of the people."[6]

In many developing countries the tendency moves in the opposite direction, toward what Aristide Zolberg calls "monocephalism".[7] This trend can be reversed if a government has confidence in the country's unity and in the ability of its field staff.[8] When potentially fissiparous units such as tribe, region, or other parochial interests pose a danger to national unity, the government will resist attempts to decentralize. The second problem is one of attracting administrative talent to the field. Many Africans, after obtaining their education, are reluctant to return to the "bush" after working so diligently to enter the modern world that is often symbolized by the city. In addition, the commitments to the extended family are a greater burden in the rural areas, where the family of a young administrative officer is likely to join him. Yet, in Malawi this urban attraction is counterbalanced by the advantages of a field station; there, an officer is able to exercise much greater authority and carry much more responsibility than would be the case in a central government ministry. For Malawians, the drawback to a career in the field is lack of promotions and the knowledge that administrative advancement lies in the capital.

The Failure of
Devolution in Malawi

African participation in government at the
local level came to Malawi in the early 1930's,
as Lord Lugard's concept of "indirect rule."[9]
Until this time the regions and districts had
been administered directly by the District Commissioners. The first step toward implementing
indirect rule came in 1929, when certain judicial
powers were handed back to the chiefs. They were
brought into the administrative system when the
1933 Native Authority Ordinance authorized the
establishment of native authorities consisting
of a chief and his councillors. These authorities
were permitted to levy local taxes, which were
supplemented by government grants to finance
local activities. The effectiveness of the native
authorities was limited. For example, in 1939
one had a budget of £16, of which £12 went to
the clerk; the native authorities soon became
identified as nothing but organs of the Government.[10] As one commentator put it, "The old
authority of the chieftainship . . . tends to
drain away from below while we pour in new authority from above."[11]
This system was patently inadequate, and in
1953 the Local Government Ordinance established
district councils to take over many of the local
services provided by the native authorities. In
an amendment to the Ordinance, the native authority was declared subordinate to the council. The
District Commissioner was appointed chairman of
the council; the chiefs were made *ex officio* councillors and composed approximately one-third of
council membership. While the native authorities
were considered a projection of the colonial Government, it was envisaged that the councils would
be more independent yet still subject to control
from the province. "In practice, however, no
very great changes appeared in the day-to-day ad-

ministration at local level. Much of the excessive
work continued to be undertaken by the District
Commissioner."[12] Some District Commissioners felt
that their duties had become onerous, for now they
had to comply with the resolutions of the council
and the strict administrative code of the Ordi- ·
nance.[13] It might be suggested that many European
District Commissioners found themselves tempera-
mentally unable to cope with the African members'
slow, time-consuming rhetoric and love of argu-
mentation; prior to this, they had exercised their
authority unencumbered.

In 1964, the District Commissioners ceased to
be *ex officio* chairmen of the councils and instead
assumed the role of advisors. Many took this opportunity to divorce themselves entirely from the
councils. The District Commissioner was replaced
by a locally elected chairman, who was often chosen
on political grounds. Soon scarcely a council was
out of debt; misuse of funds and poor administration were rampant. Vigorous attempts have been
made to revive the moribund councils. While some
progress has been made, it is doubtful that they
can soon become catalysts for future development:
their efforts are concentrated on maintaining
current local services rather than on forward-looking development projects.

Perhaps it is true that "local government because of its . . . quasi-traditional attributes
. . . is often ill-equipped to serve as the primary agency for modernization. Other organizations
possessed of the attributes of local governance
are frequently established to provide an organized means of coping with issues (to) which a
local government is ill-equipped or ill-advised
to address itself."[14] When the idea of District
Development Committees was first tabled by Aleke
Banda, the Secretary for Local Government strongly
pressed the point that these committees should be
committees of the District Council. Among other
reasons, the disrepute of the councils led to the

rejection of this proposal; but the Chairman and Clerk to Council were appointed to the District Development Committees in order to effect coordination between Council and D.D.C.s. Thus, the decision was taken that local participation in the development process would be achieved primarily through decentralization, not by devolution.

District Development
Committees in Malawi[15]

District Development Committees were approved by the Malawi Government in January, 1965. However, they did not become operational until September, 1966, when training courses were introduced for members. At this time an administrative officer was assigned at headquarters to devote his full time to the committees, and the committees were pressed to meet on a regular basis. Earlier, the committees met only when the Minister for Development and Planning, Aleke Banda, came to address them or when senior officials visited. This was by design; basic policy decisions were being made, and it was hoped to avoid an abortive start — which, despite this caution, was not evaded.

The Government recognized that the success of national development depended to a considerable extent on enlisting the latent energy and enthusiasm of the rural people, then harnessing this as practical support of development programs. The District Development Committees (D.D.C.s) were expected to be the primary vehicles in effecting grass roots participation. Initially, district leaders were asked to state the type of projects they desired. The government consequently was inundated with requests from the D.D.C.s for financial assistance for a multitude of projects. While many were sound, the government did not have the financial resources to grant these requests. In addition, the government had already committed all funds for that fiscal year. Thus, poor planning accounted for an initial failure to implement most of the schemes put forward by the districts, and there was some demoralization of D.D.C. members.

At this juncture, government policy was completely reversed; the committees were no longer viewed as sounding boards by which the government could be apprised of district priorities. Instead, the committees were enlisted to support approved programs, especially in agricultural extensions. In fact, the first D.D.C. training courses concentrated on all subjects but extension work in agriculture and other natural resources.

This reorientation of committee work into a narrow, limited area permitted a more solid foundation to be laid. Albert Hirschman concurs: "A good way for an agency to become multi-purpose is to be first securely and completely grounded in one purpose. Starting out with a specific task, the agency uses the task to make itself strong enough to overcome the inevitable opposition that will arise when it finally does spread out into functions that overlap those of existing agencies."[16] Instead of dissipating their energies over a wide range, the committees were able to concentrate on a few matters of major concern: encouraging the application of fertilizer, early garden preparation, and planting, weeding, and marketing.

At this time the D.D.C.s fell within the portfolio of the Minister of Development and Planning. The Ministry was a fledgling organization with a senior official who concentrated decision-making authority in hiw own hands and was largely inaccessible to members of his own staff. The result was a failure to develop what Alfred de Grazia calls a "group personality."[17] His juniors were not provided with an internally consistent and "ordered approach to day-to-day problems. . . . in accordance with approved perspectives yet

274

without continuous reference to explicit and formalized rules."[18] For the Ministry as a whole this had severe deleterious effects, and might have been a major factor leading to its liquidation.[19] But for the District Development Section, which was responsible for the D.D.C.s, this lack of consistency may — paradoxically — have served to its advantage. Because of the senior official's preoccupation with major development projects, and his only peripheral concern with rural development, the District Development Section was able to develop unique patterns of behavior and an individual identity. Its autonomy was somewhat diluted when the section was subsequently transferred to the Development Division of the Ministry of Economic Affairs, also under Aleke Banda, which replaced the Ministry of Development and Planning. Yet the groundwork had already been laid. By the time of its transfer, the section had already developed basic doctrines and its operating procedures were firmly entrenched. The new division head did concern himself with the work of the committees; and the section was therefore, strengthened by its more complete integration into the matrix of government. By this time, such integration was essential and served to the advantage of the D.D.C.s.

The committees include representatives of the Malawi Congress Party, the District Council, and heads of departments at district level.[20] The intention was never that the impact of the committees would be limited to the district level but that they would influence Malawian attitudes down to the village level. As Aleke Banda stressed, "It is not enough to hold a lot of meetings or discussions. Discussions or meetings should be immediately followed with action so that tangible results could be realized without delay."[21] Members were to accomplish this by mobilizing their constituencies so that committee decisions were known and implemented by villagers. For example,

the Chairman of the Malawi Congress Party for each
district was to make such decisions known to his
officials at the branch and village levels. The
Chairman of the District Council was to ensure
that all councillors knew and supported the Committees' work, and the District Commissioner was
similarly to mobilize the native authorities under
his jurisdiction. Although the concept was theoretically sound, in practice this follow-up work
was not done. Many decisions died in the committee room at the *boma*.[22]

Action Groups

It was suggested by several chairmen that a
more formal organization, below the District
Development Committee, was needed if development
was to be carried to the rural areas. These men
felt that their objectives could be attained more
readily through the establishment of more formal
lines of communication at village and area levels.
Action groups were recommended and accepted, not
as discussion groups but, rather, as executive
agents of the main committee.[23] The membership,
selection of chairmen, and organization of these
action groups varied (and still do) from district
to district, according to local conditions.[24]
The Northern Region responded most enthusiastically, and action groups spread rapidly from there
throughout the country.

Karonga District formed the most effective
groups and thus deserves comment. Its organization is based on a tiered system of three area
action groups, chaired by the chiefs of Karonga,
formed below the D.D.C. In turn, the chiefs
have formed action groups at group village and
village levels. Extension workers from the Department of Agriculture are available to give

276

advice and guidance, and a demonstrator skilled in a particular agricultural specialty is seconded to village action groups whenever it is considered appropriate to embark on some intensive campaign. The education of these groups at area and village level has been accomplished through encouraging them to attend training courses. In Karonga there is already a training center at Baka, near the *boma*. Two others are planned which will coincide with the area groups, so that each will have its own training center. If the D.D.C. feels that some major problem needs attention, a campaign is mounted through the action groups.

The concept of action groups proved to be a sound one which permits responsibility to be pinpointed. If problems arise in some locality, they can be resolved more easily by contacting one man, the chairman of that area's action group, as the responsible person. Generally, the most effective DDCs exist where there is the best organization of action groups. Figure 1 illustrates the simplicity of organization which was achieved with the formation of these groups.

By the end of January, 1967, the committees had been functioning for six months. A preliminary evaluation of their work found that they had been valuable. For one, they served as a forum through which district leaders were kept informed of the government's aims and objectives. In the committees, too, civil servants and Malawi Congress Party officials were able to meet and, in many instances, to resolve their differences. This alone is an important measure of success; although serious differences still exist, the committees have played a major part in their amelioration. With the establishment of action groups, native authorities were also brought into the picture; and they have participated, in some cases to a major extent, in the group's work.

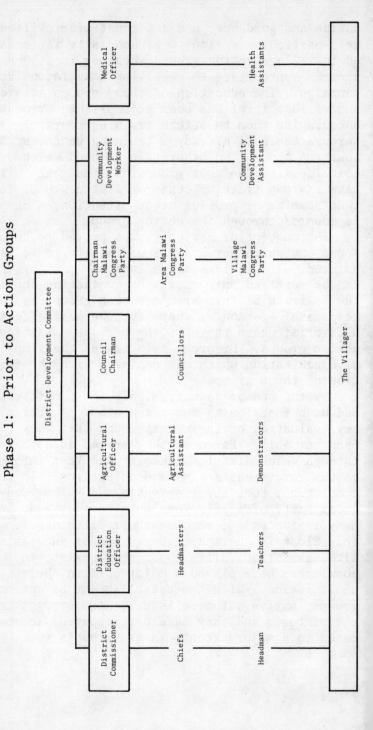

Figure 1
Action Groups

Phase 1: Prior to Action Groups

Phase 2: After Action Groups

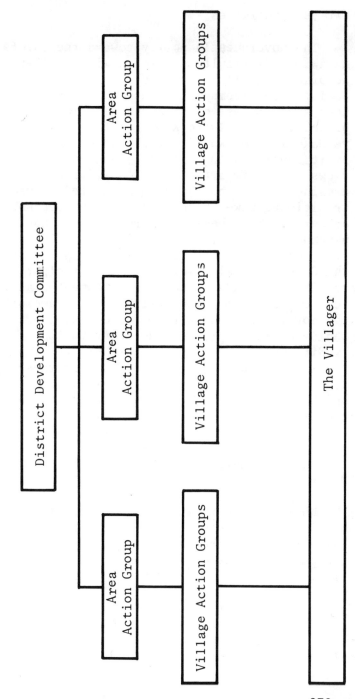

Native Authorities

The Government's policy toward the chiefs in Malawi is difficult to discern with complete accuracy. While respect is duly paid them, especially on ceremonial occasions, they have been kept more or less outside the decision-making process. Chief Mwase Kasungu of Chewa and Inkosi ya Makosi M'mbelwa III of the Northern Angoni exert considerable influence, and doubtless their views are of importance and considered so by the President. But no chief is permitted to use his traditional power base to criticize Government or party. This became apparent when Inkosi Gomani, paramount chief of the Angonis in the Central Region, was deposed in 1967. Yet it appears that the Government will welcome the participation of traditional leaders in the development plan if this can be accomplished within the framework of the Government and party. For example, one very senior official praised the contribution of the traditional leaders in the Northern Region, adding, "Public recognition of the efforts of these traditional leaders will have a significant impact on the improvement of agriculture in the rural economy."[25]

The Malawi Congress
Party

Whatever the influence of the chiefs, it is marginal compared with that of the Malawi Congress Party (M.C.P.), the country's only party. Perhaps the purpose in permitting only one party is "ultimately to promote national integration (and) prevent secessionist movements . . . which might grow up around ethnic-regional groups."[26] There are certain advantages to organizations such as the D.D.C.s in operating within a one-party state. "If there are two rival parties, it may be diffi-

cult for local officers . . . to exert any real
presence, since their political chiefs would be
afraid of losing votes. But with one-party government . . . where there is a good chance that
politicians and administrators will be pulling
together, the prospects are better."[27]

The existence of a one-party state certainly
does not ensure the elimination of strife and
conflict, which might in some cases reach an intensity and virulence within the party equal to
any conflict which might have occurred between
two parties. The result of such conflict can
be very disruptive to a D.D.C. The Ncheu committee had one of the most capable, determined, and
articulate M.C.P. Chairmen as a member. Jairos
Watford Makwangwala was a key factor in making
the Ncheu committee one of the most effective in
the country. In July, 1967, he was disbarred
from the party and his cousin, Inkosi Gomani, deposed from his traditional seat. It is likely
that their fall from official power was caused in
part by a rival faction.[28] The loss of these
men, both of whom served on the committee, sapped
the Ncheu D.D.C. of its vitality. This loss was
compounded by the brutal slaying of Makwangwala in
October, 1967. Key members of the party, such as
the new M.C.P. Chairman, Harry Karima, and the
Member of Parliament, Ledson Chidengu, *et. al.*
were arrested and later convicted.[29]

In Africa politicians are more vulnerable to
temptation than are their administrative counterparts. Administrative officers most often enter
the modern world through a gradual process of education and exposure. The politician, on the other
hand, is often catapulted into a new life to which
it is difficult for him to adapt. Chinua Achebe,
a keen observer of his native Africa, documents
the problem in his novel, *A Man of the People:*

> Perhaps the most astonishing thing Max
> told me about the new party was that one
> of the junior ministers in the Government
> was behind it.
>
> What is he doing in the Government if
> he is so dissatisfied with it? I asked
> naively.
>
> I know how you feel, said Max rather
> patronizingly. . . But we must face cer-
> tain facts. You take a man like Nanga
> now on a salary of four thousand pounds
> plus all the — you know. You know what
> his salary was as an elementary school
> teacher? Perhaps not more than eight
> pounds a month. Now do you expect a
> man like that to resign on a little mat-
> ter of principle?[30]

There is a natural tension between politicians
and civil servants that is heightened in Malawi
by an ambiguous delineation of power and authority at district level. The expatriate District
Commissioner (D.C.) maintains his position, usually by holding himself aloof from the M.C.P..
while the young Malawian D.C. often finds it
difficult to cope with the party. One bright
and energetic young Malawian D.C. rashly wrote
a vituperative letter to his district's Member
of Parliament, charging him with interference in
the work of the D.D.C., and soon found himself replaced. Perhaps the most successful are the more
mature Malawian D.C.'s, who with age and experience are best able to cope. Until lines of
authority are more clearly drawn within the districts, this problem will remain; but fortunately
many capable and committed leaders on both sides
have learned to cooperate with one another.

Once the politicians' support has been secured,
they can very usefully assist the committees:

282

> One of the principal utilities of polit-
> ical organization is its capacity to
> shield and protect administration. . . .
> Where action programs are likely to meet
> resistance from hostile interests . . .
> where the community must be encouraged to
> take some positive action in the face of
> apathy, misunderstanding, or opposition,
> the political techniques of persuasion
> and the example of a group of positively
> committed individuals may spell the dif-
> ference between the success and failure
> in the execution of development programs.[31]

D.D.C. activities, by nature not tied to one site,
with effects spreading broadly through all aspects
of community life, are impossible to insulate from
politics.[32] In the light of the importance of political support for DDC activities, the attendance
rate of barely over 60 percent for politicians at
formal meetings is discouraging. While their participation must be encouraged, care must be taken
that the M.C.P.'s participation is based on its
desire to promote development, and not the party.
If the D.D.C. becomes identified with the latter
purpose, its usefulness will end.[33]

Self-Help

Acknowledging some shortcomings on the political side, the D.D.C.'s progress continued and a
firm foundation for development was laid. The
committees were providing a valuable service to
government by disseminating information and, in
some cases, changing the attitudes of many farmers
toward new methods of agriculture. Nevertheless,
it became apparent that committee members' interest would diminish if their role continued to
be confined to supporting approved programs. Some
members felt that they had been appointed propa-

gandistic agents with little influence upon the
type of development projects in their districts.
The intensity with which committees expressed
this view led the author, as officer-in-charge
of the District Development Section, to report
the matter to the District Development Subcommittee of the National Development Committee,
which was chaired by Aleke Banda.

> While the committees for the most part
> have lent considerable assistance to
> approved programmes of Government, their
> demand for participating in the assign-
> ing of priorities is increasing. It is
> important that when members tour the vil-
> lages, they can point to developments in
> which they have played a part. This is
> required to maintain the enthusiasm of
> members, as well as to enhance the pres-
> tige of the committee in the district.
> All too often, when a committee recom-
> mends some form of district development
> the ministry concerned must reply that
> although the project deserves merit, all
> development resources have been allocated.
> This diminishes the spirit of members. It
> is recommended that the Ministry of Eco-
> nomic Affairs be provided with a limited
> allocation of funds which can be used in
> support of programmes suggested by the
> committees.[34]

The first step toward securing an independent
financial base for the committees came on December
1, 1966, at the fourth meeting of the District
Development Subcommittee. This meeting agreed
that the D.D.C.s would be responsible for aided
self-help projects. Most of the funds for these
projects come from the U.S. Agency for International Development, which has been supporting
the self-help program in Malawi at the rate of
$50,000 a year. These funds are first received

284

by the U.S. Ambassador, who, under current State Department regulations, may allocate them without Washington's prior approval.

Before this decision, self-help projects were handled through the Department of Community Development and grants were made to the District Councils. A.I.D. agreed to reimburse the councils for approved projects but, because of the councils' very insecure financial position, many were unable to advance funds. But the self-help program also failed because the responsible department exercised inadequate control and took no action either to withdraw committed funds from projects which languished for considerable periods, nor to attempt seriously to revive them. A.I.D. expressed considerable consternation. At the meeting of the Subcommittee mentioned above, the head of the External Aid Unit concluded that "under the present arrangement (the government is) in danger of losing U.S. support." Once the aid began to be channeled through the D.D.C.s, a system was arranged by which the Treasury advanced funds to self-help projects. This eliminated one major difficulty. In addition, careful control over aided projects has been exercised, and A.I.D. expressed its satisfaction with the new program. Fearful of being burdened with the old moribund projects, the District Development Section obtained permission to assume responsibility only for new projects.

As in Tanzania, strenuous efforts were made "to bring about some order to the system (by) establishing an administrative system embodying a philosophy of close co-operation between village action groups and a hierarchy of administrative units."[35] But in Tanzania the established system was often bypassed in order to speed the process of approving projects.[36] In Malawi every effort was made to build speed and efficiency into the system, in order to avoid the dangerous disregard of formal and approved processes which was devel-

oping in Tanzania. Attempts were also made to
avoid the conversion of self-help into an *inves-*
tissement humain, of using cheap labor to replace
scarce capital, for the attractiveness of this
principle "creates the danger of a slight shift
of emphasis, away from local leadership and local
needs and towards national planning. At that
point sensible technical help to harness local
enthusiasm tips over to central exploitation."[37]
Fortunately, the local character of self-help in
Malawi remained largely intact, except for a
secondary school self-help program that was fostered from the center by the Ministry of Education.

Four Peace Corps volunteers were recruited
and equipped with Land Rovers. Their main duty
is to give technical assistance to aided projects
so that scarce funds are used to best advantage.
The volunteers assist projects which fall between those which can be done exclusively by local
people and those which must be undertaken by the
Ministry of Works and Supplies. Not only has
this improved the standard of construction on
aided projects; it has also helped improve self-
help generally. As one volunteer put it:

> Each month the organized self-help pro-
> gram improves and becomes a better ve-
> hicle for the channeling of funds to
> needy projects. With each aided project
> comes noteworthy ancillary benefits. In
> fact, most self-help schemes are unaided
> by external funds. These range from the
> construction of latrines and wells to
> the housing for government staff who
> would otherwise be unable to take their
> posts at schools and clinics, to the
> building of schools and medical facil-
> ities themselves. Although the extern-
> ally aided projects are a minority, the
> way in which they are handled strongly
> influences the majority of locally fi-

nanced undertakings. Part of the organized schemes' benefit is the increased
competence of the locally based Community Development Assistant and the D.D.C.
in handling improvement schemes of any
description.[38]

The volunteers technically review each application
for self-help funds put forward by the D.D.C.s and
check the bills of material. They have been a most
valuable addition, for they have ensured that the
standard of aided self-help projects has justified
the assistance rendered by A.I.D. This in turn
has encouraged the U.S. Government to enlarge the
program.

The program's serious weakness is administrative.
The volunteers are attached to the Department of Community Development, but in fact their function is
supervised by the District Development Section of
the Ministry of Economic Affairs. Despite an agreement reached between A.I.D., the Department of
Community Development, and the Ministry of Economic Affairs, considerable resistance developed
in the Department of Community Development to using
the volunteers as assigned, i.e., on aided self-
help projects. With the agreement of the Secretary for Local Government, terms of reference were
recast to ensure that the volunteers gave absolute priority to aided projects.[39] This improved
the situation considerably, yet the difficulties
of locating the volunteers in a separate ministry
were still amply illustrated. In his final report,
the author strongly recommended that unity of
command be achieved by placing the volunteers directly in the District Development Section.[40] In
Malawi, the Department of Community Development
focuses very narrowly on the village, while the
D.D.C. organization is district and nationally oriented.[41] These approaches often conflict, thus

heightening the practical problem of relying on staff of the department to serve directly in line functions of the district development system.

The self-help program of the DDC's nevertheless soon won a reputation for efficiency and effectiveness. As one volunteer put it, " . . . self-help procedures are improving each year. Less than 50 percent of the 1966 projects can be called successes. The 1968 projects promise to be more efficient, more rapid in completion, and technically more sound than their predecessors . . . projects in the wind for 1969 seem to show even more promise."[42] The Administrative Secretary in the Office of the President and Cabinet expressed this another way:

> During my discussions with the Committee, a number of problems have been thrown up, all of which show the members' awareness of and interest in, the various problems of development. To give an example, the members of these Committees are well aware that having impressed upon the people the need to grow more crops, there is the problem of siting markets in the best places to meet the needs of the people and the need to improve feeder roads to make these places accessible. The Committees have applied themselves to such problems and in a number of cases have suggested feeder plans and assisted with self-help, in the construction and maintenance of these roads.[43]

The self-help program has become one of the main activities of the D.D.C.'s and reflects their success.[44]

Additional Funding

Another major source of funds for DDC's is the Christian Service Committee (C.S.C.).[45] An early program by C.S.C., known as the Utumiki project, had been canceled by the President because it had recruited its own field staff and subsequently failed to integrate itself fully with the governmental services. The President indicated his willingness to accept another form of assistance if it was offered through the existing governmental structure; a joint C.S.C. and Government of Malawi (G.O.M.) committee (C.S.C./G.O.M. Working Party) was established. The Development Division was the natural home for such a coordinating committee, supplying both its chairman and its secretary.[46] This gave the D.D.C.s a privileged position in competing for the scarce resources of C.S.C., and the Secretary for Economic Affairs stressed their importance to representatives of the C.S.C.: "A carefully controlled programme of district development under the auspices of the DDCs would not only increase their effectiveness, but would also assist in meeting overall national objectives."[47]

Out of the £18,000 allocated at the first meeting of the C.S.C./G.O.M. Working Party, the D.D.C.s were allocated £15,000 for the drilling of boreholes and the purchase of trucks to assist in the distribution of farmers' aids in the Northern Region. This assistance takes on even greater significance for the D.D.C.s when one realizes that, if used successfully, it opens the door to the allocation of much larger sums. The C.S.C. is especially anxious to assist in the country's development, particularly if this can be done through an organization which works down to grass-roots level. Indications were good that further aid for the D.D.C.s was to be forthcoming; the idea of allocating additional funds to individual committees was favorably received by the C.S.C.

These donors (A.I.D. and C.S.C.) and their
funds enabled the committees to participate actively in assigning district priorities. They
ceased to serve as mere vehicles for transmitting
and disseminating information and central government directives. Now, playing a more complete
role in the development of their districts, the
D.D.C.s' effectiveness and value was enhanced.
Since the first, abortive start, when Government
requested projects from the D.D.C.s at a time
when funds were not available, to the Government's
refusal to consider further proposals, a balance
was reached in which demands and information
flowed in two directions: from the districts to
the capital as well as outward from the capital.
    While this financial support has boosted com-
mittee morale and increased their competence as
planners, it has meant that they have engaged
mainly in ad hoc piecemeal development as funds
have become available. It was suggested that
they begin to deal with more comprehensive district development, since piecemeal efforts often
result in waste and ill-conceived projects, judged
in the overall context of district and national
requirements. The author's final report recommended that the D.D.C.s be authorized to put forward proposals as part of the overall national
development program and compete for available resources based on the merit of each project, rather
than procuring their own funds and thus being useful but ancillary to the overall plan. At present the national plan is confined to those projects which are suggested by the central ministries and departments. Should this recommendation
be accepted, the D.D.C.s would become an integral
part of the planning mechanism. The outcome
would be a national plan which is more realistic
regarding local conditions and local aspirations,
one to fire the enthusiasm of rural people for
its implementation.

Organization

The chairmen of the D.D.C.s are the District Commissioners, who are responsible to the Office of the President and Cabinet. This caused an administrative problem, since the District Development Section was in the Ministry of Economic Affairs but constantly issued instructions to officers of another ministry. While the arrangement received full support and cooperation from the President's Office, it was awkward. The transfer of the District Development Section to the Office of the President and Cabinet would eliminate this problem, as well as offer the advantage of providing regional officers for district development work, for the Office has already stationed Supervisory District Commissioners (S.D.C.) in the regions. The obvious difficulty of giving the committees adequate supervision and assistance from the center could be alleviated by the S.D.C.s, who would provide a direct link to the districts. In late 1968, this recommendation was accepted; and the ideal of unity of command moved closer to realization.

PART II: INSTITUTION-BUILDING

The aim of institution builders might (best) be described as social control. By building institutions, persons should be better able to control the course of change and to accomplish certain desired changes within a shorter period of time than would otherwise be possible.[48]

Any observer of reality is confronted with the methodological issue of how to transform empirical data from a specific case into ideal type concepts. This is what differentiates basic research

291

from mere description. Unless this is done, there can be no quantification or cumulation of data to facilitate comparison with similar . . . phenomena; . . . through the adoption of a common language . . . research could lead to the acquisition of systematic knowledge about institution building.[49]

Albert Hirschman has found that "each project turns out to represent a unique constellation of experiences and consequences . . . (which result) from the varied interplay between the structural characteristics of projects . . . and the social and political environment."[50] If we are to understand the dynamics of successful developmental programs, are we then obliged to examine each individual project in turn? Hirschman would agree that while each project is unique, certain common threads run through most projects; if discerned by the administrator and researcher, they can provide important clues toward understanding the general processes of development.

Accepting this hypothesis, we then must turn to identifying key variables. The knowledge thereby gained must be systematized and put into a common terminology to facilitate communication. The current proliferation of nomenclature , wherein many terms refer to similar phenomena, only increases the general confusion. Milton Esman *et al.* attached to the Inter-University Research Program in Institution Building have taken an important step toward establishing a common frame of reference.[51] While their conceptualization does focus on certain key variables in the development process, it is flexible enough to permit modification and growth as needed.

When an organization is established, one must account for the environment which it enters. This is why D.D.C.s must take their own form in Malawi; religious adherence to the system developed in Malaysia would be dysfunctional, if not outright disastrous. In biology the process of adaptation is known as homeostasis. An illustration is the homeostatic mechanism of temperature control in the individual, which is "so finely developed in man that life is possible only in a narrow range of temperature. Yet because of this temperature control, he is able to function in a wide range of climatic conditions."[52] The concept of institution-building considers the interaction between the organization and its environment as central. While the conception leans pronouncedly toward social engineering, or of using an organization to institute changes in the environment, it assumes that, in order to effect the desired changes, an organization must adapt itself to the environment in order to survive. Thus, there is a basic conflict which confronts the institution-builder: the compulsion to adapt in order to survive meets head-on the necessity of unfettered, innovative action.

As developed by the Inter-University Research Program, the concept of institution-building consists of five clusters of institutional variables which interact with the environment: leadership, doctrine, program, resources, and internal structure.[53]

Regarding resources it should be pointed out that "where the resources to support an organization come only from one point in the environment, a single decision can mean the survival or demise of the organization."[54] For example, some private organizations in the United States concerned with international affairs were supported mainly by government funds. Now that these funds have been diverted largely to domestic programs, these organizations are in jeopardy. Initially, funds for D.D.C. projects came only from A.I.D. A search for additional resources revealed C.S.C.'s willingness to participate. The recommendation that the D.D.C.s compete for a slice of the national

293

development budget, while based mainly on planning considerations, promises to promote further diversity of resources, thus increasing the strength and resiliency of the committees, whatever the vicissitudes of outside aid.

In the institution model these five institutional variables are tied to the environment through four types of linkages: enabling, functional, normative, and diffused (i.e., public opinion). These categories are not mutually exclusive and obviously overlap at times.[55] An illustrative model of the institution building universe is show below.[56]

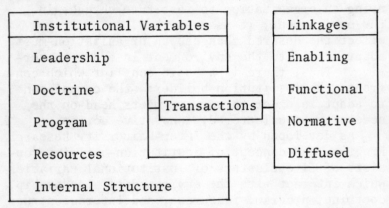

Some of the institutional variables are particularly relevant to a certain type of linkage. For example, doctrine is closely related to normative linkages, program to functional linkages, and resources to enabling linkages.

Institutionality

"Institutionality" is the desired end product of the institution-building model. It connotes that the organization has achieved some support and complementarity in the environment. Once organization has put down roots in its society, survival ceased to be its major concern. The ability to survive is a necessary but insufficient test of institutionality.

Philip Selznick suggests that institutionality has been reached when an organization has intrinsic value in society, when it has "valuation beyond the technical requirements of the task at hand . . . (and) evokes automatic rather than purely calculated sympathy and support."[57]

Such a definition is difficult to operationalize, but it is suggested that it may be possible to devise a questionnaire so structured as to measure such "intrinsic value."[58] The targets of such a questionnaire would have to include persons internal to the organization as well as those who compose its immediate environment (i.e., enabling, functional, normative, and diffuse linkages). The size of this immediate environment would vary widely with the nature of the organization itself.

The purpose of this paper is not to provide a new institution-building model. The model proposed by Esman and his associates is useful in evaluating organizations and thus fits our purposes. But before making use of this concept, one must point out its limitations. Whether we determine institutionalization intuitively or by behavioral techniques such as Polsby's, a further question remains as to whether institutionalization ensures that the innovation necessary for development will continue.

Does the attainment of institutionalization ensure the elements which permit the organization to continue to innovate, does it embody what has been called "innovative thrust"?[59] Or is institutionality a Procrustean bed which molds the organization into the status quo of the existing environment? If the organization loses the capacity to innovate while accommodating to its environment in order to survive and flourish, the test of "institutionality" fails to measure innovation thrust and instead merely measures a projection and expansion of the same environment it had first hoped to change. If this is correct, institutionality is a dysfunction of development, not its essence. Until both institutionalization and innovation are operationalized and correlated with one another, this point will remain debatable. It is not the purpose of this paper to test such a hypothesis, but in adapting the institution building model one must note that a high degree of institutionality may not be compatible with change in the context of the developing world.

Samuel Huntington argues that the very essence of institutionality, and in fact its definition, is adaptability. He asserts: "The more adaptable an organization . . . is, the more highly institutionalized it is; the less adaptable and more rigid it is, the lower its level of institutionalization," because "the more challenges which have arisen in its environment and the greater its age, the more adaptable it is. Rigidity is more characteristic of young organizations than of old ones."[60] It may be argued that a certain amount of rigidity (regarding minimal acceptable outcomes) is necessary if an organization is to put forward and successfully carry out innovative programs. A highly adaptable (i.e., institutionalized) organization would be less willing to jeopardize its position in society by taking such a strong stance.[61]

Major parties in the United States may be good examples of institutions which mirror the society rather than privide innovative thrust. Richard Hofstadter has stated that the goal of major parties has been to "bind together a sufficiently large coalition of diverse interests to get into power; and once in power, to arrange sufficiently satisfactory compromises of interest to remain there."[62] Innovative thrust has come from minor parties which have not yet reached institutional status; instead, they "have been attached to some special idea or interest, and . . . generally expressed their positions through firm and identifiable programs and principles. . . .

296

When a third party's demands become popular enough, they are appropriated by one or both of the major parties and the third party disappears."[63] It is clear that the innovative thrust comes from the noninstitutionalized structures, third parties, rather than the institutionalized, major parties.

In a highly industrialized society some innovation is acceptable and even expected. Therefore, in this environment even highly institutionalized organizations will continue to innovate. But even in this context there is some danger that such institutions will fail to innovate quickly enough to adapt to emerging problems, especially in the contemporary world, in which failure to anticipate emerging problems may be catastrophic. In such circumstances the ability of institutions to adapt to prevailing patterns may not be sufficient.[64]

In the developing world, excessive institutionalization may pose a much more serious problem. Here tradition often dominates. An institutionalized structure which adapts to and mirrors traditional mores will fail to provide innovative thrust. In this respect institutionalization may prove dysfunctional in the developing context. Therefore, the author suggests maximum innovative thrust, not institutionalization, as the goal of institution-building.

One may suggest a circular model as helpful in understanding innovation in organizational terms.[65] At the top of the circle one would find an ideal society, in which organizations are highly institutionalized. Occupying a nearby point would be a society which lacks integrated organizational structures. In one sense the two societies are similar. In a society lacking integrated organizational structures, development fails for want of any organized innovating force; on the other hand, an extremely institutionalized structure serves only to reinforce the status quo. If the latter contention is valid, the promotion of in-

stitutionality by Esman and his associates, if
carried to its logical conclusion, might paradoxically serve as a dysfunction of development, the
very opposite of their stated objective. One gets
varying, increasing degrees of innovative thrust
as organizations move toward the bottom of the
circle.

Until operationalized and tested, this model
remains speculative, but equally speculative is any
assertion that a high degree of institutionality
ensures innovation and change.

Institution-Building
and District
Development Committees

The concept of institution-building does not
offer the administrator a simple recipe which, if
he blends the ingredients carefully, guarantees
the success of his enterprise. Rather, the concept permits the administrator to focus his attention upon certain key points in his own organization as well as in his environment. By critically reviewing the existing structure of his
organization, the extent and kinds of transactions
it has established with its environment, the administrator should be in a better position to
pinpoint links in the chain which require strengthening or modification. His success will be determined by the skill and commitment which he brings
to bear on the entire network of institutional
variables and their linkage to the environment.

> The determination of tactics for each sig-
> nificant linkage, the need to monitor and
> adapt these tactics to feed back from ex-
> perience and to new circumstances in the
> environment emphasizes the importance of
> timing, capacity to bargain, willingness

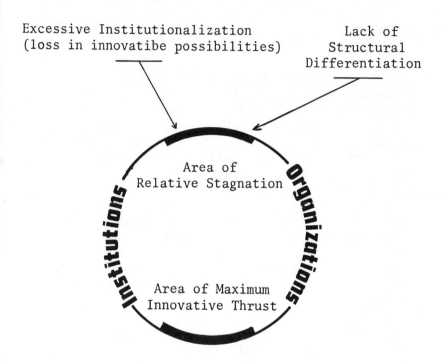

Figure 2
Simplified Circular Model of
Organizational Innovation

Excessive Institutionalization
(loss in innovatibe possibilities)

Lack of
Structural
Differentiation

Area of
Relative Stagnation

Institutions

Organizations

Area of Maximum
Innovative Thrust

This macro-model is suggestive and heuristic, not definitive. It is dynamic in that organizations may be represented as points along the circle, and their positions may change over time. Should these points cluster in the area of maximum innovation thrust, we may conclude that that society is highly conducive to change. As organizations become excessively institutionalized, innovations may still continue through the birth of new organizations or through the revitalization of existing ones. In the latter case, movement would be counterclockwise.

The actual area of maximum innovative thrust is to be determined by empirical research.

299

to adjust to changing situations — the
whole panoply of the political arts of
management — these determine the ability
of the innovative organization to make
its way in an ambiguous environment
while protecting its main pragmatic objectives.[66]

The concept does not offer a panacea for the
researcher's problems, though it does provide a
useful set of lenses of which many are "in particularly sharp focus albeit . . . crudely ground
and still unpolished."[67] The fact these lenses —
institution-building — still require refinement
demands that the researcher proceed cautiously
but imaginatively when applying them to a single
case or relating his study to the broader universe.
In particular, one has difficulty distinguishing
among the enabling, functional, normative, and
diffuse categories.[68] This confusion makes it
difficult to describe an institution in terms
of institution-building; the concept will serve
the researcher better as an evaluative tool.
Therefore, this conclusion will attempt to appraise the DDC's in terms of some concepts developed by Esman and his associates.
    Leadership is the most important institutional
variable. In the DDC hierarchy, leadership was
provided primarily at three levels. At the very
top the Minister, Aleke Banda, was the main driving
force behind the committees. In the administrative
service, the author served as officer-in-charge of
the District Development Section at the center,
while at district level the District Commissioners,
as Chairmen, were the main factor in the success
or failure of individual committees.
    Therefore, the Minister's position was most
crucial, a fact which has been emphasized by the
Secretary for Economic Planning and Development
in Kenya:

Owing to the dangers caused by the different weight of personality between
various Ministers, it follows that . . .
the Minister responsible for National (and
rural) Development must be of a stronger
personality than the others.
The obvious answer to this danger
is that the leader of the Government
should himself be directly responsible
for National Development Planning.
However, in many countries this is
not practicable and the second alternative is that the Minister responsible
should be the Deputy Leader or at least
that Minister having the greatest political prestige or having the greatest
confidence or support of the leader himself. . . . Planned development calls
for strong discipline over portfolio
Ministers as well as over civil servants
and the general public; that discipline
can only be effectively exercised by the
Government itself in the person of its
leader or of his recognized spokesman.[69]

In Malawi there is no deputy leader or spokesman of the President, perhaps purposely on the
part of the President in order to secure his position through the balancing of subordinate groups
and individuals. Yet Aleke Banda, if anyone, can
be said to have had the President's greatest confidence; this was reflected in his large number
of positions in party and government. It was
this power base which permitted the D.D.C.s to
prosper. A similar case is the College of Education in Nigeria, which developed with the active support of Asikiwe, former President of the
Republic. "Apparently, the strategy at Nsukka
(the College) during the first four years was to
'play the game' with Azikiwe in order to protect
the institution behind his powerful political

301

figure. But, if his fall from grace had occurred before the institution had moved to its second-stage strategy, the project would have certainly been a failure."[70]

In Malawi, there was no question of "playing the game" with Aleke Banda, for his genuine commitment to district development was recognized. Although the organization might have enhanced his political base in the rural areas, the main objective of increasing the viability of the D.D.C.s was simultaneously realized. But, as in the Nigerian case, had Banda departed from the scene earlier, the D.D.C.s as now constituted might well have been relegated to the archives.

In late 1968, Banda was relieved of his responsibility for the D.D.C.s, which were transferred to the Office of the President and Cabinet. Subsequently, he became Minister of Trade and Industry and is now Minister of Finance and Minister of Information and Tourism. With the D.D.C.s directly under the President's Office, the criterion that rural development be directly under Presidential control has been realized. As President, Dr. Banda cannot clearly devote his full attention to the D.D.C.s; it appears that he has delegated some of this responsibility to Alec Nyasulu, the Minister of State for National and Regional Development.[71] Still, the line of command is directly to the President; with his active support, the D.D.C.s should have a stronger power base than ever before.

The second level of leadership was at the administrative center. With an expatriate as head of the District Development Section, there is some question as to whether the changes he introduced will long endure.

In some situations expatriates may occupy leadership positions for a short period of time and bring about changes in doctrine, program and internal structure,

> which leave the organization more pro-
> ductive than before and closer to insti-
> tutionalization . . . (but) many is the
> case where "gains" made by expatriate
> leadership have been dissipated after
> their departure.[72]

The possibility that this might occur was recognized; during the author's last six months he was
assisted by a Malawian understudy. This should
not only encourage greater continuity than would
have otherwise been possible; it should also reduce the risk that gains will be dissipated, for
his successor was chosen from the most capable
local administrative officers and had gained experience during a year and a half as Chairman
of the Nsanje District Development Committee.

Finally, at district level, leadership varied
greatly in quality. Least effective were the
expatriate District Commissioners (D.C.s), who
showed little aptitude for or interest in D.D.C.
work. An exception was in Cholo District, whose
expatriate Chairman shared great empathy with his
African members and was therefore able to obtain
their full participation. It is likely that these
posts will gradually be Africanized, so the difficulty of uncooperative expatriate D.C.s will
gradually fade. Among Malawian D.C.s the most
successful were usually the older officers, although almost all of these officers were enthusiastic about the D.D.C. approach. As the caliber
of the field administrative service is improved,
committee leadership will be enhanced.

A second institutional variable is internal
organization. "We can say that the more ambitious the change goals of the institution builder
. . . the more critical is internal structure."[73]
Further, it was found in a review of several
case studies that key personnel "failed to perform their designated roles because their commitment to the new program conflicted with a pre-

existing network of linkages to other institutions in the system."[74] With the transfer of D.D.C.s to the Office of the President and Cabinet, the District Commissioners fell directly in the purview of the District Development Section. The problem of conflicting responsibilities was eliminated through unity of command.

Another focal point is doctrine and its translation into program. One difficulty might be the "inability of the institution's resources to sat-. isfy environmental demands."[75] This occurred during the first abortive start of the D.D.C.s, when project proposals from the field were encouraged though no funds were then available. With the procurement of funds from A.I.D. and C.S.C. and the possibility of other sources, this problem has been greatly reduced.

In the formation of an institution, a choice exists between building a new organization and reconstituting an existing structure. The former possibility is more feasible "when the original organization is perceived by important groups within the society as discharging its functions inadequately or as neglecting activities which it should be performing."[76] It will be recalled that a suggestion was made that the D.D.C.s become committees of the District Councils. Because of the failure of the councils, the recommendation was overruled and the D.D.C.s were established as a new organization. Further, the Department of Community Development, which is very much a part of the council structure and for some time was in the same ministry, failed to implement a successful program of aided self-help projects. The failure of community development, it has been stated, is widespread and "the record is one of general failure and only rare successes."[77] At any rate, the responsibility for self-help was transferred to the D.D.C.s, yet the volunteers recruited to assist self-help remained with the Department of Community Development. This is

apropos to the functional linkages of the D.D.C.s;
for in the Esman model, the functional linkage
complex includes "these organizations which constitute the real or potential competition, organizations which perform or seek to perform, similar functions and services to those of the institution under study."[78] The failure of the Department of Community Development to cooperate in the
use of volunteers might be one manifestation of
this competition and represented a weak linkage
in the D.D.C. system throughout the author's time
in Africa.

In the preceding section, the utility of
using "institutionality" as the final goal of
institution-building was questioned; maximum innovative thrust was put forward as a more appropriate criterion of effectiveness. The author
argued that excessive institutionalization might
prove dysfunctional for development. While institutions are necessary, there may well be a
limit in this process beyond which institutions
no longer provide the impetus for development.
John Hanson offers criteria which are helpful in
measuring institutionality, but these criteria
must also be met by any viable organization.[79]

The first necessary, but insufficient, criterion is survival. This condition has been met,
for the D.D.C.s have survived despite several
ministerial changes and the loss of the leadership
and support of Aleke Banda. Second, Hanson proposes autonomy. Here again the D.D.C.s have been
successful in maintaining their own individual identity within the structure of government. Hanson
also proposes the use of services and resources
(support) as additional standards of measurement.
When agricultural shows were approved for Malawi,
it was decided to organize and run them through
the D.D.C.s; likewise, when the concept of
"model villages" was proposed by Formosan advisers and strongly backed by President Banda, the
D.D.C.s were again tapped to run the program. The

Institute of Public Administration has formed close
ties with the District Development Section and
often asks officials of this section to help train
administrative officers. These are but a few of
the services requested of and rendered by the D.D.C.
organization. Pressures at the disposal of the
D.D.C.s, too, have increased and additional support is anticipated.

Finally, Hanson proposes "respect and approval"
as an important measure of success. "the extent
to which the programs and the personnel of the
organization are judged to be serving accepted or
emergent goals. . . ."[80] When the D.D.C.s were
first introduced, they were received with considerable skepticism by former British colonial
officers, many of whom are in the most senior
positions of Malawi's civil service.[81] Because
of their concentration at the highest levels of
the administrative service (during the period of
this study), their support and approval were of
great importance. The comments of the second
most senior expatriate officer show the increasing
acceptance of the committees at these highest
levels of government.

Prior to embarking on my tour of District
Headquarters in January, you asked for
specific information on the working of
the District Development Committees.
During my first month of travelling, I
have had the opportunity of meeting three
District Development Committees. . . .
Before meeting the Committees, my
only contact with them had been through
correspondence during my term in the
Ministry of Health . . . (and) I had a
number of doubts about these Committees
from my limited contact with them.
Having had a closer look at these
Committees in the Northern Region, I
have revised my thinking about them. At

the outset of this Minute, I wish to record that I believe the concept of District Development Committees is sound
and, given the right type of leadership
and assistance . . . they will go a long
way to effecting reforms in the economy
of the country.[82]

The fact that the D.D.C.s are now under this
official's supervision in the Office of the President and Cabinet makes it more likely than ever
that this leadership and assistance will be made
available.

Conclusion

District Development Committees, although recently grafted onto the structure of the Malawi
Government, have grown into well-established organizations for bringing change to rural areas
of the country. With the active, enthusiastic
support of Aleke Banda, the D.D.C. system has
grown from a fragile child into a sturdy adoles-
cent well able to stand alone. The possibility
of further growth is great; the D.D.C.s are
likely to become (if indeed they are not already)
a major component of Malawi's development process.
A primary reason for the success of this venture has been the decentralized nature of the
organization. Within this broad framework of
decentralization, the District Development Section and the committees have enjoyed some independence. The major thrust of the enterprise,
however, has been to develop very close relations
between the center and the committees, and in
turn between the committees and the villager.
The problem of reconciling the need for strong
central government with the need for local responsibility has been resolved in favor of a balance
between the two, but with close liaison and final

authority resting with the center. In many developing countries, the author believes, rural development will most successfully occur within the context of the central government system, not through the proliferation of a complex of autonomous local authorities which derive little support and guidance from the center.

While the D.D.C.s are now generally accepted and supported by the Government, one questions whether their increasing integration into the governmental structure may not act as a brake on their innovative abilities. Despite independence, the Government of Malawi remains largely based on the colonial model, which values law and order over development. The colonial system was highly centralized, even under indirect rule, and the continuation of this attitude places the D.D.C.s in a dilemma. The D.D.C.s require the acceptance and support of Government, but if they are too thoroughly integrated into the government structure, they may lose innovative ability; governmental pressure on the D.D.C. system may also push it toward excessive centralization. In either case the objectives of the D.D.C.s would be sacrificed.

NOTES

1. Emil J. Sedy, "Improvement of Local Government and Administration for Development Purposes," *Journal of Local Administration Overseas*, I, 1 (January, 1962), 147.

2. Aleke Banda, in circular letter from the Minister of Development and Planning, dated February 3, 1967, addressed to all Chairmen of the District Development Committees.

3. Frank P. Sherwood, *Devolution as a Problem of Organization Strategy* (Bloomington, Ind.: Comparative Administration Group, 1968), p. 9. The distinction between decentralization and devolution, which is the nomenclature adopted in this paper, has also been termed deconcentration and decentralization, with the latter term referring to more or less autonomous units. See Harold F. Alderfer, *Local Government in Developing Governments* (New York: McGraw-Hill, 1964), pp. 9 ff.

4. Ethel Albert states the case for centralization in her study of Ruanda and Urundi: "As political power in a society is strongly centralized, conformity to social and political decrees will be more effectively enforced and uniformity in behavior therefore greater . . . a traditionalistic and strongly centralized society like Ruanda can show a greater amount of actual change . . . than Urundi, more diffusely organized though less traditionalistic and psychologically more receptive to innovation." Quoted in "Socio-Political Organization and Receptivity to Change: Some Differences Between Ruanda and Urundi," *Southwestern Journal of Anthropology*, XVI (1960), 71-73. Albert points out the shortcomings of devolution in a developing country but does not, I feel, argue against the decentralization of the administration hierarchy — which might, in fact, have the dual advantage of both central control and genuine local participation.

5. Jawaharlal Nehru, *Community Development and Panchayat Raj* (New Delhi: Government of India Publications Division), p. 8.

6. D. E. Lilienthal, "The T.V.A.: An Experiment in the 'Grass Roots' Administration of Federal Functions," address before the Southern Political Science Association, (Knoxville, Tennessee, November 10, 1939. Available in pamphlet form.

7. Aristide Zolberg, *Creating Political Order* (Chicago: Rand McNally, 1966), p. 111.

8. Henry Maddox, *Democracy, Decentralization and Development* (London: Asia Publishing House, 1963), p. 40.

9. Frederick Lugard, *The Dual Mandate in British Tropical South Africa* (4th ed.; London: W. Blackwood and Sons, 1929).

10. T. D. Thompson, "Local Government Training in Nyasaland," *Journal of African Administration*, VIII, 4 (October, 1956), 197-98.

11. Margery Perham, quoted in G. B. Jones, *Britain and Nyasaland* (London: Allen and Unwin, 1964), p. 175.

12. J. W. Robins, "Developments in Rural Local Government in Nyasaland," *Journal of African Administration*, XIII, 3 (July, 1961), 150.

13. *Ibid.*

14. Fred G. Burke "Local Governance and Nation Building in East Africa — A Functional Analysis," Program of Eastern African Studies, Syracuse University, Occasional Paper (1964), p. 21.

15. Much of the discussion which follows in the remainder of Part I is from an article by R. A. Miller, "District Development Committees in Malawi: A Case Study in Rural Development," *Journal of Administration Overseas*, IX, 2 (April, 1970), 129-142.

16. Albert Hirschman, *Development Projects Observed* (Washington, D.C.: The Brookings Institution, 1967), p. 51.

17.   Alfred de Grazia, *Politics and Government* (New York: Collier Books, 1962).

18.   Philip Selznick, *Leadership in Administration* (Evanston, Ill.:   Row, Peterson & Co., 1957), pp. 17-18.

19.   For a description and explanation of the ministerial reorganization which took place on November 1, 1967, see the memorandum of the Secretary to the President and Cabinet (Brian Roberts), Ref. No. 14/01/16/4, of October 26, 1967.

20.   Full membership includes the District Commissioner (Chairman), Members of Parliament from the district, District Chairmen of the Malawi Congress Party, League of Malawi Youth, and League of Malawi Women, Chairman and Clerk to District Council, Farmers Marketing Board Supervisor, Agricultural Officer, District Education Officer, and Community Development Worker.   The Chairman has the power to co-opt the Senior District Representative of other ministries and departments, chiefs, and other influential persons who are not members of the committee to attend any meeting to provide any relevant information or assistance.   The committees varied in size but were usually composed of 12 to 15 members.

21.   Aleke Banda, address to the cholo D.D.C., minutes of the April 4, 1968, meeting.

22.   Administrative center, particularly the center of a district.

23.   Action groups were accepted in principle at the fourth meeting of the District Development Subcommittee, held on December 1, 1966.   This subcommittee, chaired by Aleke Banda, with Secretaries of Development Ministries as members, served for a brief period as the policy-making organ for the

D.D.C.s. In the minutes of this meeting it is
recorded that the Minister stated: "The policy
of the Government is in opposition to the proliferation of committees; therefore, no formal committees may be formed below the D.D.C.s. However,
in formal action, groups may be set up . . . to
aid in district development as needed." This
opened the door to the widespread use of action
groups.

24. The D.D.C.s decide on the organization
and membership of their own action groups. Therefore, membership varies from district to district.
Depending on the nature of the district, politicians may be predominant in one district, while
civil servants or traditional leaders may dominate the action groups of another district.

25. Minute from the Permanent Secretary (Administration), Office of the President and Cabinet,
to the Secretary to the President and Cabinet,
dated February 5, 1968.

26. Immanuel Wallerstein, "Decline of the
Party in Single Party States," in Joseph La Palom-
bara and M. Weiner, eds., *Political Parties and
Political Development* (Princeton: Princeton
University Press, 1966), p. 204.

27. Guy Hunter, *The New Societies of Tropical
Africa* (New York: Frederick A. Praeger, 1964),
p. 110.

28. Gomani, although deposed, continued to be
recognized as Paramount Chief by his people.

29. For an account of the trial see *The Times*
(Malawi), March 14, 1968.

30. Chinua Achebe, *A Man of the People* (New
York: Anchor Books, 1967), p. 79.

31. Milton J. Esman, "The Politics of Development Administration," in John O. Montgomery and William J. Siffin, eds., *Approaches to Development: Politics, Administration & Change* (New York: McGraw-Hill, 1966).

32. The concept of site-bound vs. footloose projects and its political effects is explored in Hirschman, *op. cit.*, p. 93.

33. In *The Times* (Malawi) of September 10, 1968, it is reported: "The Nkotakota District Malawi Congress Party Chairman . . . has appealed to the people there, through their action groups, to contribute food and other things to the following MCP Annual Convention in Lilongwe." Fortunately, as of September, 1968, when the author left Africa, the use of the DDC organization for purely political purposes was a relatively rare occurrence.

34. Robert A. Miller, *District Development Committees, Progress Report*, Zomba: Ministry of Development and Planning, 1967.

35. Garry Thomas, "Community Development and Nation Building in Transitional Tanganyika," Program of Eastern African Studies, Syracuse University, Occasional Paper (1964), p. 18.

36. *Ibid.*, p. 26.

37. Hunter, *op. cit.*, pp. 111-12.

38. For two interesting examples of self-help projects carried out under this program, see Robert A. Miller, "District Development Committees in Malawi: A Case Study in Rural Development," *Journal of Administration Overseas*, IX, 2 (April, 1970), 136-38.

39. The Department of Community Development is under the Ministry of Local Government.

40. No information is currently available to indicate whether this recommendation has been implemented.

41. The extreme village orientation of the Department of Community Development has been noted by outside observers. E. N. Burke, Social Affairs Officer with the United Nations Economic Commission for Africa, after visiting with the Department stressed the principle "of promoting the development of the whole community as an integral part of the united nation" and, implying that this was not being done in Malawi, he recommended that the department "consider slating itself more closely . . . to the Development Program." E. N. Burke, "Community Development in Malawi," Zomba: Ministry of Local Government, August, 1967, pp. 26-28.

42. From the Technical Advisor for self-help projects to the Secretary for Economic Affairs, No. CD 1/10/210.

43. Minutes from the Permanent Secretary (Administration), Office of the President and Cabinet, to the Secretary and the President and Cabinet, dated February 5, 1968.

44. Thomas, *op. cit.*, p. 29, claims: "It is generally agreed that self-help schemes are unlikely to make a significant net contribution to the country's economic development." In Malawi, the entire construction of elementary schools and teachers' houses for these schools, outside of urban areas and those undertaken by the missionaries, were dependent on self-help. This alone, not to mention other contributions of self-help, would point out the importance of self-help, for

314

if schools and other social services are not directly economic they certainly free capital, if done by self-help, which can then be used on more immediate and purely economic projects. This seems to be the case in most countries of the developing world, including Tanzania, to which Mr. Thomas refers. F. A. Byabato, of the Ministry of Planning in Tanzania, found: "Out of the shs. 776,680 which the Government contributed for the period 1/7/65 to 1/7/66 in order to assist self-help schemes, work to the value of shs. 18,921,900 has been completed," See his article "Community Development," in *Report on 1st Seminar on Development, 24 Oct.-3 Nov., 1966* (Kuala Lumput, 1967), p. 17. While these figures may be inflated, they do point out that self-help is important in Tanzania, and is perceived as such by its leadership. In Malawi, the leadership, up to and including the President, frequently stresses the importance of self-help.

45. The Malawi branch organization of the World Council of Churches.

46. The head of the division served as Chairman while the author served as Secretary.

47. Minutes of the first meeting of the C.S.C./G.O.M. Working Party held on February 26, 1968. (The Secretary for Economic Affairs, Mr. Robert Dewar, has moved to a position with the World Bank.)

48. Norman Uphoff and Warren Ilchman, "The Time Dimension in Institution Building" (University of Pittsburgh: Inter-University Research Program in Institution Building, 1967), p. 1. (Mimeographed.)

49. J. W. Eaton, "The Inter-University Research Program in Institution Building," (University of Pittsburgh: Inter-University Research Program in Institution Building, 1968), p. 6. (Mimeographed.)

50. Hirschman, *op. cit.*, p. 186.

51. The Research Program had its headquarters at the University of Pittsburgh; and participating universities included Michigan State, Indiana, and Syracuse.

52. E. A. Wilkening, "Some Perspectives on Change in Rural Societies," *Rural Sociology*, XXIX, 1 (March, 1964), 12.

53. For the sake of brevity the component parts of the institution model are summarized. For a more complete treatment of this concept see Milton J. Esman, *The Institution Building Concepts — An Interim Appraisal* (University of Pittsburgh: Inter-University Research Program, 1967). (Mimeographed.)

54. Sherwood, *op. cit.*, p. 26.

55. Hans C. Blaise and Milton J. Esman, "Institution Building: The Guiding Concepts" (Pittsburgh: Inter-University Research Program, 1966), p. 15. (Mimeographed.)

56. *Ibid.*, p. 9.

57. Selznick, *op. cit.*, p. 17.

58. Nelson Polsby has attempted to operationalize institutionality in his study of the U.S. House of Representatives. He distinguishes three major characteristics of an institutionalized organization, which he measures over time. His indices are (a) it is well-bounded (differentiated from its environment), which he measures by the degree to which leadership is recruited from within the organization; (b) the organization is internally complex; (c) the organization tends to use universalistic rather than particularistic

criteria, and automatic rather than discretionary methods for conducting its internal business.

Polsby offers no threshold above which an organization becomes an institution. Rather, he examines the House over time to determine whether and to what extent his indices decrease or increase. See his article "The Institutionalization of the U.S. House of Representatives," *American Political Science Review*, LXII, No. 1, March, 1968, pp. 144-168.

Whether the concept is operationalized based on "intrinsic value" or on Polsby's indices, it is obviously easier to measure the change in institutionality within one organization over time than to compare two diverse types of organization. Different organizations have different structures and different immediate environments. However, one of the primary purposes of the model is to compare two or more different organizations. Here "institutionality" as a comparative concept still proves wanting.

59. John Hanson, "Institutionalization of the College of Education of the University of Nigeria," in *Institution and Education: Papers and Comments* (Bloomington, Ind.: University of Indiana Publications, 1967), p. 27.

60. Samuel P. Huntington, "Political Development and Political Decay," *World Politics*, XVII, 3 (April, 1965), 394.

61. Philip Selznick maintains: "As a business, a college, or a government agency develops a distinctive clientele, the enterprise gains in stability that comes with secure sources of support, an easy channel of communication. At the same time it *loses flexibility*, the process of institutionalization has set in." Selznick, *op. cit.*, p. 7. Italics added. On the surface it would appear that Selznick and Huntington disagree,

for the former identifies institutionality with inflexibility and the latter with adaptability. Yet the disagreement falls away when one realizes that Selznick is referring to inflexibility in terms of innovation and that he would, it may be assumed, accept the proposition that institutions are highly adaptive to the prevailing environment.

62. Richard Hofstadter, *The Age of Reform* (New York: Vintage Books, 1955), p. 97.

63. *Ibid.*

64. It is on this basis that one may criticize the Nixon Administration for being short-sighted in enthusiastically espousing the "silent majority" while failing to deal with emerging patterns which may in time tear the society apart.

65. I am indebted to Dr. Clyde Ingle for suggesting that a circular, rather than a polar, model would be most suitable. Another model of organizational innovation may be conceptualized as a parabola in the form of an inverted "U." The vertical axis indicates degree of innovative thrust, while the horizontal axis indicates degree of differentiation. Such a model would be more conducive to empirical analysis, and is suggested by Leslie S. Dopkeen.

66. Esman, *The Institution Building Concepts - An Interim Appraisal*, pp. 32-33, quoting John Hanson. (Mimeographed.)

67. Hanson, *loc. cit.*

68. Guthrie Birkhead, quoted in Esman, *The Institution Building Concepts.* (Mimeographed.)

69. William Wamalwa, "The Implementation of Development — The Role of the Politician," in

*Report of First Seminar on Development, 24 Oct.-
3 Nov. 1966* (Kuala Lumpur, 1967), 23. Insertion
mine.

70.   John D. Montgomery, commenting on John
Hanson's Nigerian study, in *Institution and Education,* p. 30.

71.   See *The Times* (Malawi), February 13, 1969,
p. 4, for a report on Nyasulu's tour of D.D.C.s.

72.   Uphoff and Ilchman, *op. cit.,* p. 34.

73.   *Ibid.,* p. 18.

74.   Eaton, *op. cit.,* p. 15.

75.   Esman, *The Institution Building Concepts,*
p. 19.   (Mimeographed.)

76.   *Ibid.,* p. 47.

77.   David Hapgood, *et al., Policies for Promoting Agricultural Development* (Cambridge, Mass.:
Massachusetts Institute of Technology, Center for
International Studies, 1965), p. 16, quoted in
Henry C. Hart, *The Village & Development Administration* (Bloomington, Ind.:   Comparative Administration Group, 1967), p. 8.

78.   Blaise and Esman, *op. cit.,* p. 14.

79.   Quoted in Esman, *The Institution Building
Concepts,* pp. 28-29.   While Hanson's criteria are
used in this section, one may also use Polsby's indices in illustrating the increasing viability of
the D.D.C.s.   Leadership is being recruited within
the organization itself, the organization is becoming internally more complex with its increasing
responsibilities, and a system of procedures ensures that responses are becoming more automatic
than discretionary.   (Mimeographed.)

80. *Ibid.*

81. While the British had set up District
Teams during the colonial era, and these teams
were similar in many ways to the D.D.C.s, such
teams were composed exclusively of civil servants.
What many expatriate British officers objected
to was the merger on the D.D.C.s of civil servants and politicians.

82. Minute from the Permanent Secretary (Administration), Office of the President and Cabinet,
to the Secretary and the President and Cabinet,
dated February 5, 1968.

Lesotho: Toward Real
Independence

by Nicholas Danforth

The Kingdom of Lesotho is geographically contained within the Republic of South Africa . . .
A large portion of the absentee Basotho population (which seeks employment in the gold,
coal, and diamond mines of South Africa as
well as in the commerce, industry, and agriculture of that country) is made up of
males . . . . Most of the Basotho who leave
the country do so for lack of employment
opportunities . . . . The 1-3 percent rise
in GNP barely kept pace with the population
growth of 2.2-2.5 percent per annum. . . .
Servants are easily obtained at R8-R15 a
month. . . . A single European working in
Lesotho requires a minimum salary of R150 a
month.[1]

It is not without good reason that Lesotho
has been called "The Switzerland of Africa".
In winter with its mountains deep in snow
under vivid blue skies, and ski-runs flash-
ing with colour, there can be few more
healthy climates in the world. In the

mountain streams that run clear and clean,
the trout fishing is superb. There are
several tourist hotels supplemented by a
score or more in South Africa within easy
reach. . . . In Lesotho, the traditional
greeting for a stranger, with hand upraised
in welcome, is "Khotso!" Simple and sincere.
"Peace be with you."[2]

Colonization has always required the existence of the need for dependence. Not all
peoples can be colonized: only those who
experience this need. . . . Wherever
Europeans have founded colonies . . . their
coming was unconsciously expected — even
desired — by the future subject peoples.
. . . When the colonizer first appears, it
is not as an enemy but as a stranger, as a
guest.[3]

The intercourse of these natives with the
white race has been fatal to them from the
very beginning.[4]

Introduction

The 1960's brought the deceptive glitter of
political independence to Lesotho. Economically,
however, the small, impoverished enclave was, as
it had remained for generations, almost totally
dependent on British financial support and South
African employment. Since 1970 the Basotho people
have begun to recognize and challenge this dependency. Traditionally proud, individualistic
and self-reliant, the Basotho are gradually overcoming the economic and often psychological dependence on white society and aid which, paradoxically, has been a partial, indirect cause of
Lesotho's poverty. There are of course primary
demographic and geographic reasons for Lesotho's
economic stagnation; less known is the economic

322

effect of the persistent attitude of many Basotho toward themselves as inherently "poor" and toward whites as enviably "rich." Certainly this attitude helps explain why so much of the Basotho's energies for so many years have been wasted, from the perspective of endogenous development, in mines and factories far beyond their borders. This attitude may help to explain why, until recently, agriculture and livestock were neglected in favor of an impractical and costly "European" educational system and illusive attempts at industrial development. It may help explain why trees and topsoil were widely destroyed, towns became overcrowded, tens of thousands of families had absentee fathers, and the government became one of the most overloaded and underproductive bureaucracies in Africa.

For a century a sense of dependence on the developed world and a felt need to emulate it blinded the Basotho to their own strengths and resources. Because of political independence and the subsequent cutting of the colonial umbilical which had guaranteed aid from Britain, Lesotho has been forced to grope for national economic self-reliance to avoid becoming another South African bantustan. This essay describes the growth of the Basotho dependency complex and several manifestations of it which I encountered in various development projects as a Lesotho official from 1966 to 1968. It is important to remember that since 1968 the complex has diminished; nonetheless, too little effort has been made to understand it, its origins, and its effects on development.

Background

The first whites among the Basuto were invited to Basutoland by the tribe's first Paramount Chief, King Moshoeshoe I. One of Africa's most brilliant statesmen and warriors, Moshoeshoe had organized the remnants of various small tribes, which had been ravaged by Zulu raiders during the 1820's,

323

into a strong fighting unit under his command. After repulsing the invaders, Moshoeshoe settled his people in the lowlands near what is now Maseru, Lesotho's capital. Troubled by stories of white settlers advancing from the Cape, he decided to ask for help from European missionaries who were said to be helping other African tribes. Moshoeshoe sent an emissary with 100 cattle to "procure in exchange, a man of prayer," and soon gave a spirited welcome to three young French missionaries of the Paris Evangelical Missionary Society. The first mission in Basutoland was set up nearby. Foreign aid to the Basotho, from what they saw to be a superior white culture, had begun.

At the same time, other white travelers began to pass through Basutoland, first as traders who returned to their homes in the Cape, later as Boer trekkers intending to settle.[5] Moshoeshoe treated them hospitably; he offered land for grazing and temporary cultivation, but began to fear for his people's "existence and independence." After 1840, Moshoeshoe sought British protection by demonstrating to the British how much their help was needed and how receptive the Basotho were to the Englishman's way. Instead of the traditional, graceful stone *rondavel*, Moshoeshoe built for himself the first square house in Basutoland — an impractical symbol of the first attempts of the Basotho to imitate the white man (the remains of which can still be seen near Maseru). A more picturesque indication of Moshoeshoe's conversion to British customs was his wardrobe; sketches of the times show him wearing a dark European suit with his blanket, a top hat instead of his catskin hat, and a walking stick instead of his warrior's "knobkerry."

In 1868, when the Basuto nation was close to extinction and entirely surrounded by Boers, the King's ultimate plea was sent by emissary to Queen Victoria: Moshoeshoe pleaded with her to let his people become a "flea on your blanket." Victoria accepted. Basutoland became British territory and the Basotho, despite Boer protests, became subjects of the Crown.

Except during the Gun War of 1880-83, fought between British forces (under the Cape government, which then ruled Basutoland) and Basuto warriors led by the three sons of Moshoeshoe, subsequent years of British rule were mostly peaceful. During the Boer War, Basuto chiefs feared a Boer victory over the British and petitioned the British to remain in Basutoland indefinitely. A separate British administration was set up, and a High Commissioner drew up laws for the territory and encouraged the Basotho to establish internal self-government. For years the colonial administration numbered less than five expatriates. There were no resources in Basutoland which could be exploited by the British Empire, and Basutoland was of slight strategic value to British forces during the Boer War. The British had assumed that Basutoland would eventually become part of the Union of South Africa, on which the Basuto would inevitably be economically dependent. However, in both world wars the Basuto were known for their loyal service and brave fighting; many Basuto fought with British units in North Africa and Italy. After years of British protection and aid, during which the British and Basuto had fought side by side against common foes, the British were (and are) unwilling to hand over their protectorate to racist South Africa.

All Basotho lands belong to the nation and are allocated by the chiefs to farmers and occupants. Until recently there was little security of tenure over allocated land, and very few whites have settled permanently in the country. Most of those who did, other than missionaries, now own shops and hotels. To the Basuto children who grow up in Maseru or in a district capital, several of their town's prominent citizens are white British or South African government officials, traders,

325

and hotel owners, some of whom were born in Lesotho
and are fluent in Sesotho. Many Basotho boys come
from rural or mountain villages to town to find odd
jobs as caddies at the white clubs, washing cars
at the hotels, pruning hedges, and brewing tea in
white homes before they go to work in South Africa.
Many rural children have white teachers, often nuns
and the priests they hear on Sunday, sometimes
British and American volunteers. Rural families
may consider themselves lucky to live near a road
where they can beg or sell homemade souvenirs to
passing white South African tourists.

The white man's influence increases as the
Basotho children mature. Most young men are unable
to find work at home and must leave their families
for jobs in South Africa, where deliberate pressure is continually put on them to change their
traditional ways of life. Even those who find
work in Lesotho must play new roles:

> Today (says the advertisement by the
> Lesotho National Development Corporation)
> Lesotho has its sleeves rolled up. The
> traditional Basotho hat has been changed
> for a construction worker's helmet. The
> chatter of the drill and the rapping of
> the riveter are the music the Basotho is
> waking and working to. There are tall
> cranes reaching for the sky and the Basotho's
> brow is proud with sweat.[6]

The degree of white acculturation in Lesotho
may have been one reason for the relative indifference of the Basotho to complete independence,
once they had achieved self-government in 1965.
In contrast to those African nations which had
been at least temporarily unified by the struggle
for independence, Lesotho was virtually handed
its independence with some degree of relief by
the British. Independence was opposed for a time
by the opposition party, which boycotted the in-

dependence celebrations on October 4, 1966. Also
against independence was King Moshoeshoe II, a direct descendant of King Moshoeshoe I and titular
Head of State, whose powers were diminished by
the new constitution.

After a century of British support, in 1966
the Basotho found themselves in a predictable
African dilemma, addicted to colonial protection
and budgetary support, without a common cause or
single leader who could unite them. The opposition to foreign exploitation which might have unified the Basotho in the 1960's, as it had in the
1860's, did not appear.

Since 1965, political power in Lesotho has
been held by the Basotho National Party (B.N.P.)
and its founder, Prime Minister Leabua Jonathan,
who was strongly supported by South Africa and
Britain before and after attaining his office.
The B.N.P. was created in 1959 to oppose the Basotho
Congress Party (B.C.P.), which had called for
greater national self-reliance (even though it apparently received support from leftist nations)
and consistently opposed dependence on aid from
Britain and South Africa. The B.C.P. also de-
plored the large numbers of foreigners who worked
in the Lesotho Government. By contrast, before
1970, the Prime Minister and B.N.P. officials
brought many white South Africans into government
service. The Prime Minister frequently traveled
abroad to seek aid, telling foreign donors:

> We are not a nation of paupers. We retain
> our self-respect. . . .With the help of
> our many friends we shall be successful . . .
> Can you help? Will you help?[7]

Throughout the 1960's, the B.N.P. did not attempt badly needed educational, agricultural, administrative, and land reforms. For example, because the B.N.P. received support from the powerful Catholic Church in Lesotho, the party made no

327

appreciable effort to modernize the costly and anachronistic Catholic educational system, which controlled most of the nation's schools at Government expense. Vital land reforms to consolidate landholdings and to improve farming methods required a basic restructuring of the powers of the local chiefs. Yet many Basotho leaders and expatriate advisors continued to seek the answers to Lesotho's needs outside her borders. Because of the obstacles to modernizing agricultural and educational practices, the Government instead emphasized industrial development financed by foreign capital, primarily from South Africa.

Where white missionaries first settled, drawn by "the desire that men feel to draw near to each other, to know one another, and to live a life in common",[8] in 1970 the white investor was being asked "to put an investment in Lesotho for only one reason — to get a good return on your money."[9] Where Basotho warriors once fought invading Boers, the Lesotho Government was now inviting South Africans to take advantage of

1. Complete exemption from company income tax for the first six years of operation.
2. Free land for industry, with leases granted for an indefinite period.
3. Plentiful power and water.
4. "Intelligent" labor for a minimum daily wage of 85¢ (U.S.)
5. Travel facilities linking Lesotho with South Africa "and therefore with the entire world."

New industries built after independence included a tire retreading plant, a candle factory, a mohair carpet factory, a brewery, a tractor assembly plant, a pottery, a paint factory, a furniture factory, and several brickfields. Public works projects included government office buildings, a postal complex, and the Leabua Jonathan International Airport. In 1966 the nation had three miles of tarred road — paved for a visit by King George VI in 1949. In 1968, the 90-mile Leabua Jonathan International Highway was completed, and new dirt roads were under construction throughout the country. One diamond mine with international backing began to produce, and two more diamond prospecting operations got under way. The $40 million Oxbow hydroelectric project — involving dams, tunnels, and turbines high in the mountains — was planned to provide power and 220 million gallons of water daily to South Africa. In Maseru, a $2 million Holiday Inn, complete with gambling casino and swimming pool, opened in 1970; and a $500,000 shopping center and apartments for expatriates are under construction.

Light industries, tourist facilities, and other construction projects unfortunately will do little to solve Lesotho's massive unemployment problem. Only a few thousand Basotho, at most, will be able to find work on such projects in the next few years. For security reasons, mining companies will attempt to keep the number of their Basotho employees to a strict minimum. Building of roads, tunnels, dams, and other projects requiring heavy machinery will generally call for semiskilled Basotho workers trained in (or currently working in) South Africa — not unemployed, unskilled townspeople, who most need employment. Industries are no panacea for Lesotho's ills; in fact, they may prove to aggravate them. Farmers and young people should be encouraged to remain in their own rural areas, where they are needed to use and to teach improved agricultural methods. Instead, new urban factories will help to draw the better-educated rural Basotho to towns, where many will remain without work, away from their families, living in ghettoes where most of them must share crowded rooms.

New industries should make use of local produce. However, with the exception of mohair for carpets and mud for bricks, most of the new factories required imported raw materials for their

329

production of candles, tires, paints, etc. The
furniture factory required imported wood; Lesotho
was long ago stripped of its trees. Even clay
for pottery must be shipped 600 miles from the
Cape. Thus, only a relatively small number of
Basotho who find work in Maseru's factories — and
several South African entrepreneurs — profit from
the more than $5 million invested in Lesotho in
the past few years. Hundreds of thousands of
others will remain basically untouched by such
"development": they include farmers, the urban
unemployed, and other Basotho who cannot afford
to use the electricity from Oxbow, to gamble at
the Holiday Inn, shop in the shopping center,
drive on the highway, fly from the airport, or
play golf and polo at the club. Consequently, a
major criticism of Lesotho's recent industrial
development effort was that it did not address
the real needs of the great majority of Basotho.

Part of the problem rested with Lesotho's
economic planners, or lack of them, in the mid-
1960's. An Economic Planning Unit, staffed by
British and U.N. economists, failed to produce
a development plan acceptable to the government
and was dissolved soon after independence. Another ineffective body, the National Planning
Board, was created under the constitution and
consisted largely of Basotho businessmen and
political leaders, white missionaries, and other
laymen. Each month, casual discussions by the
Board examined the possibility of introducing such
"development" as television, commercial helicop-
ters, and cable cars to carry tourists up the
Drakensberg Mountains. No official development
plan evolved until the present Central Planning
and Development Office was set up within the
Prime Minister's Office. In 1970 the First Five-
Year Development Plan was released by the Government. Hopefully it will stimulate industries
which make greater use of domestic resources, such
as village industries, food processing, and diamond

cutting. However, the plan's greatest strength is its primary emphasis on improvement in agriculture and livestock as the most important step toward economic independence. The stress by the forward-looking Basotho planners on the local exploitation of indigenous skills and resources is a dramatic sign of the timely, necessary shift away from over-reliance on unproductive foreign aid and deceptive industrial planning.

Another central goal of the Government is to reduce recurrent expenditures, particularly Government salaries, so that more British aid will become available for development purposes. For several years an annual budget subsidy of about $10 million from the United Kingdom enabled the Basutoland Government to grow out of proportion to the nation's requirements. As the only large employer inside the country, the Government was a victim of Parkinson's Law: the bureaucracy devoured in salaries most of the funds it raised each year to keep itself in business. Little was left in the budget for initiating or maintaining productive development projects; nonetheless, a government job was Lesotho's primary status symbol. Students at the Universities of Lesotho, Botswana, and Swaziland, and those studying abroad, were intent on white-collar desk jobs; few sought training in areas of agriculture or technology where they were most needed. Voices were periodically raised to cut "deadwood" out of the Government, lower all Government salaries, reallocate funds from recurrent expenditure to development, and bolster effective agricultural and educational training — but with varying success.

On one hand, external sources of capital were necessary to create sound development projects. Yet in some cases, external aid seemed to have the effect of lessening pressure on Lesotho's leaders to search for domestic solutions to domestic problems. In the words of the anthropologist Mannoni, foreign assistance gave the leadership "a greater feeling of security while relieving them of the need to show initiative or assume responsibility."[10] The British produced in the Basotho civil servant a correct yet ineffective bureaucrat who, in Mannoni's words, "takes pleasure in performing some complicated administrative task, observing with pedantic correctness every rule and regulation, and not skipping a single formality, even if it serves no purpose at all."

During the first two years after independence there were only three references in public addresses by Government officials to the need for more self-reliance, more local effort, and less emphasis on outside aid. One speech by the Prime Minister was to welcome a group of American and Canadian volunteers to a work camp; it warned the Basotho involved to expect the volunteers to work not for them but with them. The second was a statement by the Minister of Economic Development about the need to improve local agricultural techniques through cooperatives without waiting for foreign advisors, tools, and fertilizers. The third speech, by the Minister of Finance, praised the independence of the diamond diggers who had worked hard, without much outside help, and had kept foreigners out of the diamond areas. These speeches might have been encouraging signs of the end of Lesotho's psychological dependence on outsiders — but I had drafted each one myself.

Self-Help

The disastrous results of unplanned development and over-reliance on foreign aid are dramatized by droughts and "food shortages," which have plagued Lesotho almost every year since 1965. Lesotho is "the perfect example," writes *New York Times*, "of what can be done to an ecology in less than 100 years."[11] The ecological crisis is due not so much to a lack of food as to an excess of mouths to feed — both animal and human. Too many cattle, sheep, and goats (at least 25 percent more than Lesotho's fragile ecology can bear) graze throughout the country; the grass cover has been stripped off, and most topsoil has washed away. The remaining soil lacks nutrients and is further weakened in some areas by excessive use of chemical fertilizers. The soil, moreover, does not hold the rains, which often turn to floods in springtime. With autumn come blinding dust storms. Crops have failed regularly in recent years. A picturesque Ministry of Agriculture publication for distribution abroad describes the problem as the Government saw it in 1970:

> This small country with a population of well over 1,000,000 people has been severely hit by intermittent droughts for the past five years. The state of underproduction of the staple grain and virtual starvation in some parts continued almost unabated to the present, punctuated here and there by an indifferent maize harvest and only one good wheat season. The downward trend in production was evident, as the climatic conditions became more and more unpredictable and a general desiccation of the country took place. This meant that the summer crop was wiped off and hope for winter ploughing dwindled to a point. Serious shortage of food supplies in the country loomed menacing above the horizon, and it became abundantly clear that the country's food supplies had reached disastrous proportions. . . . It is worth emphasizing that the procurement of (foreign) food supplies poses no problems. . . . The most serious problem facing us . . . is with respect to storage, transport, and distribution.[12]

In 1966 I worked in the Food for Work Self-help
Campaign as a project inspector, and later with the
Director, who had been given the politically deli-
cate job of overseeing the distribution of food aid
from abroad. Food for about 60,000 people per
month has to be distributed equitably among 800,000
Basuto — a job, as the Director himself said, that
was about as easy as dividing his last piece of
bread among his nine hungry children. The Director
was so besieged by requests for food from all over
the country that instead of turning anyone down,
he rarely came to his office. The purpose of the
campaign was twofold: to give people free food
from abroad during a drought and, in the process,
to stimulate village self-help — the building of
roads, water supplies, latrines — by giving food
only to villagers who were working on such projects.

The Lesotho Government had requested food dona-
tions from the World Food Program during the summer
of 1965-66, when the worst drought in 30 years had
caused widespread malnutrition, particularly among
children, and a few purported deaths from starva-
tion. A combination of red tape and negotiations
at F.A.O. offices, dock strikes, shipping delays,
food losses, pilferage, and spoilage prevented
the food from arriving until the following spring —
one of the wettest in years. For months rumors
had spread that food from abroad was on the way.
B.N.P. politicians, Cabinet Ministers, local chiefs,
and headmen, and District Commissioners promised
that anyone who worked on any self-help scheme
would receive at least one sack of cornmeal and
probably more — milk, eggs, even tins of meat.
Hundreds of village projects sprang up throughout
the lowlands. Women, the primary workers and
providers in Basuto families, picked up shovels,
picks, and pans, and began cutting "roads" into
the rocky, eroded soil. Politicians, anxious to
make promises in a country where sources of employment and food are decreasing as population
increases, attached no strings to their promises

334

of food. The World Food Program and the United States (which had donated most of the food under PL 480) stipulated only that the food could not be "sold or exchanged."

On paper it was an ambitious plan. The first transnational road over the mountains, for example, was to be built under the Self-Help Campaign by hundreds of villagers who lived along the way. But in fact, the program was a nightmare. Without proper planning and organization, scores of projects were undertaken which were either useless or harmful to the land, which had been parched and then flooded soon afterward. Thousands of workers, 90 percent of them women who had scraped haphazardly at the soil for months, received little food or none at all. Only a few villages, whose chiefs or representatives in Parliament were influential with the B.N.P. or with the Program Director, received their promised share of the food. Some villagers began projects, and received some food, then worked again but got nothing. The new "roads" were tracks that washed away, or became eroded gullies as the heavy rains turned to floods. In places, villagers began to expect food as payment for any work they undertook beyond their own doors. Roads, dams, and latrine pits were often abandoned and left to wash away in the rain. For who would maintain a road or dam for which he had seen no need in the first place?

As early as 1965, the B.C.P. warned its followers that food from abroad was a "bribe" by the Government to win support and a form of coercion to get them to work for almost nothing. B.C.P. leader Mokhele questioned the value of roads that would transport corrupt government officials in expensive cars. Good roads, he argued, would merely make it cheaper for the white storekeeper to drive his truck and to exploit his customers. Yellow cornmeal, he said, was a bribe from the "racist" American Government and would otherwise be fed to American livestock.

The Government's mistake in the Self-Help Campaign was not in "exploiting" free labor but in exaggerating the benefits of foreign aid and in failing to use the food to create a lasting spirit of self-help or community development. It failed to first ensure both that the local inhabitants felt an actual need for each project and that each project was technically sound. In several areas the Self-Help Campaign embittered thousands of women who had not been given the food they thought they deserved. In a few villages pipes laid for water supplies were cut at night by disappointed and bitter villagers. The Self-Help Campaign left a wake of eroded tracks, slashed pipes, and broken dams; few projects were maintained even briefly. The program in some cases even attracted workers away from their own fields where procious grain and vegetables needed harvesting.

The failure of such schemes dramatized the weakness of a system of dependency which relied on importation of resources which might have been developed within the nation itself. Before 1970, the failing Self-Help Campaign was endemic; too little effort was made by the Lesotho Government, in its preoccupation with impressive industrial plans, to emphasize the need for better farming and land use. Nothing whatsoever was done to help Basotho mothers with underfed children to limit the size of their families. None of the serious long-term implications of Lesotho's periodic droughts and food shortages were studied or publicly discussed — particularly the implications of malnutrition, hunger, and land use for population policies. To most Basotho citizens and higher officials, food shortages were no more than the chance results of natural factors far beyond their control, such as poor soil or adverse weather. The solution to the food crisis was rarely faced directly as the chronic domestic problem it actually was. Just as the Basotho farmer whose crop fails traditionally goes to his neighbor for food, Lesotho's leaders had always assumed they could go abroad for food aid. Because of such irresponsible and wishful thinking, Lesotho soil continued to wash away, food production decreased, and its population continued to explode as fast — and as dangerously — as any nation in Black Africa.

Diamond Diggers

If feeding programs dramatized the failure of dependence on foreign aid and a lack of self-reliance, the attempts of illicit Basotho diamond diggers in the 1960's to exclude all outside interference was a contrasting example of Basotho independence and self-reliance — in the extreme. Unlike the people of the lowlands, who had become accustomed to Government and foreign aid as well as white tourists and officials, the tough mountain tribesmen who dig for Lesotho's diamonds well above an altitude of 10,000 feet in the frozen Maluti Mountains get no outside help. With the exception of the one speech praising them mentioned above, they received no sympathy nor even the most basic services from their Government until after 1970. The lowlands have schools, clinics, police posts, and bus lines; in the diamond areas, these were rare. Survival there was a very constant, individual concern, for many reasons. It was illegal to dig for diamonds everywhere; in addition, most diggers bought and sold diamonds illegally smuggled in from South Africa. Contingents of Lesotho Mounted Police occasionally tried to arrest diggers and were killed or beaten. The Maluti Mountains where the illegal diggings are sited, are painfully cold in winter months: men, women, and children worked in ice and snow, often with bare feet and tattered clothes; some froze, drowned, or starved in the water digging pits. Very little dung for fuel was available in that treeless wasteland, and food was very scarce and expensive. Anyone who found a diamond was in danger of having it stolen or badly underpriced: he could show it only to a friend or to a buyer he could trust. The digger's equipment — a bucket, a shovel, and a wife or child to sort the washed gravel piece by piece — was very inefficient. Few diamonds were found in the piles of gravel, and even fewer were sold for a fair price.

Despite such obstacles, from 200 to 2,000 Basotho dug Lesotho's three large open diamond pipes during the 1960's. Only a few grew rich; many diggers who sold gemstones to licensed buyers had obtained them second- or third-hand from South Africans who smuggled them in from South African mines to avoid the ubiquitous officers of the Diamond Branch of the South African police. The unspoken policy of the Lesotho police was to encourage diamonds smuggled in from South Africa to be sold legally to one of Lesotho's dozen licensed buyers. The buyers export diamonds after Government inspection and pay a tax of 15 percent of the price paid. (One smuggler reasons that since Basotho men must leave their homes to work at low wages in the South African mines, it is only fair that some diamonds be smuggled back into Lesotho for its benefit!) In this way over $1 million worth of rough gem and industrial diamonds are exported annually from Lesotho.[13]

All these pressures forced the diggers to become independent, suspicious, and distrustful of the Government. Although their activities had annually brought the Government some $200,000 in taxes, the diggers became violently anti-Government.

In 1967, negotiations were opened between the Government and various international mining companies to arrange for modern mechanical prospecting and mining. The first agreement was signed in 1968 with the Rio Tinto Zinc Corporation (R.T.Z.) of London and South Africa. This was to be R.T.Z.'s first attempt at diamond prospecting, but the

Lesotho Government promised the nation that R.T.Z.'s multimillion-dollar Rand investment was sure to bring much more employment and revenue to the nation than could the primitive diggers, who only scratch the surface of the diamond pipes. The R.T.Z. agreement stipulated that the diggers would have to leave the pipe before prospecting could begin. Unfortunately the diggers' representatives, well-known as outspoken supporters of the opposition, were not first consulted in the matter.

Later, when local chiefs and the King had signed the necessary land leases, the Minister of Finance, then in charge of mining, flew to the diggings to explain why and how the diggers would have to remove themselves within a few weeks — without any compensation — if they did not wish to be removed after the deadline by force. Guarded by a phalanx of helmeted Basotho commandos of the select Police Mobile Unit, armed with machine guns and hand grenades, the Minister addressed a tattered, frightened group of 100 diggers who represented many others. Most diggers carried knobkerries, the old war clubs shaped like fists which are the party symbol of the B.C.P. and the sign of defiance against the Government and the white man. Some had pistols bulging beneath their blankets. After the Minister's departure, a gunfight broke out and several men were wounded.

This was typical of several violent confrontations between the diggers (most of whom either refused to budge or returned to the diggings when the police left) and the Government, which was very anxious to prove to international investors that their Lesotho ventures would be safe and profitable. R.T.Z. insisted that their operation would end abruptly if it caused any violence. In 1969 a foreign white geologist prospecting for the company was clubbed to death by diggers who refused to allow him near "their" diamonds; prospecting was temporarily discontinued. Months later, a white Rhodesian geologist was kidnapped by diggers. During the chaotic 1970 election, thousands of the diggers held protest meetings against the B.N.P. The Police Mobile Unit flew over the diggers' homes in planes piloted by white South Africans and dropped grenades, killing and crippling from 100 to 150 men and women.[14]

This and similar bloodletting have resolved none of the basic issues. Although the impoverished diggers could not have been a direct threat to the government, particularly since they were so far from the capital, they were nonetheless a psychological threat and a humiliation because of their independence and autonomy. No political disagreement has more dramatically illustrated the clash between dependence and independence in Lesotho, or has led to so much violence.

Summary

In order to achieve local economic growth, Lesotho must avoid extremes of excessive dependence, exemplified by the misnamed Self-Help Campaign, and uncompromising isolation, shown by the diamond diggers. Without more individual responsibility among Basotho farmers, teachers, and administrators, foreign assistance will continue to bring only very local short-term benefits, and may discourage local incentive. Outside aid is urgently required as well: programs for agriculture, family planning, preventive medicine, and nutritional education must be expanded as soon as possible with the help of foreign equipment and teachers wherever necessary. Practical training related to the needs of a rural economy must replace traditional "European" education: modern tools and methods for farming, animal husbandry, tanning, handicrafts, and other potentially profitable light industries must be adopted before the Lesotho economy can begin to catch up with its population explosion. Neither total self-reliance nor overdependence on aid can be sufficient.

Too many Basotho have not yet reached the stage of awareness which Professor Goulet would describe as that point when citizens of a developing nation realize that they are themselves primary agents of change. The preoccupation of the Basotho in the past with the white man's influence too often blinded them to the economic potential on their own doorstep: the foods and fruits they can grow and process and preserve; the wool and mohair output they can double; the carpets, blankets, baskets, clothes, souvenirs, and pottery they can make in their homes and sell to the world. Most important of all, the Basotho, and particularly their political and spiritual leaders, must recognize the central need for an ecological balance between population and resources which will be the only path to true self-sufficiency. Until every Basotho woman has the right, the responsibility, and the means to make an informed choice whether to bear children, all attempts to attain economic, political, and psychological freedom will eventually fail.

NOTES

1. Barclay's Bank, *Lesotho — An Economic Survey* (London: Barclay's Bank, 1970), pp. 3-30. Pamphlet.

2. Lesotho National Development Corporation (L.N.D.C.), *The Sky is the Limit in Lesotho* (Maseru: L.N.D.C., 1970).

3. Dr. O. Mannoni, *Prospero and Ciliban* (New York: Praeger, 1964), pp. 85-86.

4. Rev. E. Casalis, *The Basutos* (London, Nisbet 1961), p. viii.

5. Historical material in this section is based on Hugh Ashton, *The Basuto* (London: Oxford University Press, 1967), Ch. 1.

6. L.N.D.C., *op. cit.*

7. From a speech by the Prime Minister, quoted in Agricultural Information Service, *Drought Relief in Lesotho* (Maseru: Agricultural Information Service, 1970). Pamphlet, p. 3.

8. Casalis, *op. cit.*, p. 5.

9. L.N.D.C., *op. cit.*

10. Mannoni, *op. cit.*, p. 70.

11. *New York Times*, May 12, 1970, p. 14.

12. Agricultural Information Service, *op. cit.* pp. 1-2.

13. The most famous diamond was the "Lesotho Brown," weighing 601 carats, then the seventh largest diamond ever found.

14. *Johannesburg Star*, April 8, 1970, p. 2.

Administration in the Malawi Government and Its Relation to Social Change

by Henry J. Richardson III

This essay covers administration in the Government
of the Republic of Malawi, primarily focusing on
that portion connected with Malawi's foreign policy, as perceived by a black American serving in
the Ministry of External Affairs and living in
Malawi for two years.[1] Several background factors
which condition governmental administration are
considered first. Next, the administrative process is examined more closely in a functional
analysis of decision-making within the government.
In a final section, four policy implications are
drawn from the earlier discussion of administration and social change within the Malawi Government and Southern Africa.

If Malawi's foreign policy is thought of as
partly the arrangements which facilitate the flow
of resources necessary to its future development,
a relationship between administrative behavior in
this sector and social change relative to development becomes probable. Further, a working

343

premise of this inquiry is that, although the closeness of Malawi's relations with white South Africa and, to some extent, Portugal have rendered it the "odd man out" in the Organization of African Unity and other African forums, its administrative difficulties in foreign policy and other areas are similar to those of other African states, especially in Southern Africa. This is particularly true of the expatriate problem, endemic to Southern Africa. This assumption is plausible from the fact that the underlying governmental organization in all the independent black states of Southern Africa is drawn from the British model, subsequently flavored by local modifications. Proportionately large numbers of expatriate administrators, mostly British, work in those governments. On this basis, a survey of Malawi's governmental structure is in order.

Conditioning Factors
in the Malawi
Government

Authority Factors
    The substantive business of the government is carried on in some 11 ministries, each headed and represented in the Cabinet by a Minister or the President.[2] Reporting to the Minister as the civil service head of each Ministry is a Permanent Secretary (P.S.), followed in some cases by a Deputy Secretary, and then by one or more Under Secretaries (U.S.). Then come the Senior Assistant Secretaries (S.A.S.). In the Ministry of External Affairs, First, Second and Third Secretaries follow, each holding the civil service rank of Administrative Officer (A.O.), of which there are three grades. Next come the clerical and supportive ranks (as distinguished from the above policy-making ranks), beginning with the Executive Officers of several grades, and then the Clerical Officers of several

grades. This essay is concerned with interactions among policy-making officials.

Any discussion of administration in the Malawi Government must hinge on the position of the first and only President of Malawi and Life President of the Malawi Congress Party, Dr. H. Kamuzu Banda. Under the Malawi constitution of 1966, the Government is parliamentary in form, featuring a strong Executive. In fact, it might be more accurate to say that the Executive power dominates and the Parliament plays a ratifying role. The constitution gives the President substantial autonomy to take a wide range of action without reference to Parliament; it was seemingly drafted with this result in view. Furthermore, Parliament never dissents from the President's reports of past and future action but endorses both overwhelmingly. Finally, under the constitution, Cabinet Ministers are appointed, reassigned, and dismissed by the President (three need not be Members of Parliament), and the Cabinet as a body has only an advisory role in policy-making authority vis-à-vis the President: he is not obliged to accept its recommendations.

As for the relationship between the Malawi Congress Party and the governmental process relative to making national policy, the President seems to hold the same kind of authority with respect to the Party that he does in regard to Parliament.

The President's relationship to his Ministers was doubtless influenced by the attempted coup d'état of 1964-65 led by four younger dissenting Ministers, including the then Minister of Education, Henry Chipembere, the only other figure in the Cabinet with demonstrated national appeal. We need not explore in detail here the reasons for the split. Suffice it to say that they included both reasons of political substance — whether to accept an offered 18 million development loan from the People's Republic of China — and reasons of style and personality conflict — the President's habit of referring in public to his Ministers

345

(almost all of whom were a generation younger) in a generally paternalistic manner. The attempted coup was forcibly crushed in early 1965 and the dissenting Ministers fled to Zambia and Tanzania, whence they attempted to rally opposition to Banda while maintaining their base of support within Malawi in preparation for a possible return to power. This has not yet happened, and its probability grows more dim with time.

There is some reason to believe that Dr. Banda reacted to this attempted overthrow not only as a political threat but also as a personal betrayal, at least partially analogous to the feelings of a father toward a wayward son.[3] He was thought to be very close personally to at least three of the Ministers, and all had supported his return to then-Nyasaland in 1958 to unite the territory in its drive to independence. On the basis of this closeness and of the fact that they had generally supported him prior to Malawi's formal independence on July 6, 1964, Dr. Banda might well have felt personally betrayed by their resignations and attempt to oust him. As a result, the President conceived a deep distrust of most Malawi politicians and policy-making civil servants. A majority of the latter in Zomba, the capital, had supported the attempted coup. The President was then disposed to surround himself with British expatriate administrators seconded to the Malawi Government. This was not the sole reason for the presence of many such officers in the upper echelons of the government, but it appears to have been an important contributing factor.

The President's distrust seems to have persisted for approximately two years, from early 1965 to mid-1967. During that period the Cabinet established in October, 1964, remained generally constant in personnel except for the addition of two Ministers, though there were reshuffles of portfolios. The Cabinet was of unquestioned loyalty and did not dissent from the President's poli-

346

cies; with two or three exceptions, members tended to defer their legitimate decision-making authority to that of the President if the question entailed the least political or economic risk. As a result, the President — partly by design and partly by the chain of events — has tended to decide not only those governmental questions flowing to him from his constitutionally delegated functions and formally assumed ministries, but also many questions from other ministries as well.

However, there were indications in 1967 that the President's apparent general distrust of Malawians in policy-making positions was abating. The first Malawian Secretary was appointed as Secretary for External Affairs, to be followed shortly by similar appointments to the positions of Secretary of Education, Secretary of Local Government, and Secretary of Trade and Industry. Again, the President's attitude is not the sole explanation for these appointments, but it seems to have been a contributing factor. During the same period, other Malawians began being promoted to the ranks of Senior Assistant Secretary and Under Secretary in a visible incremental pattern.

The President's complete political dominance casts broad administrative reflections within the government. Anyone known to have access to his ear and to give advice that he respects — notably the Attorney-General and Secretary to the President and Cabinet, who is a British Queen's Counsel — immediately acquires substantial influence on a particular issue, especially if he plausibly purports to be acting on or conveying the President's wishes. For the Attorney-General this is the case on a broad range of issues, as it is with several other expatriates, perhaps two Ministers and at least one of the Malawian Secretaries. Within the government, whatever Dr. Banda says, goes.

When translated into governmental terms, however, his authority and directives must be seen as a large rug under which several rabbits might play undisturbed unless they threaten the basic position of the rug. Even though the President personally involves himself in many relatively minor matters, he obviously must rely on his Ministers, advisors, and subordinates to carry the basic burden of executing his policies. As mentioned, most of the key high-middle-level administrators in the government (as opposed to the Malawi Congress Party, M.C.P.) who thus have access to the President are British expatriates, though as noted, an increasing number of Malawians are entering these positions. Therefore, most of the officials who recommend new or revised policies, or the termination of policies, are the same expatriates or few Malawians, as are those who are charged with reporting the President's policies to the rest of the government and interpreting their meaning, and who hold prime responsibility for their implementation. In practice, once a policy is laid down from above in general terms, this group of officials (especially the British expatriates) is in a position collectively or in part, if they wish, to delay its execution, to modify it within plausible limits, to shade its meaning, and over time (unless the President keeps a close personal watch over its execution) to convert the original directive into a different policy.

One example will suffice to illustrate the problem. In early 1968, the President and Cabinet decided after considerable deliberation that the basic salary scales of expatriate and Malawian civil servants should be equalized. Acting under the Cabinet directive, the Establishments Division drew up revised requirements for promotion which were supposed to correspond with the new policy. But the actual and calculated effect of these new promotion scales was to make the promotion of Malawians holding the posts of Senior Assistant Secretary up to the post of Under Secretary considerably more difficult and lengthy than for ex-

348

patriate officers. These scales were drafted solely by expatriate officers without reference to the President or any Minister. When they were published in the Government Gazette, the actual effects of the new scales became apparent. The result was raw outrage among Malawians throughout the government. It is safe to say that all top-ranking Malawian officers, even fervent believers in cooperation with expatriates, felt the most intense hostility and resentment that their careers were put in jeopardy by aliens acting on the basis of outright prejudice. Ultimately, the scales were revised in a more equitable fashion, but not before the matter, against stiff expatriate opposition, was carried to the President in the strongest terms by one Minister who has no love lost for the British. However, the same or similar expatriates remain in a position to attempt similar (though perhaps more subtle) schemes in future.

Localization
     Some background on localization policy is useful here. Current Malawi policy originated in a committee established for that purpose in August, 1960, under the chairmanship of A. L. Adu, then head of the Ghanaian Civil Service. At that time in Nyasaland, out of fewer than 2,000 senior service posts, 104 were held by Africans; none had reached the superscale level; nine were in the Administrative or Professional grades, of whom eight were in an administrative cadre of 95. It was clear that the colonial administration was racist in structure.[4] The primary recommendations of the Committee were
     1. The localization of the civil service at the greatest rate compatible with acceptable standards.
     2. The training of technical and specialist staff through schemes to be drawn up by the ministries.

3.   The establishment of an Institute of Public Administration, to train local cadres for the Administrative and Executive grades.

These recommendations have since been carried out in the main. From the beginning the then Prime-Minister-designate Banda insisted that localization must not become a fetish and emphasized the need of expatriate civil servants for some years to come. Nevertheless, by Independence Day (July 6, 1964) about 40 percent of the expatriates in government had left or indicated their intention to leave. At the beginning of 1966, below the superscale level, there were 570 Malawians in the Public Service, as compared with 901 expatriates. The superscale level remained dominated by expatriates. Some 420 Malawians abroad in 1966 returned as trained men at varying times up to 1969. In 1968, there were 248 expatriates listed in the Malawi Government Directory serving as principal officers in the central Government (including the boards of the statutory bodies but excluding the Municipal Councils), out of a total number of 409 principal officers, approximately 61 percent. Below the Under Secretary and superscale level in the ministries there were 32 Senior Assistant Secretaries, of whom 15 were expatriates, and 49 Administrative Officers, of whom 14 were expatriates. At the present a qualification for entry to the Public Service as an A.O. is the completion of a nine-month training course at the Institute of Public Administration at Mpemba, which will soon be superseded by a diploma in public administration from the University of Malawi.[5]

Under Malawi's localization, the expatriate officer retained full authority and perquisites so long as he held that government post. Supposedly the rationale for his holding it was one of strict merit. But so long as he was registered in the Public Service at a certain grade, that post could not be localized until either the expatriate's tour ended and he chose to leave (often unwillingly) — sometimes a difficult process when only a few years remained until his retirement (with the British government preferring that he finish his career in Malawi instead of shipping him back home) — or another post at the same level was found in the Service. These two factors slowed localization considerably and introduced influences other than merit: the provision of as much sunlight as possible at the end of old colonialists' careers and the amount of influence which British expatriates as a group could mobilize. Recently, however, there has been evidence of a slow but steady upward movement of Malawians within the Service; seven now serve as Permanent Secretaries. This general policy must be contrasted with that carried out by some other African governments of localizing key posts immediately after independence, thus giving Africans the authority and perquisites of the post while retaining expatriates as advisors, where needed, outside the civil service line of seniority.

The expatriate problem must be seen in light of the handwriting on the wall in Malawi. Ultimately expatriates will not be needed or will not be allowed to serve in the Government except in limited advisory capacities. The timing of Africanization of governmental and commercial posts is one of the most emotive problems in all Africa, certainly in East and Southern Africa. This is in part true because of widespread suspicion (well-founded in Malawi) that expatriates — especially British and increasingly South African — continue to try to run the government and expand their influence as much as possible even though it is not "their" government.[6]

A closer look at British expatriates as a group, especially the older ones, is in order. Their loyalties are almost inevitably divided, for they are British subjects on loan to the Malawi Government, and they are paid by both the Malawi Government as their employer of the moment and

351

"topped off" by the British Government which has
loaned them to Malawi. Since they remain dependent on Her Majesty's Service for their career
advancement, seniority, and pensions, they retain
professional, emotional, and social ties to the
United Kingdom and to similar groups in both white
and black Southern Africa. One result is that the
British High Commission in Malawi (the British
embassy) has in certain situations strong though
informal influence on the high civil service level
of the Malawi Government in the formation or implementing of policies. These ties are not the
sole source of such influence (e.g., Malawi is the
world's third largest recipient of British aid),
but they are a recognizable factor and cause considerable resentment among Malawian civil servants
and Ministers.

A related factor is that meritorious service
in Malawi can qualify such men for honors (e.g.,
Commander of the British Empire) given each year
by Her Majesty's Government. Since most of the
officers in line for such honors tend to occupy
important posts in the Malawi Government, one
can stongly suggest that they would be reluctant
to formulate or implement any Malawi policy causing
discomfort to Britain even though it might be in
Malawi's best interests. An additional, related
characteristic of some of these officers is to
seek to connect their names with the largest possible number of government projects and committees,
without accomplishing much of substance. This
tactic, conscious or unconscious, aims to give
London the impression of great service and achievement to consider for the next Honors List.

Still another characteristic of many such expatriates is their desire to make a second career
or to retire in South Africa after their tours in
Malawi. This assumes added significance in view
of increased South African influence in Malawi.
For instance, at the time that the Labor Agreement
was concluded between Malawi and South Africa in

1967, the Secretary for Labor was a British expatriate; around that time he was also negotiating
a job in labor affairs with a private company in
South Africa, to begin at the end of his tour in
Malawi. As civil service head of the Ministry
of Labor, he was regarded as the natural initiator
and coordinator of the approaches to the Agreement to be made with the South African Government.
In fact, however, there was notorious reticence
by the Labor Ministry to provide the necessary initiative; ultimately the required coordination
came from the Ministry of External Affairs. A
conference with South African officials to resolve
outstanding problems on the Agreement was tenta-
tively scheduled for the date of the Secretary's
departure from Malawi Government service. Un-
abashedly, he suggested that since he was driving
to South Africa to take up his new job and would
be in the Republic at the scheduled time of the
meeting, he should arrive and represent Malawi
in those discussions (receiving salary, per diem,
etc.), send his report back with another Malawi
official, who would fly to those discussions specifically for that purpose, and then immediately
end his Malawi career and continue on to Capetown.
Fortunately, his kind offer was refused.

In this case it was apparent that his coming
employment is South Africa, in the same field in
which he served in Malawi, seemed likely to dissuade
him from making strong representations to the South
African Government on labor questions, although
these had the President's approval. Further, this
apparent reason for his reticence was noted, in
some cases bitterly, by all concerned policy-making
Malawian civil servants. Finally, he seemed ob-
livious to the conflict of interest likely in such
an arrangement.

Three further points should be made regarding
expatriates. The ex-colonial expatriates seem to
have an incredible degree of loyalty toward Dr.
Banda personally, perhaps because they feel their

security of tenure is greater so long as he is in
power, but also perhaps because of their gratitude
for the lack of what they consider the officially
sanctioned racism present in Zambia and Tanzania
against white expatriates. Second, relatively
few of these expatriates uphold the highest traditions of government service. They are competent,
in some cases exceptionally so, and work many hours
overtime. They work with the best interests of
Malawi's future as an independent African state
at heart, with a sincere appreciation of the challenges facing their Malawian co-workers, without
the air of "superior civilization" or heavy pa-
ternalism so distressingly prevalent, and relate
to them as fellow men with a number of shared
problems. Finally, on a few occasions, expatriate
civil servants have criticized government policy
in ways with which their Malawian colleagues sym-
pathized but evidently did not dare say so. This
criticism was sometimes motivated not solely by
antagonism to ministerial or Presidential policies,
but also by certain antagonisms within the British
expatriate group. For example, some older expatriates feel somewhat hostile toward the Secretary-
to-the President/Attorney General. They consider
him a "new boy," a kind of parvenu who, without
paying appropriate dues in terms of length of
service or background, has attained his present
position by personal brilliance, luck, and perhaps
other factors and has thus denied an opportunity
for influence to an "old boy."

The President's Moods
     The daily moods of Dr. Banda are of central
concern because he is the decision-making center
of the government, the one point at which a bottleneck of any duration cannot be afforded, given
the government's present structure. These moods
were a subject of daily conversation among top
Malawian and expatriate policy-making officials
who often reported directly to and received in-

structions from the President. This group also included all Ministers and Ambassadors resident in Blantyre. Doubtless such information was passed by telephone or face-to-face by those among the first to have an audience on any given day.

When Dr. Banda was known to be in bad humor, questions of policy which even on the best days would receive doubtful assent or sharp questioning would be postponed in their presentation until later, except in an emergency. One of Dr. Banda's hallmarks is a notable temper and an ability to tongue-lash those who disagree with him at the wrong time or whose mistakes or incompetence become known to him. It was, according to those in a position to know, an experience that few cared to risk. One school of thought also held that on questions at the tipping point, in the penumbra between receiving a Presidential "yes" or "no," their presentation when he was in a bad mood would surely produce a negative. Consequently, adherents of this school arranged their appointments with him accordingly, if at all possible.

The Lack of Money

An overriding factor inevitably present in the attitudes of government administrators was the constant, notorious, all-consuming lack of money. This perhaps overstates the case, but the situation in the government of a desperately poor African country goes beyond the mere tyranny exercised in other situations by penny-pinching administrators in conjunction with a fanatical finance ministry or accounting office. Here, the attitude of "no money available" stalks the corridors like an angel of death, dulling the imagination and seriously reducing the perceptions of all concerned relative to what is or is not possible. In the Ministry of External Affairs this angel prevented Malawi representation at several international conferences from which she might have benefited, and in time prevented serious

consideration of sending such representatives to
many promising international gatherings. It
reached all the way down: to limiting the number
of new books to be ordered for the Ministry library to fewer than 10 per year, and to a government-wide campaign to reuse envelopes for inter-
ministerial communication. This is not to complain
that these measures were unjustified — they were
not — but to convey the resulting attitudes inside
the government.

One of the outcomes of this pall on the general
spirit was a reticence in some ministries to think
seriously about interministerial planning in ex-
pansive terms requiring increased future expenditures. This was especially true in terms of acquisition of new posts at the A.O. level. Such
planning was done; but the atmosphere was rarely
conducive to the increased expenditure being seriously discussed with the Ministry of Finance or
the Office of the President, unless a way was
found to cover that expenditure by foreign aid
from outside governments or under previously allocated expenditures. Therefore, imaginative initiatives in this category tended to be filed
away rather than examined fully on their merits.
It is perhaps worth noting that factors supporting
this pessimistic fiscal attitude were the visible
reduction of British budgetary and development
aid, and a phasing out of assistance from U.S.A.I.D.

In more development-oriented ministries, however, the problem was just the opposite: too much
imagination in the face of rampant poverty produced a profusion of plans for projects, administration, and growth. Departmental ambitions were
often confused with the welfare of the country as
a whole; many projects were advocated in the interest of expanding a particular administrative domain.
It was perhaps to force penury to affect development planning that the President set up a planning
unit of economists and created the Ministry of
Economic Affairs. It was hoped that the planning

unit would achieve an overarching perspective on development to determine the priorities of specific plans, and that the latter would force top administrators to think in government-wide terms and grapple with ordering priorities between development sectors. Both of these techniques seem to have been unsuccessful.

The Administrative Process

There are several possible approaches to analyzing the administrative process of the Malawi Government. For a small government where the number of policy-makers and available resources is limited, where authority is concentrated in a visible elite, and where the focus of inquiry is generally the top policy-making stratum of a wider process, the most useful approach is a functional analysis of decision-making. Such a methodology has been developed by Myres McDougal and Harold Lasswell.[7] Decision-making can be conceptualized as a process in terms of seven decision functions in policy-making: intelligence-gathering, recommendation, prescription, invocation, application, appraisal, and termination. We will consider Malawi Government behavior under each, keeping in mind that functions may overlap and be performed by the same official(s) almost simultaneously.
Subsequently, the administrative process will itself be considered as an arena of social change, especially relative to the problem of localization and the general question of the expatriates' role in Malawi national life.

Intelligence-gathering
We include the gathering and processing of information for making decisions and future estimates. The lack of reliable information on the component factors of decisions to be made is often pervasive.

In the Ministry of External Affairs this lack evidenced itself, for example, in the response of other African states to difficulties about diplomatic privileges and immunities; in uncertainty as to the amount of money available for future ministerial expansion; in uncertainty whether the Office of the President or other ministries had presented policy recommendations within the legislative responsibility of External Affairs to the President — and whether he had adopted or rejected them. Lack of an adequate library meant there was insufficient background material on many international issues, particularly on African response to such issues. Two examples are the paucity of information available regarding the operation on the continent of the Madrid Convention on Patents and Trademarks, and the work done by various international organizations on many development issues.

Information was persistently lacking on the administrative responses of other African states to many problems. Information on (and sometimes coordination with) the foreign policies of other African governments was provided by the Mission at the United Nations, from direct correspondence using diplomatic channels, and through infrequent personal contacts. But there was little sharing of extended administrative experience and problems, perhaps caused by Malawi's position as "the odd man out." The need for this sharing was impelled by a general desire to develop an African way of meeting challenges and formulating solutions in light of African experience. There was an implicit realization that most of the information relied upon for decision-making even about trends in Africa originated from non-African sources. Which brings us to another characteristic of intelligence-gathering.

One aspect of the expatriate problem was the general tendency of those who had served tours in former British colonies outside Africa to present uncritically policy precedents from their former colonial experience as guides for Malawi policy. Frequently the net effect was a reluctance to demand or search for data for a decision rooted in current Malawian needs, but instead to argue that British colonial experience must provide the guiding precedent. Thus, in drafting a model air services agreement for use in future negotiations, available African precedents were consistently downgraded by the then expatriate-dominated Ministry of Transport and Communication, in favor of British-negotiated air agreements in Malaysia.

Intelligence-gathering must be seen as a spectrum of greater or lesser availability of information on a given issue. Data from international organizations were available on some development questions. Some needed books were provided by embassies and foundations. Insights on foreign policy matters were sometimes available to the President from Party and other sources. But recognizing this spectrum did not eliminate the prevalent shortage of information. Consequently, available information tended to be regarded as more valid than prudence perhaps dictated, precisely because it was often the only information.

The information shortage was also accentuated by a relative lack of intelligence-gathering technology. The phone system between Blantyre, the commercial center and site of several governmental ministries, and Zomba worked sporadically and had limited capacity, impeding communication between government ministries. Within ministries there was a shortage of photocopying machines, impeding the processing and dissemination of information.

Much available information came from other government ministries, both orally and in writing. Available tabular data was welcomed, but the pressures of decision-making in an understaffed and overworked ministry (a fair description of most Malawi government ministries) led to a preference for receiving conclusions supported by the briefest necessary account of the underlying data; this preference seemed to be Government-wide.

A special problem for the Ministry of External
Affairs, probably shared by all ministries for
which the President either acted as Minister or
relative to whose subject matter the President had
strong opinions, was that the President had his own
sources of intelligence on domestic and foreign
events. This information was often unavailable to
the officials upon whom he called for policy recommendations. The result was that the information
which underlay the Ministry's recommendation might
be superseded, reducing its relevance and sometimes
generating a sense of futility and frustration in
the authors. At other times, however, private information would come down from the President's
Office with a request for a new policy recommendation.

A direct connection of the Ministry of External
Affairs to the administration of social change was
its involvement in negotiating technical assistance
arrangements. This involvement arose after External
Affairs made it clear that it could not advise on
the adequacy of such arrangements for intergov-
ernmental negotiations without policy-making participation in preparing Malawi's proposals. In
this context, the Ministry played the role of in-
telligence-gatherer relative to the requirements
and attitudes of the foreign government, and intelligence dispenser to other governments on
Malawi's wishes. Information was shared in both
written and oral form, often at interministerial
meetings at the Under Secretary-Senior Assistant
Secretary level, on the one hand, and negotiations
at the official level with representatives of
foreign governments, on the other.

Recommendation
       "Recommendation" refers here to proposals and
their promotion for one or several future prescriptions from lesser to more authoritative officials. or between officials of equal rank.

The form of most policy recommendations, including those from the Secretary up to the President, was a "minute" — a written memo of one or two pages entered on a file addressed to another official. Recommendations were formulated by several combinations of officials. Those for decisions on important matters went through the Secretary, who decided whether the matter should be referred to his Minister or the President. The outstanding exception was an interministerial committee established by the Cabinet. These committees operated at the level of Secretary-Under Secretary and included other relevant officials, and recommended action directly to the Cabinet through its chairman or through the concerned Minister.

There was a key exception to the general rule that the Secretary reported directly either to his Minister or to the President. On issues involving the Office of the President, or which had a component in which the President was known to be continually interested, the Secretary reported both to his Minister and to the Secretary to the President and Cabinet. This enhanced the latter's influence; he could report back the President's directions and remand policy recommendations from other parts of the government to himself, a Minister, or the President.

Within each ministry the Secretary might devise several arrangements to provide him or the Under Secretary(s) with policy recommendations. One was to assign a question to a Senior Assistant Secretary or below, with instructions to report a recommendation directly back to him and not through the Under Secretary or other intervening official, except perhaps to "keep them in the picture." Another was to assign the question *en gros* to the Under Secretary, who in turn could make his own arrangements, with the intent that it be resolved at the lowest possible level. External Affairs, for instance, had several A.O.'s responsible for specific areas, such as European affairs.

Incoming questions would normally go to them first
for action at the lowest level. They in turn
would report to either the S.A.S. or U.S. and up
to the P.S. if necessary. Combinations of these
two methods were also employed.

Financial and personnel administrative questions were generally advised on in each ministry
by a Finance and Establishments Officer (F.E.O.),
who usually reported directly to the P.S. Each
P.S. took care to insure that final decisions
on these matters effectively remained in his own
hands. In the Malawi Government this post carried
added social significance, since advice was given
on questions of promotion in rank and of Africanization of posts held by Europeans, and since for
the first few years after independence this post
was generally held by a European.

This latter fact must be seen in the context
of the close cooperation inherent in the F.E.O.
post in each ministry with the Establishments
Division — the department in the Office of the
President responsible for personnel matters throughout the government — which is expatriate-dominated.
An African P.S. was in danger of being outflanked
should his European F.E.O. disagree with his opinion and attempt to mobilize support among his social cronies at Establishments or elsewhere in the
Office of the President and Government. This was
especially likely when the P.S. attempted to Afri-
canize a post in his ministry held by a European
who was well-entrenched and wished to remain there
until his retirement. Such confrontations echoed
throughout the government. Often they were resolved by the Secretary to the President, who
seemed inclined to retain the expatriate, all
other things being equal. Many Malawians feel
that his bias went further than this. On these
questions the top Malawian officers in the government maintained close communication to counter
maneuvers by expatriates who were often supported
by the British High Commission. The morale of

Malawian officials from A.O. and above depended significantly on the outcomes of these confrontations.

Recommendation and intelligence-gathering offered perhaps the greatest opportunities for the penetration of foreign influence into the government. Aid agencies, hired experts, and embassies provided policy recommendations on various issues. For instance, the British Government granted Malawi its third largest amount of development aid, including the seconding of expatriates to the Malawi Government as administrators.[8] These administrators held Malawi Government-established posts with titles and perquisites; they were also British subjects residing in a foreign land. Long British experience in administration fixed in their minds a weighty presumption as to patterns of future administration. Accordingly, the situation was a natural one for the British High Commission to recommend on Malawi governmental administrative problems and to be concerned about the happiness of its citizens. This concern was enhanced by social and sometimes familial ties. The expatriate community in Malawi remains decidedly separate from Africans, except for token social contacts and a few genuine friendships. While the British presence is most familiar, other countries have similar positions of influence due to aid or other relationships, notably West Germany, South Africa, France, and the United States.

Prescription

"Prescription" refers to the articulation of policies as general requirements of future decisions, by persons expected to have the authority to do so.

It is necessary here to consider the relationship of law to the administrative process. We have already noted the dominance of the President over the Parliament and Cabinet. Since all Ministers, save possibly three, were Members of Parliament, they sat when it was in session and with the President proposed the majority of legislation. This made the approval of the President or Cabinet the critical step in the legislative process: generally, all else was prologue.

The administrative authority of each ministry was fixed by legislation, but frequently there was overlap, especially concerning responsibility for administering specific laws. Lawmaking in Malawi, and perhaps in any African country at this historical moment, seems a less deliberative process than in, for instance, the United States. The time span between the felt need by the Executive for a new governmental policy and a legislative enactment to implement it or to justify what is already being done is shorter than in countries where the roles of the Executive and legislature have been defined and separated by crisis and by history. This was true in Malawi, whether a question involved drafting new legislation or amending old. The substance of new legislation was proposed within individual ministries, to pass for approval through the P.S. via a Minister to the Cabinet or to the President. Sometimes it was proposed by Members of Parliament, but never in opposition to a known wish or policy of the President. Upon his approval it was drafted by the Ministry of Justice.

A key role in this approval was played by the Secretary to the President, wearing his Attorney-General's hat. His approval of the subject matter of the proposed legislation and his recommendation to the President that he grant approval were critical. His opposition was usually conclusive unless the President chose to disregard his advice; how often this happens is not known.

Thus, the interaction between legislative and administrative policies was often lively and intense, especially in ministries such as Finance, Development and Planning, Trade and Industry, and the Office of the President. Law was seen

364

not only as a series of communications prescribing policies, but sometimes also as a series of un-wanted restraints on actions for which there was a need strongly felt by individual ministries or the President. Often the administrative response to the President was to seek to interpret the legislation so as to accomplish as little as possible of the desired policy while remaining within its substance, and at the same time to demand its amendment or repeal. This was some-what enhanced by the absence of lawyers officially attached to ministries, except External Affairs, to aid in this interpretation. Legal interpre-tation was the responsibility of the Ministry of Justice for all save questions of international law. But this referral arrangement suffered from the general unfamiliarity of Justice with the cur-rent policy concerns of the referring ministry, and from the inevitable lapse of time required for an answer.

This relationship between law and administra-tive policy owes much to the preeminent position of Malawi's President. But the intensity of this relationship seemed also generated by (1) Malawi's being a poor African country with enormous devel-opment problems for which law-as-legislation is perceived as one solution; (2) the initial burst of legislation immediately after independence, now being appraised by the Government in response to demands from the people and to some perception of the efficacy of its enforcement locally; and (3) a better appreciation by the Government of its own needs and goals. These three factors seem to be Africa-wide.

Another problem was that of ascertaining what guidance or command the law gave on a particular issue. This belonged to the Ministry of Justice, but its problems in finding the law are revealing. A decreasing but significant amount of law of several origins was in force simultaneously in Malawi. First, the received acts of British leg-

365

islation were incorporated into the laws of the
former Nyasaland under the authority of various
Orders-in-Council. Next, the enactments of the
Governor-General of Nyasaland and the Territorial
Legislature became Malawi law. This situation continued until 1953 and the formation of the Federation of Rhodesia and Nyasaland; the legislature
at Salisbury produced superseding legislation for
those areas in which it had plenary authority.
In December, 1963, the Federation was dissolved;
the Territorial Legislature and the Governor-
General again became the local sovereign authorities. On July 6, 1964, Malawi became independent, with effective sovereign authority passing
from the British Crown to the Malawi State, a
process symbolically completed in 1966, when
Malawi became a republic. The Parliament began
to enact legislation in 1964 which both repeated
colonial legislation on a temporary basis and took
new directions. By 1968 much, but not all, of the
colonial legislation had been reconsidered and
superseded. Consequently, the "law of Malawi"
included a backlog of five kinds of legislative
enactments plus African customary law in areas
such as rights of succession and criminal law.[9]

To answer a question of law under these conditions required a thoroughly cross-indexed and
updated legislative compilation; few were available outside the Ministry of Justice, and even
those were suspect because of the loose-leafed
complexity of updating. Therefore, authoritative
versions of law-as-legislation-plus-precedent were
relatively unknown in the Government except by
hearsay among officials. The situation was
alleviated somewhat by written requests for legal
interpretations and by provision of partial com-
pilations in other ministries. To remedy this
confusion, a Commissioner for the Revision of
Laws worked for two years in conjunction with
Justice and the Cabinet to repeal remaining colonial legislation and prepare a definitive, updated version of the Malawi laws. This is now
complete.

In Malawi legislation, delegations of power to the Executive are made by reference to the authority of the President or Minister to take or refrain from taking certain action. Therefore, much of the Secretary's authority derives from these delegations to the Minister, to be implemented by him under the Minister's general instructions, as civil service head of that ministry. Not surprisingly, a certain amount of tension existed between the Cabinet and some members of the upper echelons of the Public Service. This tension was grounded partly in their different areas of concern: the Minister was concerned with political pressures on him in the context of the Party, his local constituency, and his relationship with the President, as well as with the merits of the issues facing his ministry. The P.S. was concerned primarily with issues and events in his ministry and with solving problems according to the best knowledge available. Tension resulted if the Minister decided an issue arising out of the ministry on political grounds little related to the merits of the problem. Depending on the Minister, the P.S. might be concerned when the former sought to intervene directly in the administrative process, fearing that the latter, not appreciating the nonpolitical subtleties of the problems, would make a disastrous decision difficult or impossible to reverse.

The imported tradition of the Public Service is that of dedicated service to the State with complete noninvolvement in political affairs. While it is quite possible for a Minister in an African government to head a ministry, the substantive issues confronting which he has little or no expertise to deal with, it is probably impossible for the top officials in the same ministry to be unaware of the political currents and pressures within that government and of how their actions would affect them. They may choose to refrain from acting in an overtly political manner and abstain from overt participation in political maneuvering. But they cannot be said to be isolated from politics, as they would tend to be in the larger, tradition-bound bureaucracies of Western governments.

The Secretary of the ministry is known within and outside the government as the person to see "to get things done," primarily because of his general range of discretion in implementing prescribed policies, and because the weight of his policy recommendations is accepted often enough on routine matters to be virtually a policy prescription, if it does not sharply depart from previous policies or action. This prescription-equivalent would not generally be true if the Minister, or especially the President, were personally concerned with the success of the policy. Usually the P.S. is the authoritative spokesman on a policy for his ministry vis-à-vis the rest of the government, or for the government vis-à-vis the public.

Invocation

"Invocation" means the making of a preliminary demand or appeal to a prescription in the hope of influencing the results of governmental action to meet a particular situation. Our concern is to identify the arrangements for making these appeals. To invoke a policy already prescribed implies an audience or target group(s) to which the policy is invoked. Target groups include such groups within the government, e.g., officials and Ministers in other ministries, and those outside the government.

Relative to both groups, not every instance of invocation is motivated by problem-solving objectivity. A policy may be invoked to fulfill a separate interest of the invoker or of some group with which he is connected, or to preserve consistency within the government and in the actions of a Minister or the President (though for the latter this must be seen as an advisory reminder and not as a limitation of his power).

With respect to government groups, invocation often takes the form of a demand in the name of the President or a Minister for action to apply the policy involved (application will be subsequently considered). Sometimes the President will select the policy to be invoked in particular circumstances. Often, however, a policy will be invoked by the officials who gathered the intelligence on which it is founded, recommended it to the authoritative decision-maker, and drafted or otherwise suggested the form in which it was prescribed. The demand at the core of the invocation is made by that Secretary or Minister charged by the President, Cabinet, or legislation to implement the policy, to the ministry he heads, to other ministries, to the business community, quasi-government corporations, and the public at large. This demand may be accompanied by an authoritative instruction from a higher level that necessary cooperation be forthcoming from other officials.

Often it is both a prescribed policy and the authoritative directions for its implementation which are invoked; this is especially true at the level of Secretary vis-à-vis other ministries. A demand by one Secretary to another for partial implementation, accompanied by an authoritative instruction for cooperation, produces considerable leverage. Herein lies a major source of the Secretary's influence upon the President and Cabinet: he has access to the President, from whom he can receive instructions on various policies to be transmitted by him to several Secretaries. Alternatively, those instructions might be given by the President directly to the relevant Minister or Secretary.

A policy is invoked by a Secretary to his ministry generally to implement the requirements of that policy. The imperative for others within the ministry to act is generally backed with the Secretary's own authority: this would seem to be increasingly true the lower the level allowed for

ministerial implementation. Thus, a Third Secretary will generally respond to the invocation
of a policy from the knowledge that it is the
wish of his immediate superior or of the Secretary that the policy be implemented but without
knowing the feelings of his Minister or those
of the President. Although the desires of both
the Minister and the President are often known
throughout the A.O. corps in the ministry concerned, it is the efficacy of the chain of command that guarantees the execution of the policy.

For the Secretary vis-à-vis the Under Secretary, the invocation of a questionable policy
or one which the latter strongly opposes may not
be adequate on his sole authority: confirmation
of the wishes of the President or Minister may be
required before the Under Secretary is moved to
act. Similarly, on a lower level, analogous confirmation of the wishes of the P.S. may be sought.
This problem in the latter context is ameliorated
by the system of filing by subject-policy headings,
so that the lower officers, on receiving the file,
will have before them the comments and instructions of their superiors. In fact, much invocation by the President and Ministers is also in
written form, often as memos or notations of approval on memoranda of recommendation.

The area of those outside the government is
more diffuse. The process and criteria for deciding which policies would be invoked to Party
functionaries and which would utilize governmental
channels — often there are combinations of both —
is unknown, but almost certainly the key decisions
are made by the President. However, some coordination in this area was provided by the Minister of
State, who is also the Administrative Secretary of
the Party. On a higher level, the President often
invokes policies directly to the people by means
of speeches in Parliament, at Party gatherings,
and on the radio. This method (as opposed to others,
such as publication in the *Government Gazette* alone)

emphasizes the gravity of the policy, often underlined by the President's sometimes graphic description of penalties for violations. This was
the case with the announcement of price-control
measures imposed immediately after the 1967 de-
valuations of the British pound and subsequently
of the Malawi pound.

Application
"Application" means the actual implementation
of a policy already prescribed and invoked. Part
of this process has already been described in the
conveying of the President's instructions to his
Ministers and Secretaries, in written and oral
form. The Secretary's subsequent instructions to
his ministry are generally in the form of written
"minutes" giving instructions on a particular file
addressed to specified officers. There may be an
instruction to "keep him in the picture" if the
matter is sufficiently important, this to be done
by sending the file back to the Secretary in mid-
application with copies of the relevant correspondence and perhaps an explanatory "minute."

The application of policies by the Ministry of
External Affairs involved communication with the
international community, on the one hand, and communication with the President (who is officially
also Minister of External Affairs) and other ministries, on the other. External Affairs was not
involved in applying policies directly to the
Malawi public, with one exception. Most contact
with the public was on the basis of a request for
information of an international nature (e.g., the
interpretation of a treaty with respect to a potential licensing agreement with a foreign company)
or a request to approach a foreign government on
a specific matter, (e.g., the visa requirements for
travel to that country).

The exception concerned diplomatic privileges
and immunities, for which the Ministry was legally
responsible. This included interpreting the rel-

evant legislation as well as recommending new policy. A significant question was whether non-dip-
lomatic personnel were to be granted diplomatic
privileges (immunity from arrest, customs duties,
licensing fees, etc.). There was steady pressure
from resident embassies that, for example, technical assistance personnel should have these
privileges, which was resisted on general instruction from the President. A ministry official refused to concede this point in negotiations on a
technical assistance agreement with representatives of a Western government, and approval was
refused another ministry to allow Malawian employees at an embassy tax exemptions or to allow
technical assistance personnel to be granted am-
bassadorial immunities.

The extent of privileges accorded was significant in symbolically indicating the degree of
independence of Malawi from outside governments,
and the demands of their embassies for such privileges were generally resented by Malawians in
the government as indicating neo-colonialist
attitudes. This resentment traveled with that held
by many Malawians against all expatriates, who as
a group were seen as demanding special privileges
while in Malawi.

In External Affairs, much policy application
was done by letters to other ministries and embassies or by conveying a policy orally in the
context of meetings. Vis-à-vis other governments
and international organizations, the Ministry
sought to ensure that the government spoke with
one voice, and therefore sometimes refused to apply policies until their substantive and administrative inconsistencies (e.g., no one Ministry
recognized as holding the overall coordinating
responsibility for a project or program) were
resolved.

Policy was also applied to wide-ranging matters of complexity and importance by inter-ministerial committees as well as by ministries. This

was the case with the negotiation of the Labor
Agreement with South Africa, for example. The
decision on whether or not there was to be an
agreement was made by the President in conjunction with the Cabinet. The latter prescribed
Malawi's basic requirements for such an agreement
and established an inter-ministerial committee
chaired by the Secretary for Labor to recommend
specific policies and to clarify objectives. This
committee was then reconstituted, subsequent to
Cabinet approval of policy, as the team to nego-
tiate the agreement with the South African delegation, the chairman keeping the President informed
throughout. Subsequently, the Secretary for Labor
retained coordinating responsibility for implementing Malawi's obligations under the agreement,
c.g., the provision of Malawi passports to all
Malawi workers within and en route to South Africa.

Inter-ministerial committees were also con-
vened at the lower U.S. or S.A.S. level to handle
matters of continuing but lesser importance.
Thus, policy on several technical assistance
agreements was decided in the context of the Ministry of Development and Planning or the Ministry
of Finance with an S.A.S. or U.S. chairing a committee representing necessary ministries, the
chairman reporting to his own P.S. or higher, if
necessary. Often one of these ministries sponsored
the committee even though continuing administrative
responsibility for the substance of the agreement
might subsequently devolve upon another ministry
or the Office of the President upon the agreement's
entry into force. A similar committee would be
reconstituted for the next such agreement, in effect producing a floating negotiating team composed of about half expatriate and half Malawian
officials.

Appraisal
      "Appraisal" means the comparison of the levels
of performance in the implementation of a policy

with the set objectives of that policy, so that adjusting measures may be taken to augment or maintain its success, or so that the policy may be terminated. The President was known throughout the government to become quickly and strongly displeased if key policies (i.e., policies in which he took personal interest) did not yield the results promised him by officials within the predicted time span. Therefore, a close watch was kept on such policies, especially by Ministers, Secretaries, and Under Secretaries.

More generally, the appraisal function was performed by most officers above the rank of S.A.S., and certainly by all superscale officers. Included in "appraisal" are the questions of who is the continuing custodian of the policy's objectives, and of deciding whether those objectives have been modified after application of the policy. There is often an interplay between somewhat unrealistic objectives and the appraisal of policies designed to meet them. Perhaps this interplay is more intense in an African government because of its fundamental need to prescribe new solutions, whose imperatives and effects are unknown without the passage of time, to urgent far-reaching problems. For this reason, much of the ministry's appraising function rests with the P.S., who almost alone can survey both the various political and other imperatives surrounding the original definition of the objectives and the success of attempts at implementation under those objectives.

Also, much policy appraisal is done in the inter-ministerial committees. The necessity of this function's being performed on a relatively high governmental level is apparent: for an appraisal to be useful, its findings must produce recommendations weighty enough to influence whoever first prescribed the policy, or those who presently have the authority to amend or terminate the original policy. Thus, subsequent to the con-

clusion of the South African Labor Agreement, an
inter-ministerial committee at the Secretary level,
chaired by the Secretary to the President, met to
appraise labor migration policy relative to Rhodesia and South Africa in the light of present
policies in those countries, domestic Malawi policies, and regional conditions.

De facto appraisal capacity was also exercised by the Ministry of Finance and all Secretaries faced with tight budgets in light of the per-
petual scarcity of money. Specific appraisal
authority was vested in such government departments as the Inspectorate Branch of the Establishments Division, the service commissions (e.g.,
Judicial Service Commission), the Commission for
Revision of Laws, the Natural Resources Planning
Unit, the Industrial Development Office in the
Ministry of Trade and Industry, the Inspectorate
of the Ministry of Education, the Department of
Community Development in the Ministry of Local
Government, and the Farmers' Marketing Board.

Termination

"Termination" means the putting an end to
authoritative prescriptions and arrangements
arising within them. A rule of thumb might be
that the more likely it is that a substantial
dislocation of men, procedures, money, and administrative effort will be involved, the more likely
that a Minister or the President alone will be
seen within the government as having the authority to terminate that policy or policies. An indicator here is that the Ministry of Justice demanded the approval of either the President or a
Minister before it would draft new or superseding
legislation.

A difficulty arose if the policy was one to
which the President was publicly (or even explicitly within the government) committed. There
was a felt need to protect his prestige as Head
of State and Government and to avoid any situation

375

where he would be seen to have noticeably recanted that policy. At least for the public record, as in most governments, great efforts were made to find continuity rather than to make known a reversal. The procedure for this relates in part to the influence of the President's daily mood on governmental decision-making: on some days it was better to suggest revision (termination) of policies than on others. Often steps leading to termination were taken through the Secretary to the President, if he agreed with their substance; he was a clearinghouse for many such proposals, on which his recommendations were weighty.

Policy Implications

While no definitive axioms can be formulated on the basis of the foregoing examination, four policy implications can be suggested for considering the administration of social change in Africa.

Government as Arena of Change

In a small African country the governmental process itself is an arena of social change. That is, the positions, relative influence, and degree of authority held by certain groups and individuals in the government may well have significance for the attitudes of people in the surrounding society regarding the existence or promise of social progress. The Government is the largest, most structured organization in the country except the Malawi Congress Party. Other private groups do not approach it in power, wealth, or scope of national influence, nor do they publicly compete with it in the formation of opinion. Therefore, the Government and the Party are the most visible organizations, all the more so because they are simultaneously headed by a very strong Head of State, Government, and Party. Most of the country's educated elite are connected in some way with the

Government or have close ties with those who are. Among this group especially lively interest in Government policy exists generally, and in Government personnel policies, especially who is in favor and who is not, and in the speed of advancement of Malawians vis-à-vis expatriates. This interest is further related to the fact that foreign-owned commercial firms take their localization cues from Government policy.

The localization question finds its focus in the governmental process. The wide interest in localization on the part of the majority of urban-educated Malawians plus many others in direct contact with the Government in rural areas reflects the sensitivity of the general question of the role in national life that should be played by expatriates. This in turn reflects even more profoundly the fact that African independence was as much a racial movement as anything else.

The concern with localization in Malawi was made even more intense by the "merit" policy adopted by the Government immediately after independence, which also caused some continuing criticism of Malawi by other African countries. Although this is officially ignored as Malawi goes her own way, a certain strain is involved in the acceptance of this policy by many highly motivated and educated Malawians within and outside the government.[10] Finally, the localization question is spotlighted by the continued predominance in power and wealth of the white enclaves in Southern Africa with which, at least for the present, the government feels it must cooperate. The personal ties between whites in those enclaves and many expatriates within the government (and the commercial sector) are known or suspected by many Malawians, and this heightens the general concern.

Therefore, it can be implied that the Government's policy on localization will not be viewed outside of the Government merely as an internal personnel matter, but as an indicator of the Government's and the President's feelings about the general role of white expatriates in Malawi society, the availability of influence to qualified Malawians in public service, and the future role of Malawi vis-à-vis the white enclaves. This is indicated by the President's feeling it necessary to announce at the 1967 Party convention (and therefore nationwide) the appointment of the first Malawian Permanent Secretary and to spell out his plans for similarly elevating three others in the near future.

In the same speech he also announced the opening of formal diplomatic relations with South Africa. These two key announcements may well have been made in the same major speech in an attempt to separate the question of relations with foreign whites from that of the position of local whites by indicating that contacts with the white South were not expanded at the expense of localization. With visible parallel growth in both areas, the latter seems so far to be true.

If this implication is valid, then personnel measures taken by the government relative to expatriates can be seen as affecting national atitudes about social change in the country. Should effectiveness in this area be seen to falter over any substantial period of time, the government's effectiveness and willingness in other areas and issues of social administration might well be affected.

President as the Center

A second implication concerns the central role of the President in government and the effect on the administrative process of his inevitable replacement by a lesser figure. As has been discussed, the President is currently the decision-making center of the government and wields vast power over all its sectors. His successor, whoever and whenever, will almost certainly be under severe pressure to relinquish some of these prerogatives. Signigicant decision-making power on government matters might then fall to Ministers; alternatively, if the Cabinet continues to include some Ministers who do not fully administer the subject matter of their ministries, Secretaries may experience an analogous increase in de facto power and authority. Their recommendations to a Minister unable to pass the decision off to a dominating President might well become de facto prescriptions if they tended to be ratified by that Minister.

Should the latter occur, however, there would arise the possibility of an increase in existing tension between politicians and the Public service. This tension is reflected outside the capital as conflict between representatives of the Government and Party functionaries. Currently this conflict is kept within manageable limits by the President, but it is a continuing problem and is frequently the subject of his public exhortations. Should a less commanding figure assume the Presidency, however, one result of this conflict both within and without the Government might be renewed attempts by the Party to reassert its control over the Public Service by more direct intervention into policy matters at all levels. It is impossible to say whether this conflict would be intense enough to disrupt, for example, the administration of development projects or the prescribing of development policies, but certainly it would hinder these activities.

It has been persuasively argued that effective government in a modern African state depends on the retention of leadership and firm policy guidance by the Party over the bureaucracy to provide a governmental process politically representative of the people (which the bureaucracy is unable to do); to provide effective policy direction over government departments; to curb corruption, destructive infighting and other bureaucratic abuses; and generally to prevent a breakdown of government

379

service. This need for Party leadership comes at
a time when Party structure has atrophied and
the competence of its personnel has been weakened
because a relatively small number of capable people enter government service, a major cause of a
general decline of national parties as an institutional source of political authority.[11] Up to
now strong control has been exercised simultaneously over government and Party by President
Banda, thus generally fulfilling the above prerequisite for effective government. It seems unlikely that this simultaneous control could survive a change from the present regime to one headed by a less commanding figure. Further, it is
uncertain whether public order could be maintained
following such a transition.

Patterns of Governmental Decision-Making

     A third implication relates to the patterns of
governmental decision-making. As noted, each ministry is set up in a roughly hierarchical policy-
making structure with a chain of command generally
operating from Administrative Officers up to the
Secretary. The decision-making patterns in this
particular structure seem generally unilinear:
up and down the chain of command, with the intelligence-gathering and recommendation functions
particularly related to outside sources. The
President's dominant position over the Public Service, plus the functional division of bureaucratic
responsibility into ministries and departments,
with consequent problems of coordination and infighting, indicates Malawi's somewhat personal-
istic decision-making patterns, especially around
key issues. Otherwise those patterns tend toward
fragmentation between ministries, but not destruc-
tively so. It is therefore risky to rely on a
concept of "the Malawi government bureaucracy"
without carefully specifying time factors, surrounding circumstances, and particular problems.

The overall question is whether the retention of this structure six years after independence represents its adoption as an African administrative structure, or whether it represents a transitional phase toward some other kind of structure more reflective of traditional African patterns of decision-making. For present purposes these latter patterns are characterized as generally communal, with maximum participation by the group to which the policy is to be applied, the policy emerging from intensive discussion within the group as a consensus rather than being consistently prescribed by an authority figure.

Several implications are involved in adapting this tradition to the requirements of modern government. One is the closer structural integration of Party and Government discussed above. Another is that decision-making within the government includes not only the Public Service but also representatives of major groups in the society. It can be suggested that the tradition of an autonomous, apolitical public service of trained administrators to run the government is discordant with the declared objectives of many governments to create more egalitarian African societies. Such a tradition creates a continuing elite tending towards consciousness of its own expertise vis-à-vis the general public and resentful of all interference with bureaucratic forms and procedures. These wide-ranging questions are continuing ones in Africa, in the context of the relationship between party and government, and are noted as such here.[12]

Government the Transmitter of Outside Influences
The governmental process itself is perhaps the primary transmission belt whereby outside influences enter African countries, especially those that are small, poor, and out of the way, such as Malawi. "Outside influences" means primarily extra-African influences in terms of technical and other advisors, literature, and printed material

from other continents. The government cannot, of
course, hermetically seal off the country from the
outside world; but to overcome barriers of language,
cultural tradition, race, and general unfamiliarity
with the society, the cooperation of the government
is generally necessary.

If this premise is valid, it implies that the
approval of key government officials is a critical
element in validating outside recommendations about
how Malawi should develop and about what criteria
measure "progress" in its social change. Such
outside advice is all too readily offered by foreign
governments and international groups. The perspectives of key government decision-makers about what
social change is or is not desirable in a particular development situation may be critical in de-
termining (1) whether outside assistance is needed
in that situation, (2) whether particular types
of assistance will be accepted, and (3) the indices of success in that situation. If this is
so, it is suggested that it is even more important
in a small African country than elsewhere for
politicians and administrators concerned with
foreign policy to grasp thoroughly their country's
domestic economic and general development needs.

This, of course, is not a complete statement
of the role of a governmental decision-maker in
an aid situation, because many donor governments
have developed subtle techniques of literally in-
filtrating an African government and attaching
numerous conditions to the granting of aid so as
to severely limit the range of decision. But it
does indicate that since the Government is the
most structured group (along with the Party) in
a country with few countervailing social organizations, without the cooperation of those officials — coerced, induced, or genuine — foreign
governments and other purveyors of outside influence would find it very difficult to influence
local attitudes about development goals and standards of progress.

382

Malawi and American Aid
Policy in Southern
Africa

Administration and development in almost any
African country cannot be divorced from the policies of the major aid donors. The same is true
for Malawi, in part because of the aforementioned
tactics of donors' representatives who attempt to
influence the Malawi administrative process, and
in part because Government administration is affected by events in the Southern African region.
The aid policies of several major donor countries,
including the United States, are influenced by
and in turn influence these same events. Accordingly, a look at United States aid to Malawi and
its aid policies in the surrounding region, from
the vantage point of that region, is in order.
    Through A.I.D. the United States furnished
Malawi approximately $3 million per year, mostly
in project aid for rural development, the provision of teachers through the Peace Corps, and some
technical advisors.[13] The annual value of such aid
has now sharply declined preparatory to being
phased out entirely in a few years. In fiscal
1970 the total technical assistance aid in "self-
help funds" for 23 African countries, including
the five in black Southern Africa, amounted to
$1,750,000.[14] Malawi is a staunch member of the
Western bloc. All her aid comes from Western
countries and her foreign policy reflects Western
interests, e.g., support for Israel in the Middle
East and for the United States in Vietnam. Other
symbolic, tangible ties to the United States are
visible. Blantyre is the sister city of Independence, Missouri; Malawi is one of two countries in
Africa whose citizens need no visa to enter the
United States for limited visits; and an Investment Guaranty Agreement has been concluded between
the two governments.

It is an unfortunate axiom of international
behavior that official aid from a donor country
is provided as an extension of its foreign policy
principally to assist in meeting political objectives. This is especially true of the United
States. But if United States aid embodies this
political content in decisions about who gets
aid and how much or who does not, and if Malawi
is in the Western camp, as it demonstrably is,
then under the rules of this gigantic game, the
United States is playing most unfairly by not
paying for what it gets. To the extent that
Malawi has suffered abuse because of her support
of American policy, for example, on Vietnam, she
should be compensated by the beneficiary accordingly, certainly more than at the current level of
less than $1 million annually.

If, on the other hand, United States aid is
not to be directed toward the satisfaction of political objectives — at least not directed toward
the donor's political objectives, as much official rhetoric proclaims — then the amount of U.S.
aid to Malawi, when the wealth of America is compared with the needs of Malawi, is too little by
almost any standard. Worse still, this paucity
is attempted to be camouflaged in Africa under
the umbrella of the "regional aid" concept.[15]
From the vantage point of black Southern African
governments, this particular American policy
either was devised for the purpose of, or permits,
several trends.

The most serious such trend is the evolution
of the Southern African region into a Greater South
African Co-prosperity Sphere. South Africa's current "outward-looking policy" toward the black
Southern African governments is a combination of
highly attractive offers of official loans for aid,
military blustering, government-instigated private
investment, favorable technical assistance arrangements, and liberal economic and trade arrangements. Examples of the latter are the 1966

Trade Agreement with Malawi and the 1969 renegotiated Customs Union Agreement with the former
High Commission Territories. In the latter, the
revenue to those three countries from South African
customs collections tripled from the amount under
the 1910 Agreement, at the same time providing a
larger percentage of each of the annual budgets
that is subject to South African revocation. South
Africa is consolidating its economic influence in
the region; Botswana, Lesotho, Swaziland, Malawi,
and, for purposes of trade, Zambia are currently
drawing closer to the Republic in economic terms.
Simultaneously, South Africa is suspected of having ambitions to find outlets in markets and investment opportunities, as well as politically
(and, some say, militarily) as far north as Tanzania,
and of having already cooperated in covert trade
arrangements with several African countries north
of Zambia. These events must be seen in the context of the current military sluggishness of the
Southern African liberation movement (but not in
Portuguese Guinea) and some confusion as to the
governmental attitudes of Zambia and Tanzania
toward liberation strategy, as illustrated by the
current dispute over the meaning of the Lusaka
Manifesto. All of the above give plausible reason
to believe that current economic dynamics show the
"White Redoubt" expanding its economic influence
steadily throughout the region by co-opting the
economic options of the four southernmost black-
governed states and attempting to hinder Zambia's
turn to the north, while taking an increased
share of her trade.
    Washington cannot be unaware of these prevail-
ing dynamics. A primary tenet of its regional aid
policy is that available resources go to individual states only insofar as they will be used to
further a regional development scheme that is
"economically viable," as opposed to a national
development scheme.[16] Generally, the only regional arrangements in Southern Africa that prom-

ise to meet this stringent criterion are the arrangements being orchestrated by South Africa. The denial of substantial aid to these states, unless it is used for regional development schemes which would inevitably center upon white South Africa as the dominant participant, strengthens South Africa in the region by making closer ties of the black Southern African states to the Republic a condition of receiving United States aid. To some extent A.I.D. has recognized this inherent conflict without taking measures to resolve it, though it has agreed in principle to finance the building of the Botswana-Zambia road.[17]

In conjunction with other instances of United States economic cooperation with South Africa, this represents the imposition of an aid policy for purposes that might be racist, producing a result that is demonstrably racist. With respect to purposes, there is some indication that the United States would oppose, or look most unfavorably on, a black revolution in South Africa (and implicitly in Rhodesia, Southwest Africa, and the Portuguese territories) for both economic and geopolitical reasons. George Ball, disarmingly cast as an Establishment liberal by the Vietnam War, stringently warns in *The Discipline of Power* that black control of South Africa would turn the region into an "economic slum," which would be unacceptable.[18] The conclusion is that some form of white power must be preserved into the future. This is not presented here as a conclusive indication of the deep thinking of the United States Government, but as a highly plausible indication of what it may be.[19] If so, aid policy in the region seems likely to be prescribed and implemented in order ultimately to serve this more comprehensive policy. With respect to the result, the only apparent way to reverse the South African-promoted economic trends in the region is for resources to be provided to generate stronger economic countertrends. Currently, South African policy, by forging Republic-centered links throughout the region, is helping whites to perpetuate their domination over black Southern Africans. The only possible available basis for countertrends would seem to be the general success of the liberation movement (which the United States is on the record as unwilling to promote), or outside aid to provide leverage for the economic disengagement of black South African states from South Africa. Probably both will be necessary.

The latter is our focus here. The goal would be to foster cooperation of black governments and peoples in the region around the theme of economic disengagement from South Africa. They would rely on outside aid imaginatively conceived to give them leverage against South Africa, to cushion them against South African economic reprisals, and to enable them to look elsewhere for the majority of their aid and trade needs, with the ultimate goal of creating a new economic regional framework not dominated by South Africa, into which liberated territories could be brought. Of necessity this does not force these five governments to sever all economic ties to South Africa, but it would substantially reduce their dependence on the Republic while simultaneously expanding their ties to outside countries. Botswana and Swaziland are currently attempting to establish economic relationships to the north; Malawi continues to maintain her contacts with Zambia and Tanzania, despite periodically strained relations. The willingness of the United States to back Botswana in resisting South African diplomatic pressure on the building of the road link is a hopeful sign, so long as it continues. However, the depth of South African opposition to the scheme is uncertain, as is the length to which she would be willing to go to block its completion. Similarly, the depth of American commitment to Botswana is unclear, although the Secretary of State has said that the United States wants to help "provide alternative sources of assistance and means of access" to black countries caught in South Africa's economic web.[20] If this American policy is to take priority over heavy South African opposition and is to be implemented with perseverance for Swaziland and Lesotho, for example, with substantial financial backing, it is just possible that the goal of black regional disengagement from South Africa can ultimately be realized. If this goal is not met and current trends continue, it is likely that the region's black people will slide deeper under white South African domination.

The needed influx of aid could perhaps begin with resources for feasibility studies to determine the quickest, most efficient ways to meet this goal. Key also will be a redefinition within U.S.A.I.D. of how aid may be used, and certainly a radical redefinition of cost-effectiveness standards as applied to a justification for future aid in this context.

A second general trend is fostered by using a regional aid concept in Southern Africa. Such a policy lends itself easily to becoming another cloak under which to apply traditional Western cost-effectiveness standards to evaluate projects key to the development of a particular country, but projects susceptible neither to regional standards nor to economic valuation: i.e., it offers another way to say "no."

An example of such a project for which United States aid was denied is the current Malawi project to move the national capital from Zomba to the central region city of Lilongwe. Whatever one thinks of the merits of this controversial project, there seems no disputing the historic, legal, and indeed assumed right of any government, including that of Malawi, to implement such a project if in its judgment the future of the country would be served by it. The basic issue here is not whether the project is economically sound in terms of giv-

ing a certain monetary-equivalent return per
dollar loaned, but whether an African government
(or governments of other developing countries)
will be permitted to define its own development
needs under criteria basically its own — without
de facto coercive pressures through aid and other
regulation of resources by outside powers. This
question is especially relevant with respect to
the provision of aid, because generally the necessary resources for development, particularly financial capital, must be provided in part by other
countries. The doctrines to protect here are
those of sovereignty and national self-determination, counterpoised against "economic feasibility" and "prevention of waste of aid by self-help."
The struggle between the pairs is fierce and may
in some cases be a matter of national life or
death.

The Lilongwe project is currently being financed by a combination of private and official
capital in the initial amount of $11 million from
South Africa. Before accepting the South African
tender, Dr. Banda exhausted all Western aid possibilities, including the international agencies
and aid agencies in the United States, France,
Great Britain, and West Germany. In every case
he was turned down on the grounds of economic
infeasibility. There was some agreement that an
economic growth point was needed in the Central
Region, but all potential donors felt that moving
the capital was unnecessary to achieve this and
that other projects should take the first priority
given the same amount of capital. Banda had
never stated the problem as primarily one of economics, but as a national development problem in
the fullest sense of the term. The move was being made to unify the country be redressing the
concentrations of services, population, wealth, and
authority away from the Southern Region, where
they had been over-concentrated under the colonial regime. Moving the capital would give the

North and Central Regions a greater stake in the
entire country politically, economically, and
psychologically, thus enhancing national unity.
This is perhaps least an economic question; posing
it as such vitiates most of its substance and
perverts attempts to understand it. It is a question to be both asked and answered by those of
the land, those who are of the people and do not
merely research them. It is a question of fine
judgment which a government must make by its own
sensors, and which cannot be made primarily from
existing empirical indicators.

Many major development questions in Africa
are of this stripe, e.g., the Tan-Zam rail link.
But generally they are not conceived as such by
American and other Western aid officials or policy,
and have thus been denied aid. Yet an African
government's right to make such decisions without
international penalty of withdrawal of aid and
capital lies at the core of the concepts of national self-determination, sovereignty, independence, neo-colonialism, and colonialism. African
governments must determine their own destinies;
the attempts of the West to do so colonially were
not only wrong — they failed. Our task is to try
to establish aid policies that will accelerate
the fulfillment of their future as they define it,
and not as we wish it for our convenience. Such
policies, if implemented, promise to give governments such as Malawi's substantial assistance in
creatively meeting the administrative problems
created by the need for development and therefore
for social change.

NOTES

1. The author wishes to thank Professors Michael Lofchie and Richard Sklar of U.C.L.A., and Selby Joffe, for valuable criticism at different stages of this essay. The opinions and conclusions herein are, of course, entirely my own.

2. The Ministries are generally External Affairs, Finance, Office of the President, Trade and Industry, Development and Planning, Agriculture, Education, Works and Supplies, Transport and Communications, Labor, Local Government, Justice, and Natural Resources. The number of ministries may vary from time to time as they are consolidated and governmental responsibilities are rearranged. Thus, in mid-1967, Trade and Industry, Natural Resources, and Development and Planning were consolidated into the "super-ministry" of Economic Affairs, with planning functions being placed under the Office of the President. This reshuffle was intimately connected with the President's desire to rearrange the Cabinet, create three new posts of Regional Ministers, place Aleke Banda at the helm of Economic Affairs, and give more rationality to the government's planning process. This arrangement lasted for about a year, when again, for a mixture of administrative and political reasons, there was another Cabinet-ministry reshuffle, with Economic Affairs dissolving in favor of the status quo ante with the addition of a Ministry of Agriculture. Precision is also thwarted by a single Minister sometimes holding more than one portfolio, or a shift in the President's portfolios.

3. For a generally straightforward, though slightly pro-Banda, history of the events surrounding the attempted coup, see John G. Pike, *Malawi: A Political and Economic History* (London: Pall

Mall Press, 1968), pp. 163-70. There is considerable indication that in the critical months of
1964 before the actual armed rebellion, the dissenting Ministers did not want or expect to remove Dr. Banda, and even that they feared his loss.
Therefore, "attempted overthrow" as a description
of the events leading to the split might be impre-
cise. However, subsequent to Henry Chipembere's
speech of resignation in Parliament, the political
imperatives in the confrontation gained their own
momentum, the situation rapidly polarized, and
coexistence between Dr. Banda and the dissenting
Ministers within the same political arena became
impossible. From the longer view, therefore (including the armed rebellion), it is more nearly
correct to speak of this sequence of events as an
"attempted overthrow."

4. *Ibid.*, p. 162.

5. See M. J. Bennion, "Training for Localisation of the Public Service in Malawi," *Journal
of Local Administration Overseas*, V No. 1. (January, 1966), pp. 23-24. The statistics were compiled from the *Malawi Government Directory* as of
February 1, 1968, plus an Establishments circular
of July 1, 1968, reviewing Senior Administrative
and Administrative Officers Posts as of July 1,
1968.

6. For a more detailed examination of the relationship between Malawian and expatriate civil
servants within the government, especially concerning racial factors, see H. J. Richardson III,
"Malawi: Between Black and White Africa," *Africa
Report* (February, 1970), 18.

7. This mode of analysis has been adapted
from their formulation of decision functions in
international law. See Meyer McDougal and Harold J.
Laswell, "The Identification and Appraisal of Diverse

Systems of Public Order," in Richard A. Falk and Saul H. Mendlovitz, eds., *The Strategy of World Order* (1966), pp. 45, 53-54. For further discussion of decision functions in other contexts, see generally "Materials on Law, Science & Policy" (Yale Law School Library, 1965). (Unpublished.)

8. In 1967 this aid amounted to approximately $23.07 million. O.E.C.D., "Geographical Distribution of Financial Flows to Less Developed Countries, 1960-64, 1965, 1966-67." Paris: Organization for Economic Cooperation and Development, 1968, p. 168.

9. For a wider view of the African affliction of legal overlap, see Ann Seidman, "Law and Economic Development in Independent English-speaking Sub-Saharan Africa," *Wisconsin Law Review* (1966), 999, at 1005-15.

10. Pike, *loc. cit.*

11. Michael F. Lofchie, "Representative Government, Bureaucracy, and Political Development: The African Case," *The Journal of Developing Areas,* II (October, 1967), 37.

12. Zambia, for instance, has recently introduced a set of administrative reforms designed to increasingly politicize provincial and local governmental administration. See William Tordoff, "Provincial and Local Government in Zambia," *Journal of Local Administration Overseas,* IX (January, 1970), 23. And, more generally, see Lofchie, *op. cit.*

13. O.E.C.D., *op. cit.*

14. Charles C. Diggs, Jr., *Report of Special Study Mission to Southern Africa, Aug. 10-30, 1969,* House Report. No. 91-610 (Washington, D.C.: U. S. Government Printing Office, 1969), p. 177.

15. The emphasis of the regional A.I.D. office in Lusaka is described as "to develop regional and multidonor programs which would help foster the economic independence and political stability of the Southern African region." *Ibid.*, p. 25.

16. *Ibid.*, p. 26.

17. By the end of fiscal 1969 funds had been obligated for four new regional projects — based on increased cooperation between the region's black-governed states — which, however, totaled less than $1 million. These were mostly in the area of education; the most significant is a provision to survey an all-weather road link between Botswana and Zambia. See *Ibid.*

Subsequently, the United States announced that it expected to build the $6 million road link and a new ferry complex across the Zambezi River. Also, it is evidently giving Botswana diplomatic support against South Africa's opposition to the scheme. This opposition has so far taken the form of a denial on legal grounds by South Africa, through diplomatic channels to Botswana, that the latter shares a common border with Zambia. See *New York Times* (June 1, 1970), Sec. C, p. 16, col. 1. But neither the nature of the projects nor the amount of funds is sufficient to dent, much less reverse, the aforementioned regional dynamics — though the road link is a step in the right direction. As Diggs, *op. cit.*, notes on p. 25, A.I.D. is "faced with the formidable task of selling the regional approach and of convincing (the black Southern Africa states) the new A.I.D. policy has relevance and that it is not a covert way of abandoning Southern Africa."

18. George Ball, *The Discipline of Power* (Boston: Little, Brown, 1968), pp. 257-59.

19. Diggs, *op. cit.*, describes American foreign policy towards Africa as "schizophrenic" (p. 3). Schizophrenic in a dynamic policy situation tends to reinforce the prevailing policies by presenting them with no coherent opposition. Further, the pro-black African side of the ledger, relative to the liberation of Southern Africa, has been primarily verbal, while links and aid to South Africa and Portugal have been tangible and of an economic nature. Further, "schizophrenic" might be too mild a term to encompass the strength of the United States-South African-Rhodesian lobby in Washington and its alliances with white racism in this country.

20. See *Los Angeles Times* (June 18, 1970), Pt. 1-A, p. 1, col. 1.

PART IV

Theory, Practice, and Development Administration: Lessons from Africa

A Behavioral Approach to
Development Administration

by John D. Montgomery

In this age of challenge, even the tarnished wisdom of public administration theorists is not ex-
empt from attack. Perhaps if the efficiency can-
ons of public administration as taught for so
many years at Syracuse University and elsewhere
had been less interesting academically, less successful ideologically, or less conspicuous in
world affairs, they would not be so vulnerable
today. Who among us finds it rewarding today to
reproach French legalism, British pragmatic elitism, or Soviet rigidity as influences on the
presently developing world? American public administration has proved too inviting a target to
pass up. Somehow the other versions of modern
public administration are less worthy of attack
than the more systematic, more universalistic,
more pretentious principles developed in the
United States during the first third of this century. And so it should be: the Peter Principle
protects the less ambitious who choose not to rise
above the level of their competence. American
public administration, too, was safe enough in

its cozy precepts until it ventured forth to organize and rationalize the "non-Western" world.

One of the curious features of this collection of essays has been a consistency of thought that transcends the different vantage points of critics who have worked the American, European, Asian, and African beats — whether as sociologists, economists, political scientists, or men of affairs. They agree on the relevance of the Western experience; even Mr. Orewa's critical analysis of African experience stresses that fact. Professor Esman's thoughtful paper emphasizes important theoretical deficiencies of recent approaches to development administration, both in its cultural assumptions and in its technical derivations, but he works from American experience. Professor Goulet's insights introduce important dimensions drawn from French experiments with the politics of development administration; but he, too, is trying to deal with a body of theory that is essentially American. Professor Swerdlow correctly demonstrates that we know more about productivity than about development, but most of what we know about productivity we learned from the capitalist experience. The African papers, too, share some common concerns of which I shall speak later.

Out of this array of challenges — discreet, professional, and even gentle as they appear — three distinct themes seem to emerge with a truly revolutionary, though happily not martial, sound. The first is the challenge to the static model, the convention that treats administration as a stationary engine gobbling up inputs and spewing forth outputs. The challengers of this obsolete physics remind us that we are dealing with change. They call attention to an important fact: once change is conceded, nothing remains fixed. The governmental engines that power development must themselves change. A new physics takes over. The question is no longer only who uses the machine, or even whom does the machine use, but what happens to the machine as it is used?

400

The second challenge attacks the notion that administration is an inert, colorless, and even odorless chemical. It rejects the view that a bureaucracy is a politically neutral instrument or catalyst selflessly serving whatever policy amalgam society transmits to it without absorbing anything or otherwise changing itself. Again, this challenge is not a startlingly new discovery, even in the Western context. Long before Parkinson, astute observers knew that bureaucracies perpetuate themselves by growing if they can; and if they can no longer justify that, by finding new ways of stagnating. Even before the Institution-Building Consortium explained how an administrative unit functions as a subsystem of society, successful bureaucratic leaders had figured out ways of adapting by linking their institutions to external sources of support. Now the institution-building theory raises this practice to the level of doctrine; but if we are to help bureaucracies learn to survive, we need to answer some new questions: why, or when, should an institution survive at all? Which institution should be introduced, or strengthened? Is survival a social utility? By what fruits shall we know our institutions of change?

The third challenge is against the simple subject-predicate view of the administrative process. It discards the interpretation of development as a predetermined goal to be achieved by a self-determined elite. It prefers instead to treat development administration as a compound-complex sentence, which constantly changes subjects, objects, and verbs. For none of the papers in this volume is satisfied with measuring developmental progress for administrators by counting up the miles of roads built or paved, the thousands of acres newly irrigated, the added school rooms built, or even the numbers of persons made literate. There are new questions for development administrators to consider: What new standards of

performance do their citizens require of society?
How much of an investment in modernization do they
make of their own volition? What instruments and
processes do they employ in resolving conflicts
arising out of development? The manner in which
the development administrator discovers, and influences, the behavioral responses that citizens
actually make to new opportunities is at least
as important as the conventional dimensions of
bureaucratic performance heretofore used to evaluate effectiveness.

The three challenges tell us important things
about development administration: it is dynamic,
it is political, and it must look as much to citizen responses as to bureaucratic behavior.

Policy Choices

The import of these questions is not for research scholars alone. If the Age of Technology
is to serve the public in Africa and Asia better
than it is in America and Europe, policy choices
have to be made on some basis other than the pure
rationalities of macro-economic or macro-technical
development. These choices are of two orders:
first, among programs or service sectors, and
then among alternative means of implementing them.
The first-order decisions will determine which elements of the public will benefit the most from
modernization,[1] and the second, how whatever benefits there are in the process will be distributed. Other dimensions are involved in both
choices, of course, but I see these two as those
most closely related to the emergent theories of
development administration.

Western conventions have circumscribed both
orders of decisions made in the underdeveloped
countries. Those of the first order — which sectors or programs deserve the investment of capital, leadership, and energy — have been made in

402

the past along "growth" and "profitability" lines.
Decisions so made tend to favor whatever classes
possess the capital or other resources required
for the initial investment. One of the consequences of this approach, along with the desired growth
of productivity and output, has been the uneven
enrichment of different sections of the population,
to a point where the rich-poor gap has actually
widened, even in countries whose developmental
progress is most encouraging. Another consequence
has been the neglect of other problems and the
woeful inadequacy of the criteria by which choices
are made in the nonmarket sectors of development.

The second-order choices — the distributive
choices — are commonly interpreted as administrative rather than political. They have convention-
ally been made according to standards of efficiency,
again narrowly interpreted by reference to economies
internal to the sector or operation involved. One
consequence of this approach has been to focus the
attitude of policy-makers upon the rather frail
human resources most immediately available to planners — the bureaucracy — to the virtual exclusion
of the vast human resources external to the government — the client citizens, whose attitudes, energies, and interests are the ultimate objectives
of development.[2]

It is now possible, within reason, to determine who benefits, and how much, from various program choices made in the public or private sectors (the first-order decisions). It is also
feasible, at least for selected samples of citizens,
to observe behavioral responses to developmental
opportunities that are made available to the public (the second-order decisions). These two lines
of inquiry belong to different, but compatible,
forms of political research: group theory and
political psychology, respectively. Group theory,
including both studies of interest aggregation
and political coalitions, helps explain how different elements of the public make their desires

known to political leaders and how decisions are
made in the face of conflicting claims. The techniques and findings of such research, though not
extensively applied to the L.D.C.s, are familiar
enough not to require restatement here. But political psychology has not yet addressed itself
extensively to problems of development administration, and I should therefore like to suggest here
how it might be possible to study citizen responses to various policies and procedures used to
influence public behavior. One advantage of this
approach is that it can be applied in all sectors
of development, whether in market or noneconomic
spheres of modernization.

Responses to Opportunity
     At least three forms of behavioral response
to development opportunities can be used as indicators of citizen commitment to modernization.
The categories I propose to use as a basis of observation can also be used to test a fundamental
assumption of modern democratic theory: that
passive acceptance of a government's developmental
efforts contributes less to the achievement of its
political objectives, and of modernization itself,
than does active participation in them. They also
assume that active participation is not a single,
undifferentiated form of behavior. If these assumptions are true, it should be possible to measure citizen participation in developmental change
across sectors, and to aggregate observed behavior according to an implied scale of commitment
to modernization. It should also be possible to
make comparisons of citizen response to developmental opportunities over both time and space.
The categories I have found most useful for these
purposes are, I believe, relevant to the findings
brought forth here from the African experience:
     1. Behavior reflecting the acceptance of a
rational discipline or standards which must pre-
cede active modernization programs. Such behav-

404

ior is usually a response to new influences coming from sources outside the traditional system, although in some cases it may be a continuation of traditional standards. For farmers, for example, it might involve the changed patterns of cultivation required by new seed varieties; for merchants, adjustments to new taxes or laws; for villagers, the acceptance of unfamiliar standards of health and education; for civil servants, procedural innovations and new professional ethics. The discipline imposed by modernization is one of its most obvious hallmarks: modern workers, managers, and clerks lead lives demonstrably different from those of their predecessors, and these differences seem to be so universal as to be imposed by the requirements of the new productive system. The discipline may not be the same in all societies, but it is always different from what preceded it. In agriculture, as well, modernization adds new disciplines to those imposed by nature; and these disciplines are easily observed in behavior at the farm level, at the mill, and among middlemen. As we have argued here, even bureaucracies, seemingly as impervious to change as the Law of the Medes and Persians, depart radically from tradition as civil servants begin to act as change agents. The standards of good bureaucratic behavior are not the same in a static as in a dynamic context.

2. Behavior representing individual investments of time, labor, or capital in developmental programs. Such behavior indicates a deepening commitment to the goals of the government and the other forces for change in society. It includes capital outlays to purchase improved supplies or productive equipment, or additional labor, or time allocated to acquiring new skills related to development. It may also mean deferment of immediate consumption for a more desired future end. The risk-taking farmer who tries out new seeds or invests his limited capital in fertilizer is just as necessary to the government's development pro-

405

gram as the laborer who attends trade school in order to enter the modern sector, or the entrepreneur who invests capital in textile machinery. Again, similar investments may also be identified among civil servants who choose to make arduous, time-consuming visits to the countryside in order to promote family planning, community development, or local health measures, or to conduct Mr. Orewa's site audits.[3]

3. Behavior indicating a citizen's acceptance of civic means of resolving interest conflicts arising out of development. Such behavior is closely associated with the two other developmental activities just described. It recognizes the social obligations incurred when men benefit from developmental programs. Since traditional grievance-settlement processes have presumably been established for resolving traditional disputes, the presumption is that development-related interest conflicts may require new instruments for achieving new levels of accommodation. Traditional means will often seek to resolve new forms of conflict as they begin to arise, but they gradually lose their value as new issues prove to resist resolution by earlier processes. Issues of this kind would include increases in farmland values as irrigation becomes available and as new varieties produce greater yields, giving rise to disputes over the allocation of profits, creating conflicts of interest among members of a credit cooperative, and otherwise generating political problems that were unknown in earlier times. Slash-and-burn cultures suffer such tensions when new farming practices increase the importance of plots of ground whose ownership is indeterminate. In commercial and industrial sectors, new issues arise when the public interest is threatened by unrestrained exploitation of such community resources as radio waves, breathable air, and drinkable water. The civic resolution of such issues is as essential to the continued well-being of the

polity as the original acceptance of productive
standards and individual investments were, especially when the Government itself is associated
with the developmental changes responsible for the
conflict.

Measures of citizen participation in such con-
flict-resolving instruments include submission of
adversary interests to public arbitration, membership in community tribunals, the registering
of protests and complaints through lawful channels,
and the acceptance of legitimate judgments subject
only to political redress. Violent behavior,
disregard of duly expressed public interest concerns, and membership in and support of unlawful
protest movements may be interpreted as negative
behavior under this category, at least in cases
where suitable conflict-resolution instruments
are present. One of the tasks of development administration, broadly conceived, is to provide such
instruments in order to reduce friction losses in
the processes of modernization.

Crises and Development

It is the current political fad to treat every
deficiency in society as a crisis. Whether this
notion derives from the media, to which a non-crisis
is non-news, or whether democracies really can function only from crisis to crisis, we hardly notice
anything lower than a crisis. Now that so many
political scientists have given up the idea that
they can identify stages of development in any
really discriminating way, some of them have seized
upon the "crisis" or the sequence of crises as
the best way of classifying political behavior.[4]
Following this fashion, it would be possible
to identify "crises" that occur when developmental programs fail to induce the citizen behavior
I have just described. First, for example, villagers might not accept the externally derived

standards of modernization: a whole village is, let us say, in a "crisis of apathy" because it has failed to reach the first rung of the ladder of development. Farmers see no reason to grade their produce, merchants decline to pay taxes, parents prefer not to send their children to school, and unused latrines remain as fresh as the day they were dug by diligent Peace Corpsmen. Exhortation has failed, and example stands unimitated; shall the government send in troops, set up community radio-listening posts, dispatch civil servants back to school, or create some kind of incentive system? Which administrative response will alleviate the crisis, and which will create worse ones? These become problems in development administration as soon as responsive citizen behavior is perceived as a legitimate goal of modernization.

The difficulty Lesotho has encountered in motivating its disheartened civil servants to perform a modernizing function in a society dominated by white South Africa and lacking in both self-knowledge and self-confidence illustrates an acute crisis of apathy.[5] And even in countries where civil servants are themselves prepared to undertake the task of mobilizing the citizenry, especially in the elitist style of a post-colonial bureaucracy, they may only arouse hostility if they persist in their traditional attitudes toward the public.[6] For the task of development is to assist citizens to "gain control over the processes of change," not to exhort them to abandon their traditions for the sake of some political abstraction dreamed up in a far-off capital city or to build up an economy that benefits only the rich.[7]

The traditional way of converting civil servants to change agents is through training. That is the hope of the new institutes of public administration in Nigeria, Tanzania, and Ethiopia: that by refocusing the bureaucratic attention on citizens, the apathetic behavior of both parties can be invigorated.[8] Sending accountants to the field is expected to do more than improve bookkeeping practice: it implies new standards of output for both the auditor and the audited. Reorganizing government services should produce better flow charts, but in Nigeria it may also explore new ways of reconciling ethnic indifference to developmental goals and the requirements of nation-building.[9] And in Uganda an even more ambitious effort to bring the public and private change agents together into a single development administration career service reveals the high expectations of political leaders for a rejuvenation of the sclerotic bureaucracies involved.[10]

A second form of administrative "crisis" of development might emerge when modernizing standards have been accepted but the participating citizens see no opportunity for investment, either because there are no development activities to which they may contribute their capital or labor, or because they have no access to surplus resources for investment purposes. Farmers might continue following traditional techniques of cultivation even if there were profits in the new ways, either because they lack the capital to purchase new inputs, or because they have no access to land on terms that would justify the effort to change. They may be unable to invest because the government has refused to finance agricultural research except for export crops, leaving the ordinary farmer with insufficient technology for improvement.[11] The "crisis of investment" is, if anything, sharper than the "crisis of apathy" because it represents society's frustration of the individual's desire to modernize. Similar frustrations are felt by parents who are willing to send their children to school, even at some sacrifice to themselves, but find no place open to them; and by citizens who are prepared to pay for modern medical care where none is available. Even efforts to stimulate local investment in much-needed housing, using

409

foreign capital under government guarantees as a
lever, may fail if local administrative resources
cannot be brought together for the purpose. The
mere fact that such programs had worked in Ethiopia,
Ivory Coast, Senegal, Kenya, and Tunisia did not
prove that they would succeed in Tanzania. The
bureaucracy may find no incentive sufficient to
induce them to abandon the safer traditional procedures. Development administration begins with
administrators, but it does not stop there. To
the development administrator, the crisis of investment becomes a crisis of inadequate service.
It cannot be resolved by arousing the citizens, as
the first crisis can: but only by providing cit-
izen-clients with access to opportunities.

A third crisis occurs when development takes
place rapidly enough to generate conflicts of interest among private groups or against the public
interest. The "crisis of interests" is potentially
the most serious of all because of the scale of
conflict that occurs when a society is on the road
to development. It signifies that interests created or enriched by development have become powerful enough to defy existing arrangements for the
resolution of their conflicts. Crises of this
order may seem too important to leave to administrative remedy;[12] but they are so intimately
related to the administration of development programs that they can frequently be headed off before
they become serious political issues if the programs are wisely conceived and judiciously administered.[13] Such was the purpose of the conflict-
resolving District Development Committees in
Malawi;[14] and thus the land settlement program in
Kenya was designed in part to gain support among
Africans whose interests would presumably become
counterrevolutionary once they were freeholders.[15]
If a program to introduce new high-yielding varieties of rice takes place simultaneously with a
land reform program, means for establishing equitable values of the land must be built into both

410

programs or the rising conflict between tenants and
landlords may destroy the prospects of both. Industrial development plans that make no provision
for technological unemployment are only inviting
trouble.[16] Indeed, the provision of adequate
plans for local adaptive research is becoming increasingly a condition of licensing for foreign
industrial investors.[17] Nigerian experience in
drawing together all interested private and public parties, including unions, has confirmed the
wisdom of planning to accommodate predictable
conflicts of interest.[18] And finally, if new
instructional methods or curricula are introduced
before teachers are prepared to change or parents
to abandon their claim to high-prestige traditional forms, both groups are likely to come after
the government with fire in their eyes and uncom-
plimentary ballots (or worse) in their hands.

Treating administrative inadequacies as a
background to crisis is nothing strange to students
of African development. So much attention has
been given to governmental capabilities in post-
colonial Africa that we sometimes overlook the
fact that crises of tremendous proportions in
other parts of the world can also be traced to
these three kinds of inadequacies in development
administration.

Thus examples of the first crisis — apathy —
are provided by traditional areas of China in the
1940's which voluntarily defected to the Communists;
of the second — investment — by the presently unemployed intellectuals of India, whose personal
investments in modernization find no opportunity
for productive activity; of the third — interests —
by the robber barons and their successors in the
United States whose exploitation of developmental
opportunities made them so powerful that by the
time of the Great Depression, when the public was
finally aroused, they were all but uncontrollable.

These examples might suggest that the crises
are sequential phenomena, reflecting the patholo-

gies of various stages of development. This is probably true only of the great crises, however; in their lesser manifestations they are more likely to be cyclical. They are probably all present to some degree wherever society is in transition. In any modern polity, standards are changing, new investment opportunities are emerging, and interest conflicts strain the existing resources for civic adjudication. Any government may face crises of any order, presumably on a continually rising level of sophistication and expectation.

In Africa, where these crimes may still be manageable, it is urgently necessary to consider how recent administrative experience can help us understand them. These papers illuminate very well the potentialities of the behavioral approach to development administration.

Conclusion

If development administrators begin applying the behavioral approach to their task, they will immediately become vulnerable to two incompatible charges: the liberal's complaint that they are manipulating citizens, and the radical's objection to their efforts to keep ahead of public demands in order to short-circuit popular revolution. To the first charge I would respond that development administration is a two-way avenue to modernization: it requires change on the part of both the government and the citizens. Each should manipulate the other. To the second, we all must plead guilty. One of the objectives of development administration, under any system, is to make revolution unnecessary and even irrelevant.

Politicians want to make choices that will enable them both to survive the next election and for the sake of the one after that, perhaps, to improve the polity itself. When resources are clearly limited, as they are in most underdeveloped countries, these choices do tend to be made on a crisis basis. The political leader's task then becomes one of identifying the areas, sectors, and social groups whose continued loyalty or active support is declining or in doubt, and to serve them best. The resulting choices tend to give certain constant characteristics to the political process in such countries: it screens out the demands from sources whose support is either guaranteed or unimportant, and it amplifies the demands of two other groups: those possessing greater access to the decision-makers and those representing recognizably important political constituencies.

The politician's rationality in these cases permits him to avoid action when he perceives no threat to his survival. Thus, when he can tolerate stasis, he does so; where governmental apathy can be safely permitted, it is; and where diversionary politics can satisfy the participation desire of potentially restless groups, these tactics prevail over more costly programs. Governments are not necessarily indifferent to social needs because they respond to priorities in this fashion: indeed, they prefer to identify themselves with modernization whenever they can, especially when it seems inevitable. Representing these facts to politicians is an important task of development administration. But again, resources are limited; however much governments may desire development, they cannot provide all of the funds and leadership required for it. Where ideology permits it, therefore, politicians must make use of many other sources (including private enterprise) which seek ends compatible with their own objectives. At the same time, they continue the political strategy of using public resources to benefit those elements of society whose demands are most insistent and those that are most promising. The rationality for allocating scarce administrative resources in such cases is based on the anticipated multiplier effect to be derived from citizen behavior responsive to the opportunities for development.

To the extent that developmental objectives can thus serve both the purposes of politicians and the desires of citizens, they can be made compatible with both the democratic theory and the presumed political objectives of Western countries offering development assistance. It is not necessary to assume either that Westerners have the answers to these ultimate problems of modernization, or that African governments have. We must make some assumptions, however. We have to assume, as Westerners characteristically do, that most developmental problems are amenable to resolution or at least to improvement. No doubt such solutions will generate other problems to be resolved in an endless progression of cooperative effort: progress may not be the inevitable consequence of change, but new problems are. But any practicing politician knows this. The other major assumption we must make is that resolving these problems is not a matter of goodwill or morality, but of politics. Development administration ought be be prepared to use citizens' responses as a test of the opportunities society creates for them, and thus as a test of society itself. In this sense, its aim is to make revolutionary change unnecessary by creating the conditions for self-improvement before dissatisfaction rises to crisis proportions.

NOTES

1. The transition from groundnuts to tobacco and from plantations to smallholdings to cooperatives illustrates this problem, as suggested in Kenneth L. Baer, "Administrative Structure . . . Urambo," pp. 236-42.

2. Milton J. Esman, "Administrative Doctrine
. . ., " pp. 34-35; Denis A. Goulet, "Development
Administration. . .," pp. 61-66; and J. M Waiguchu,
"The Politics of Nation-Building in Kenya," pp.
214-16, illustrate this.

3. G. O. Orewa, "Some Aspects of Development
Planning and Administration in Africa," pp. 115-16.

4. Leonard Binder, James S. Coleman, Joseph
LaPalombra, *et al.*, eds., *Crises of Political Development* (Princeton: Princeton University Press,
1971).

5. Nicholas Danforth, "Lesotho: Toward Real
Independence," p. 327.

6. Waiguchu, pp. 222-23, 226-27.

7. Goulet, pp. 48-49, 51-52.

8. Orewa, pp. 106-07, 125-27.

9. W. Bediako Lamouse-Smith, "Complexity and
African Development Administration," pp. 162-62.

10. *Ibid.*, pp. 151-53.

11. Orewa, pp. 116-20.

12. Baer, p. 249.

13. *Ibid.*, pp. 253-54.

14. Robert A. Miller, "Institution-Building
and Rural Development in Malawi," pp. 279-80.

15. Brian Van Arkadie, "Planning, Plans,
and Planned Economics," pp. 180-81.

16. *Ibid.*, pp. 174, 180-81

17. Orewa, pp. 121-23.

18. *Ibid.*, pp. 110-11, 113-15.

Index

Malthus, T., 148
Management Service Unit, 124
Man of the People, A, 281
Mannoni, O., 316
manpower planning, 184
masses and politics, 192, 204
Massachusetts Institute of Technology, 37
Mboya, Tom, 200, 202, 205, 213
McDougal, Myers, 356
Merlman, Seymour, 42
Merton, Robert, 136, 155
missionaries, 324
mobilization, and elitism, 198, 205
modernization, 4, 34, 271–272, 404
Mokhehle, 335
Moshoeshoe, I, 317, 318
Moshoeshoe, II, 321

nation building, 166–167, 189–190, 192, 195, 218, 220
national consciousness, 189–220
national plan, use of, 86, 87, 95
National Planning Consultative Committees, 95
native authorities, leaders among, 280
Ncheu Committee, 281
Nehru, Jawaharlal, 270
nepotism, 151
Ngei, Paul, 201
Nigeria, 90, 95, 96–104, 106, 112–113, 300
Nkrumah, 148
Nyasula, Alec, 302
Nyerere, Julius, 177, 197–198, 201, 255

Obote, A. Milton, 136
Organization of African Unity, 147
Orewa, 400
Overseas Food Corporation (OFC), 237
Oxbow hydroelectric project, 329

Pakistan, 100–101
Pan Africa, 202
Pan-African Institute, 115
para-statal enterprises, 139–140
party, role of, 191, 211
Parson, Talcott, 156
Peace Corps, 286
Pearson Report, 174
personnel management, 111–115
Perroux, Francois, 51–52
planning, role of, 88–187
political leadership, 143, 174, 195

political mobilization, 191–192, 216–219
political organization, and administration, 283
political parties, 189–192
political psychology, 403
Popper, K. R., 131
POSDCORE, 66
power, analysis of, 189–190, 217–218
Pratt, Cranford, 169
public administration, 65, 72, 77, 79, 80–81, 131, 134, 399–400
public rector, 176, 179
public service, 111, 141, 151, 195

reform, need for, 118, 125
regional development, balance of, 167
research laboratories, 109–110
resource management, 98

Sartori, Giovanni, 45
Selznick, Philip, 295
Senegal, 33, 103
Sherwood, Frank, 269
Sierra Leone, 99, 100, 104
Socialism, 176, 178–179
Somalia, 95, 100
South Africa, 352–353, 384, 386–387
Southern Africa, 378
state, 180–183
structural change, 181
Sudan, 92, 103
Swaziland, 92
Swerdlow, Irving, 133

Tanganyika, 174–175, 238, 253
Tanganyika Agricultural Corporation (TAC), 238
Tanganyika Tobacco Board, 253
TANU, 244
Tanzania, 31–38, 61, 89, 92, 99, 101, 104, 145, 159–160, 167–168, 170–175, 176, 179, 185, 187, 235, 261, 285
third world, 31–32
tobacco, 236–237
tribalism, 151

Uganda, 139–140, 168, 179, 186
Ujamaa program, 186
Ujamaa Village Development, 177
underdevelopment, 27–31, 52–53
United Arab Republic, 92–94, 100, 102, 107, 109
United Nations, 31, 89, 92, 147
U. S., Congress, 37

419